For YANKEE FANS ONLY!

Wonderful Stories Celebrating
the Incredible Fans of the
New York Yankees

RICH WOLFE

International Standard Book Number: 978-0-9800978-3-2

Printed in the United States of America

10 9 8 7 6 5 4 3 2 1

Photos provided by, and used with permission of Rich Wolfe, *Sports Illustrated,* and the individuals whose stories appear in this book.

Cover design: Dick Fox
Cover art: John Kovalic
Interior design: The Printed Page, Phoenix AZ.
Author's Agent: T. Roy Gaul

Page Two. In 1941, the news director at a small radio station in Kalamazoo, Michigan hired Harry Caray who had been employed at a station in Joliet, Illinois. The news director's name was Paul Harvey. Yes, that <u>PAUL HARVEY</u>! "And now, you have the rest of the story...... ➡️

DEDICATION

To:

Jerry Butterworth
of Newton and Falmouth, Massachusetts,
the king of all New York Yankees fans in New England

ACKNOWLEDGMENTS

Wonderful people helped make this book a reality, starting with Ellen Brewer in Edmond, Oklahoma, and Lisa Liddy at The Printed Page in Phoenix—wonder women who have been indispensable sidekicks for many years. Ditto for Barbara Jane Bookman in Falmouth, Massachusetts.

How about a big thank you to the erudite Mark Schiff and his buddy, the talented Ritch Shydner, who wrote the killer book *I Killed,* and how about Rick Phalen out in Santa Barbara ... even if he is a Cubs fan.

Special thanks to Rob Taylor and the good people at the University of Nebraska Press, especially Peter Ives, Jeffrey Hammond, and Delmer Davis. And let's not forget the indispensable Matthew Donnelly; the brilliant Rob Lucas at Gray & Company; Gene Cervelli in Paradise Valley, Arizona; and the world-traveler, Dale Ratermann in Indianapolis.

A tip of the hat to all those interviewed who missed the final cut—we just flat ran out of time and space. Three chapters were cut indiscriminately due to space limitations. It was close, and we're gonna do it again next year. Thanks, everyone!

Sample Excerpts From This Book

. . . The luxury box was very small—might seat twenty-five people. Yogi and Whitey and their wives and Murcer were there—you could read on their faces and see them thinking to themselves, "Who the hell are these guys? How did they get in with us?" They treated us very nicely. I didn't have anything in there with me for them to sign and was going to go get a ball. Instead I just got a dollar bill signed. I had Whitey and Murcer and Berra sign the dollar bill. Then Gene Michael came in, and I didn't want him to sign that same dollar bill so I pulled out another one, and he signed it. . . .

. . . It was Chuck, the landlord's son. He said, "Did you hear about Thurman Munson?" My first thought was he was traded. Nobody remembers this, but there were rumors at the time that he wanted to end his career with Cleveland, his home. He wasn't going to be catching much longer. His last game with the Yankees might have been at first base. He was starting to transition away from catching and it was clear that his best days were over. So, thinking he'd been traded, I said, "No, no, I didn't hear it. What's up?". . .

. . . Besides the three ball games, the excursion package also included a night at the Hotel Piccadilly and tickets to the Jack Carson Show at Radio City Music Hall. Unbelievably, the entire package, including train fare, cost the princely sum of $20. It was the only time I ever got to see the great DiMaggio play. He retired after that season. . . .

PREFACE

You are about to be swept in the genius minds of New York Yankess fans, awe-struck by their farsighted scheming, stricken dumb by their wonderful stories as they lay bare their sordid love affair with the Yankees.

In 2003, I had an idea for a sports book. It was to be a book where fans would tell their neatest stories. Over the years, I could always identify when a fan would tell a great story about getting into a sold-out game or growing up listening to games on the radio, etc. I approached several publishers with this idea and was turned down by all of them . . . so I decided to self-publish the book. Entitled *For Yankee Fans Only,* Yankee fans told their fondest stories about growing up with the Yankees, going to Yankee Stadium, meeting a player, and other wonderful memories. The book was released for Father's Day 2003 . . . sales were very slow at first. It was disappointing because I was quite sure the concept would work. Traditionally, sports books never sell in July, August, or September. Usually sports books are bought, not by men, but by women. They're bought for Christmas or for Father's Day. That's pretty much the ball game.

Lo and behold, in September most of the retail accounts reordered. By Christmas, the book was sold out—all 30,000 copies. The world of mouth from Yankees fans is what did it. It started a string of many other fan books . . . from the dreaded Red Sox to the Chicago Cubs to the Green Bay Packers to Notre Dame fans and over a dozen more teams.

I am the least likely person in the country to write a book. I can't type. I've never turned on a computer, and I've never seen the Internet. I refuse to sit in press boxes and corporate suites. I have a belief that "the cheaper the seat, the better the fan." I really don't know why I picked the Yankees to be the first fan book I would do. Perhaps I remembered my first trip to New York during a college freshman trip from Notre Dame. There, standing on top of the

Empire State Building, the first thing I wanted to see through the telescope was Yankee Stadium. When Jerry Jones, the Dallas Cowboys owner came to New York City for the first time ever, before his first business meeting, he took a cab to the Bronx, got out of the cab, walked over, touched the side of Yankee Stadium, and got back in his cab. That was his dream as a child growing up in Arkansas—to go see Yankee Stadium someday . . . the dream of every young baseball fan.

Before doing the initial volume of *For Yankee Fans Only*, I wasn't really a Yankee fan. I wasn't really a Yankee hater. I was a National League fan, having grown up following the St. Louis Cardinals. I'd heard awful stories about Yankee fans. After doing not only the Yankee book but also many other fan books, I realize that most of the fans of every team are *great* fans. The fly in the ointment are the drunks. If you take away the drunks from almost any team—Major League Baseball, the NFL, college football—the fans are great. The truly good fans respect the other team and respect the other fans.

I never thought I'd see the day when I would ever say nice things about Yankee fans. But after dealing with Yankee fans in an objective way for these two books, it's a pleasure to say that Yankee fans are terrific . . . very enjoyable, very knowledgeable, fun, funny and, best of all, passionate. I'm glad that I chose the Yankees.

From one baseball fan to another, I truly hope that you enjoy this book. If you don't or you have any comments just call me at 602-738-5889.

Get your estate in order, you may not see another dawn . . . because hopefully you might die laughing from reading *For Yankee Fans Only, Volume II*.

Go now.

CHAT ROOMS

Chapter 1

Sweet Home
Yankee Stadium

Goodbye to the
Field of Screams and Dreams

NOSTALGIA'S NOT WHAT IT USED TO BE

Mark Braff

Mark Braff, a resident of Glen Rock, New Jersey, grew up in Fair Lawn, New Jersey, and attended Rider University, Digger Phelps's alma mater. He currently owns Braff Communications, a successful business-to- business public relations firm.

There used to be an annual game called the **MAYOR'S TROPHY GAME***, between the Yankees and the Mets. It was an in-season exhibition game. This was in the days way before interleague play. It was a big deal to the fans for the Yankees and Mets to be playing . . . and to be during the season so they had their regular rosters. It wasn't like spring training. From what I understand from years later, the Yankee players couldn't care less, but to the Mets, it was a big thing because they were horrible, and it was their chance to beat these "mighty" Yankees.

The first game I ever went to was the 1965 Mayor's Trophy Game. It was a ten-inning game the Yankees lost 2–1. We were sitting on the first base side in the lower box. I remember looking across into the Met dugout and seeing Casey Stengel. It was like, "Oh my God! Casey Stengel." It was just like—if you ever saw *City Slickers*, and you listened to Billy Crystal in that movie talk about how when he went to his first Yankee game he couldn't believe it because it was the first game he ever saw in color. That was true. We had a black and white TV. I went to that game . . . it was the first Yankee game I ever saw in color—that game I went to in person. I was so amazed at how lifelike the players were.

In 1994 the White Sox recalled Michael Jordan from Double-A Birmingham to play against the Cubs in the **MAYOR'S TROPHY GAME at Wrigley Field. Jordan singled and doubled against the Cubs.*

The Yankee uniforms were so white and crisp. The Mets with their road uniforms—the road grays. Looking in the dugout and seeing Casey Stengel—live and in person—that was him! He was right there . . . in the same place as me. I just couldn't get over it. It was a great experience. I was a kid so by the time the game was over, I was exhausted. I probably slept all the way home. Somewhere in my attic, I still have that scorecard. I used to keep all that stuff when I was a kid.

When I first went to those Yankee games, my father used to take me. I went to work with him in the summer two or three times a year, and we'd go from there to the Yankee game at night. I just couldn't wait for the day to end so we could go to the game. Then, when I got a little older, I was able to go with friends. As the years went by, I now go with my son. I have my whole life invested in that ballpark. I know a lot of people are in the same situation. It's like, "Oh my God. Now, they're going to be ripping that place down."

> . . . the old park has all the memories. It won't be quite the same.

I still go to games. I have a Friday night plan so I go to twelve to thirteen games a year on Friday nights, usually with my son. I know the problems with the ballpark, and I have to say I'll be as excited as anybody going into the new place for the first time because I'm sure it's going to be far more comfortable, easier to get in and out, better food—I'm sure everything about it will be better from the fan experience.

But, of course, the old park has all the memories. It won't be quite the same. The old park is the place I went with my dad. It's the place I saw my first game. It's the place I took my kids to their first game. You can't replace that. So . . . good idea . . . bad idea—it's hard to say. I guess that's progress and times have to move on. It will be a very sad day when they take the wrecking ball to that place.

That's a good way to look at it because if I have grandchildren and they go to their first game at the new Yankee Stadium—when they get older, to them, that's the place they'll have their memories. I guess it's all relative, as far as memories go. I'll be sad, but I guess there will be other people building new memories with their kids. Time marches on, unfortunately.

I was born in '55 so I don't remember the Brooklyn Dodgers or **NEW YORK GIANTS*** so much. I was always a Yankee fan. I started really following baseball in '64, and I remember it because Mel Stottlemyre had just come up to the Yankees that summer. Maybe that's why I became a Yankee fan because everybody was talking about them so I started watching them on TV. I remember when the Dodgers used to come into Shea Stadium and play the Mets. That was a big deal. To me, at that time, the Brooklyn Dodgers might as well have been in the prehistoric times. I didn't remember them at all. I look back on it and I think to myself, "Oh, wow, 1965 or so was only seven or eight years since the Dodgers left Brooklyn. The Dodgers would come to Shea Stadium and the Mets would sell out, and the city would be in an uproar—THE DODGERS ARE COMING TO TOWN! The Mets were so bad, and the Dodgers were so good—for the Mets to beat them was almost like time to have a parade.

I just bought for my den, from a sports memorabilia shop, a picture that was taken in the Yankee clubhouse after Game 6 of the '64 World Series. It's a picture of Maris, Mantle, and Joe Pepitone. Pepitone hit a grand slam in that game and the Yankees won to force a Game 7. It's the three of them in the clubhouse in their Yankee uniforms, with their arms around each other, with the most effusive smiles and faces of joy that you have ever seen. The reason I like this picture—Pepitone signed it, but that's beside the point—is that to me it was the last happy moment of the old

---

*In 1952 the New York Yankees, an NFL team, moved to Dallas and were called the Texans. They scored their first touchdown in Texas after **NEW YORK GIANT** punt returner Tom Landry fumbled at his own 22-yard line. Do not confuse this team with Lamar Hunt's AFL Dallas Texans who later became the Kansas City Chiefs.

Yankee dynasty. They lost Game 7 so that was certainly not a happy day.

Then, that was it. After '64, it was a dark period for the Yankees. Those were the years I started watching the team so that Game 6 clubhouse picture was the end. It was the final moment of joy. I bought that because it really struck a cord with me. There was something about that particular World Series.

At the 1968 Old Timers Day, the Yankees played the Twins in a regular game. That was Mantle's last season, and in that regular game, batting right-handed, he hit two solo home runs—one in the first and one in the ninth—off Jim Merritt, who was a left-handed pitcher with the Twins. Those were the only two Yankee runs—they lost 3-2. It's one of the great thrills to me to think back and say, "Wow, I was at a game where Mantle hit two home runs." I've never missed an Old Timers Day since. I've been to every one since 1968. I've often wondered if anyone else has been to forty straight Old Timers games. It's like I'm an old-timer myself now.

> I've never missed an Old Timers Day since. I've been to every one since 1968. I've often wondered if anyone else has been to forty straight Old Timers games.

The reason I remember those home runs—the inning he hit them in and the pitcher he hit them off of—Old Timers Day drew a big crowd, probably 50,000-plus. I was with my father, as he was wont to do, with the Yankees losing—I think it was 3-1 around the eighth inning or so, said, "Why don't we leave to beat the traffic?" I said, "But dad, Mickey's due up in the ninth inning. I want to see the Mick." So, he agreed to stay. Then, Mantle hit the home run, and I was so thrilled that we stayed and I got to see it. The reason I remember that the other run was in the first inning, about a year ago, I stumbled on a Web site called retrosheet.com. You could look up box scores from old games. I started picking out games I'd been to when I was a kid, and I thought of that one. I found it. Looking back and remembering, I thought that was just typical of the Yankees in 1968 that Mantle hits two home runs and it's the only two runs they get. They were one of the worst-hitting teams ever.

I remember one of the Old Timers games from when I was a kid, those first several years I went, they used to have the great Yankees line up on the first base side of the field and they had great opponents who would line up on the other side. Now, it's all Yankees so it's lost something in that regard. The opponents would be guys like **BOB FELLER***, Willie Mays. The thing I remember specifically was one of the last guys introduced every year, for that first few years, was always Roy Campanella. I remember vividly Campanella being wheeled out and the fans giving him a tremendous ovation every year. That was always the highlight for me, and it's something I still remember. It was sad in a way, yet, really touching to see how the fans remembered him.

The Old Timers back then, to me, were real old-timers. I had never seen most of them play—I had just read about them. It was exciting to me to see them come out in their old uniforms. Now, fortunately or unfortunately, when I go to the Old Timers games, 99 percent of the guys are guys I saw play . . . in fact, most of them I saw when they were rookies. That tells me I've been around a long time.

In one of Mantle's first Old Timers appearances, he hit a home run, batting right-handed. I remember that because he would never bat lefty in the Old Timers game. I think that was because his right knee bothered him too much so he couldn't stride on it. So, he hit a home run into the leftfield seats, which made the fans go wild.

When you are passionate about something, you naturally tend to remember all this more. I will say I'm pretty good with math even

*Between his junior and senior years at Van Meter (Iowa) High School, **BOB FELLER** struck out 15 St. Louis Browns in a regular season game. Two years earlier, Feller's catcher in American Legion ball was Nile Kinnick, the 1939 Heisman Trophy winner.

though I don't use it as part of my job. I've always been good with numbers, and I know it's because of baseball statistics—stats when I was a kid, just being able to do numbers in my head and percentages and things like that.

I don't remember a lot from those two-inning Old Timers games that the guys play. Elston Howard hit a home run one time—not over the fence—he ran around the bases. One of the Old Timers games was the year the Yankees announced that Billy Martin was going to come back as manager. That was a stunner. Remember he had been fired about a week before. Here we are at Old Timers Day, and people were bringing in Billy Martin banners, WE LOVE BILLY. The ushers were confiscating them. I was beside myself, thinking, "Who do they think they are? Why can't people have banners about Billy Martin?" Wouldn't you know, they make this announcement at the end of Old Timers Day. Talk about a shocking thing. Everybody was stunned—just absolutely stunned.

> It was Chuck, the landlord's son. He said, "Did you hear about Thurman Munson?" My first thought was he was traded.

I'm pretty sure they also retired Casey Stengel's number on Old Timers Day way back—the '70s maybe. The Guy Lombardo band was playing before the game. Then, they called Casey Stengel over and presented him with his uniform. He was on the "outs" with the Yankees because he was bitter about the way he had been fired. But, he was very touched, and he made a speech, to the effect that "Now that they've given me my uniform, I'm gonna die in it," or something to that effect. It was really pretty touching.

In 1979, I was working at a local cable system in New Jersey. I was driving home. I guess I didn't have the radio on so I was oblivious at that point. I came into our apartment—I'd been married about a year. We rented an apartment in a house, and the landlord lived downstairs. The landlord had a son, who was a couple of years younger than me, who used to come up and talk to me all the time. I walked up the stairs to our rooftop apartment and before I got in the door, I heard somebody running up the steps behind me. It was Chuck, the landlord's son. He said, "Did you hear about Thurman Munson?" My first thought was he was traded. Nobody remembers this, but there were rumors at the time that he wanted to end his career with Cleveland, his home. He was slowing down. He wasn't going to be catching much longer. He was already playing some other positions. I could be mistaken but I think his last game with the Yankees might have been at first base. He was starting to transition away from catching and it was clear that his best days were over. So, thinking he'd been traded, I said, "No, no, I didn't hear it. What's up?"

> "We can go out on the field before the game. I've got the press pass. You can be my assistant."

Chuck said, "He was killed." I thought he was making it up. I thought, "There's no way. What do you mean he was killed?" He told me he'd been in an airplane crash. I went inside and turned on the TV, and, sure enough, it was on all the channels. It was shocking. The thing was, a few days later they called up a guy from Triple-A by the name of Brad Gulden to take Munson's roster spot.

At the cable system I worked with, one of the guys used to do a local news show. Somehow he finagled his way into getting a press pass for the season to Yankee games. He asked me if I wanted to go to the game with him. This was a few nights after Munson was killed. He said, "We can go out on the field before the game. I've got the press pass. You can be my assistant." I said, "OK, let's do that." Also, security wasn't what it is today. They gave press passes to anybody. We went in, and we went on the field. We went into the Yankee dugout before the game. My friend brought a cassette recorder and we interviewed Brad Gulden. We didn't have any use for the tape. It was just a pretense for being there. We talked about his coming up to the Yankees and how it felt under the circumstances. We spent about ten minutes talking. He was just a kid, and, at the end, he said, "Where's this going to run?" He was all excited. Bob, my friend, hemmed and hawed and said, "We do freelance for radio stations and so it will probably air on some of the local stations in New York." Unfortunately I don't still have that tape.

There was a real pall around the Stadium that night. You got the feeling that the players and, even to some extent, the fans, were going through the motions for a while. . . .

Now, what the Yankee fans did to **A-ROD*** is what they did to Maris. After Maris hit 61 home runs, he could never do enough. The guy was a terrific, all-around player. He was a great right fielder. He hit a lot of home runs, but they ran him out of town— he could never do enough. And, it's the same with A-Rod. . . .

If the Yankees don't make the postseason this year, that's OK. Again, I draw upon my experience from when I was a kid, and the Yankees were so bad, the highlight of my season was watching the All-Star game and seeing Bobby Murcer or Mel Stottlemyre and hearing Curt Gowdy talk about these guys and how good they were. I would be in awe that the whole country was listening to this—about Bobby Murcer and what a good season he's having— that was a highlight because that was how bad the Yankees were. I think back to that, and I don't want to be spoiled. I don't want to be a spoiled Yankee fan. You can't do it every year. I mean, come on! If they don't do it, that's OK. I'm not jumping ship, believe me.

Between seasons, when I was a kid, the Yankees used to make an occasional trade. When they would make a trade for a new position player, I would take out a piece of paper and start doodling what I thought the starting lineup would be—the batting order. I would look at it and say, "Oh, my God. They're really gonna be good this year. Really good. They've got Rich McKinney playing third base. . . ." I used to delude myself. "There's no out in that lineup, no sir, not with Jerry Kenny leading off. Whoa! Horace Clarke will protect him for sure. Steve Whitaker looks like he's going to be a big power hitter, so . . . things are looking good."

*Bill Gates makes more money in a week than **A-ROD** makes in a year.

I have such great memories of going to games with my dad when I was a kid. The starting time of those night games back then was eight o'clock. They could play a game in two hours and fifteen minutes, not four hours, like now. I'd go to work with my father to his office in the summer. He'd give me some odd things to do around the office. By noon, we'd go to lunch and then I had nothing to do the rest of the day. All I did was look at that clock. They used to open the gates at six, two hours before the game. I would make him take me to be there to be waiting outside when they would roll up those metal gates. We'd be two of the first people in the park. I wanted to be there for batting practice so I could get autographs. I've got to say, looking back, my father was so patient and so nice to me to do that because he would sit there for two hours—two hours, from six to eight—with nothing to do while I was down by the rail getting autographs. He was a Yankee fan, but not a rabid fan like I was. He's seventy-eight years old now. His office was in Manhattan on the west side. He owned his own company making printing ink.

> "Where did you get that?" He said, "I gave the usher $10 and he took it in the clubhouse for me."

One time I remember I was down by the rails for an hour and a half trying to get autographs on my scorecard. I got back to the seat and my father had an autographed baseball with a bunch of Yankee signatures on it. These are the Yankees of the '60s. I said, "Where did you get that?" He said, "I gave the usher $10 and he took it in the clubhouse for me." You could do that then. First of all, there were no fans there. There may have been nine kids by the dugout. I remember I was shocked. I still have the ball.

Standing there by the dugout trying to get those autographs, the two nicest guys I could ever remember, and there were probably others, were both on the Orioles—Elrod Hendricks who later played for the Yankees—what a nice guy. He signed and talked to me and other kids. The other was Brooks Robinson. I was by the Oriole dugout and went down just before or just after the

"National Anthem," so we're talking about game time. He could have easily blown me off at that moment when the game was about to start, but he signed it. I really appreciated it.

There were a lot of guys who would not make eye contact and would walk past you. I was at a Yankee-Braves game, an interleague game several years back, and my younger son was probably eleven or twelve. We got there early and were in the leftfield stands watching batting practice. My son was hoping to catch a home run ball or something. **GREG MADDUX*** came walking by in the outfield. He was doing his running and was throwing a little bit. He came by and he had a baseball. All the kids were yelling for him to throw them the ball. He tossed it into the stands, and my son caught it. I was standing ten or fifteen rows back. My son came bounding up the steps, and he was literally jumping up and down that he had caught this ball from Greg Maddux. He still has that ball. It's just a baseball. It's not signed. But he knows it's from Greg Maddux. If he lives to be one hundred, he will never forget Greg Maddux flipping him that baseball. To Greg Maddux, it was just a throwaway moment, but my son—he'll remember it forever. I wish these guys would all realize the kind of impact they could have just by saying hello to a kid or signing an autograph or throwing them a baseball or something. These kids never forget it—they remember it forever.

I hate saying it only because I feel like one of those old-timers who I remember when I was a kid. They would be saying, "When I was a boy . . ." or "Ballplayers today are not what they used to be." I try not to say that, particularly around my son, because I don't want to sound like one of those crotchety old guys who think it was better in the old days . . . even though I know it was.

---

*In September of 1986, **GREG MADDUX** made his debut with the Cubs as a pinch-runner in the 17th inning . . . In 1989 Ron Darling won the N.L. Pitcher's Gold Glove. Maddux won the next 13.

IF YOU'RE LUCKY ENOUGH TO BE A YANKEE FAN, YOU'RE LUCKY ENOUGH!

Matthew Donnelly (left) and his father, Jerry Donnelly (right)

Matthew Donnelly

Matthew Donnelly is a travel agent for goods, not people. He works with Eagle Transport Services and is also a history teacher at St. John's University where he teaches the History of New York City, and yes, his curriculum does include the New York Yankees' place in the History of the City of New York. Donnelly, 43, graduated from St. John's, grew up in New Hyde Park, and now lives in Great Neck, Long Island.

T o me, Opening Day in baseball was and always will be like Christmas. There's so much excitement, so much anticipation, so much to look forward to. It's the greatest in the world—whether your team finished the previous season in first place or last place, everyone is optimistic and looking forward to Opening Day.

I don't like the Yankees moving to a new stadium. To me, Yankee Stadium is home. It's like hearing that one of your grandparents doesn't have much time left, and you want to spend as much time with them as you can now and appreciate them before they're gone. That's the way I look at Yankee Stadium. I'll miss it tremendously when it's gone. I don't think they're going to recapture the same mystique, the same historical character in a new Yankee Stadium—it's just not going to work.

Probably one of my greatest regrets, when it comes to sports in New York, would be missing the Yankees in the old Yankee Stadium. Seeing the famed short porch in right field, and the original Death Valley in left-center and just missing the old copper facade they had that was ringing the Stadium. That's something I missed. It's just unfortunate. I remember the last sporting event at the old Yankee Stadium, December, 1973, the New York **GIANTS*** were playing football in the snow. That was how it closed down. . . .

After going to Yankee games at Shea, in the mid-'70s—then suddenly the games were back at Yankee Stadium—and the first thing I noticed was how much closer the Yankee seats were as opposed to Shea Stadium. I'd been to many Jet games as a child with my dad at Shea, and the field-level seats are on a track, and they move them so they can be better acclimated for football. In baseball, you have a whole bunch of foul territory on the first- and third-base sides. This was

> At Shea, you feel like you're not part of the game, you're so far away from the action.

before they added the additional seats in subsequent years. At Shea, you feel like you're not part of the game, you're so far away from the action. The higher you go to the loge, the mezzanine and then to the upper deck, you're even further away so your view is very long range. At Yankee Stadium, even in the upper deck, you're right on top of the action. You see the game better. You're part of the game. The players can sense the fans being so close and being part of the game. . . .

One game, I saw an unassisted triple play by Randy Velarde, Memorial Day, 2000. The Yankees had runners at first and second. Velarde was playing second base for Oakland. No outs. Joe Torre decided to hit and run to stay out of a double play. As the runners took off, a line drive was hit right in the vicinity of second base on the first-base side. Velarde was going over to cover the bag and caught the ball on the fly, tagged out the Yankee runner running to second and stepped on the bag. I remember all the fans looking around, "What was that?" You look up at the scoreboard, the "Outs" went "0" to "1" to "2" to "3"

*In 1978 Bill Parcells was head coach at the Air Force Academy. His record was 3-8.

and to "0" again, as all the players ran off the field . . . as if nothing happened! I'll never forget that. The fans, all at the same time, were awestruck and dumbstruck. Everything got quiet. It happened so quick, "What the heck just happened?" Nobody realized what had happened, and then I realized that was an unassisted triple play. Randy Velarde had been a Yankee previously in '96, and then he came back again in 2001. We were sitting in the upper boxes in the upper deck closer to the balcony looking over. It happened right in front of us. It was just like bang—bang—bang—done! I remember Randy Velarde just jogging off the field, as if nothing happened. Most ballplayers, when they do something great, it's like, "Aw! I do this all the time. No big deal." . . .

Game 1 of the 2000 World Series—the Subway Series—Mets versus Yankees went to extra innings. Mike Stanton was pitching for the Yankees. There was a guy standing behind me yelling before every pitch, "Seeds, Mike, throw seeds." I thought this guy was crazy . . . but, every time he'd say that, it'd be a called strike or a swinging strike. All of a sudden, *everybody* started saying, "Seeds, Mike, throw seeds. Throw seeds." Like a seed from an orange—so small you can't hit it. Stanton pitched beautifully in relief and the Yankees won.

Also, that night, there was a guy in front of us who'd had enough beer for maybe ten people. He wanted everyone to spit in his hat for good luck. We all did, and he put it on his head, and he wore it. He said that was his version of the Yankee Rally Cap.

One Friday night against Baltimore, this guy jumped out from the upper deck right onto the screen behind home plate. All of a sudden, he jumped and he's just laying there. I saw him just as he hit the screen and said, "What was that?" I thought maybe a jacket or something had fallen. People were not paying attention to him until he hit. Play hadn't stopped. Suddenly, people started standing up and looking and pointing their fingers. The guy wasn't moving. Logically, he might have broken his neck or he could be dead. At that point, the home-plate umpire turned around and looked up, and he motioned all the players off the field, thinking this was a really serious accident. The guy must have passed out, and, all of a sudden, he comes to. The people applaud like, "OK, he's OK." Then he starts doing some kind of weird dance like he's the San Diego Chicken. Then the people start booing. He starts crawling back to the upper deck where the NYPD, New York's Finest, are waiting for him and quickly hustle him off. I remember shaking my head and saying, "Only in New York."

The Yankees are the *team* I root for. I emphasize "team"—I root for all the guys. I root for them as individuals, and I root for them as a team. I think George Will probably described it best when he said, "It's the background music to my life." It's going on as I'm living my life, as I'm doing so many other things—my career, raising my family— it's more than just a hobby, it's a passion. I never miss a box score in the newspaper. I never miss reading about them. I try to catch them on TV and radio when I can. Of course, I go to the games, but, it's more than just going to a ball game. It's a chance

> ... it's more than just going to a ball game. It's a chance to spend time with my dad. And, a place to have a good time! I never leave the ballpark unhappy.

to spend time with my dad. And, a place to have a good time! I never leave the ballpark unhappy. Whether they win or lose, I'm still happy to be there and experience the game. Leaving the ball-park, I can always find something to recall fondly.

Oddly enough—talk about strange occurrences in Yankee Stadium—people go to the games and some are there for the baseball, and some are there just to make trouble. On Opening Day, 1999, there were two drunk guys fighting in the back of the bleachers—they didn't serve beer in the bleachers anymore, so these guys must have either snuck beers in or they got ham-mered before they came. The police officers were running over to break it up. One guy swung wildly, probably not realizing the guy he was fighting with was already in the grasp of the police. He missed the guy he was swinging at, and he caught a police officer right in the face. I remember the police hauling him off—God only knows what was going to happen to him after that. Everybody was laughing about that. There was a police officer who had been standing in front of me who came back down to his post. I looked at him and go, "What the heck was that?" He shook his head and said, "Unbelievable."

You always hear about fights and everybody in the Stadium turns and looks and you always see the police running up, but I've never seen a fight really near me.

In August of 1999, one guy in the upper deck must have had money to burn or maybe he was told he didn't have long to live—he was buying the entire tubful of stock that vendors walk around with and just throwing them up to people in his section in the stands. The place was going wild. He was a big burly guy. He looked like a professional wrestler. He did it the second time, and the place was going wild. People were going crazy—clapping, cheering, screaming. Just throwing the boxes everywhere. After the third time, I saw a cop go up to him and motioning as if to say, "Look. You can't do that. Stop it. Stop it." They were probably afraid people would get hurt or riot to get to these free boxes of popcorn and peanuts. . . .

> She had covered her poncho with World Series tickets from Yankees games from the '90s, from '81, from the '70s, from the '60s, the '50s, and the '40s. It was the most amazing thing I've ever seen.

In the 2001 World Series, I went to Game 5 the night Scott Brosius hit the two-out, two-strike home run off Byung Hyun Kim of the Diamondbacks to tie the game. It landed about 10 feet from where I was sitting. As Brosius came to the plate—he'd be the last out of the game, I was thinking, "Well, you know what. It's been a pretty good Series, and we're about to go down three games to two, but we'll win it back in Arizona." All of a sudden, he swings his bat—I hear the crack of the bat. All I see is the ball, against the black of the night, coming right at me. I'm like, "This can't be happening!" It tailed off a little to the left of me, and some college kid with long hair and a goatee caught the ball. Pete Gammons, from ESPN, was looking over at him and giving him the thumbs-up and a big smile from the ESPN platform they had constructed right behind us for the World Series in 2001.

Prior to the game that night, there was an elderly woman walking around wearing what appeared to be a black poncho, but it was stiff. She had covered her poncho with World Series tickets from Yankees games from the '90s, from '81, from the '70s, from the '60s, the '50s, and the '40s. It was the most amazing thing I've ever seen. She was walking around, and people were looking at her just awestruck. They were safety-pinned onto the poncho, all in perfect neat rows surrounding it. They were tickets like they had just been torn coming through the turnstiles. I've seen her subsequent years—the 2003 World Series as well. She's an institution at Yankee Stadium. She wears the same thing—I guess she's superstitious as well. . . .

I was at Yankee Stadium in 2001 for Game 5 against Seattle in the ALCS. My dad and I were in a huge traffic jam trying to get to the ballpark. The NYPD and the state police had closed off four of the parking garages. There must have been some threat. We were told to park anywhere we wanted in the Bronx. Park on the sidewalk . . . park anywhere. If you can find a space, park there. We parked in a small park that had swings and benches just off the Grand Concourse. We walked about fifteen minutes to Yankee Stadium. People were parked on the sidewalks, in parks, in the middle of the Grand Concourse—industrial areas, everywhere.

It was so different that night because of what had happened September 11. This was something that made New Yorkers feel good about themselves once again. That night, this sent chills up my spine. These two guys were walking around the upper deck with a banner that said, "Remember the Towers!" It was like a big screen—like a silver screen—just two big cut-outs where what would have been the Twin Towers. As they would walk by, people would get very quiet and nod their heads, yes, as if in agreement.

My dad and I went to a Yankee game after MLB had resumed playing in September 2001, and we brought our American flag with us to the game. We were standing in the upper deck right behind home plate. In the middle of the seventh inning, they played "God Bless America," and my dad and I were holding up our flag, which was 5-by-8 feet. As we were holding it, they showed us on the Diamond Vision. I saw that we were on the Diamond Vision and I gave a thumbs-up. Everyone starts applauding. I look around wondering what they were applauding—what was going on? My dad said, "I think they're applauding you giving the thumbs up." I do a thumbs-up again, and they start clapping again. I'll never forget that.

> . . . I will share my love of baseball and the New York Yankees with my children with all of my heart and soul.

Every game I go to, I always see the vendor selling peanuts. The brand of peanuts sold at all Yankee home games is Bazzini. I'm a big fan of the movie, *The Godfather*, where Don Corleone, played by Marlon Brando, at one point, says, "I should have known it was Bazzini all along." The first time I see a vendor with "Bazzini" spelled out in huge red letters on his box, I look at my dad and point to the box and always say, "I should have known it was Bazzini all along." My dad always waits for me to do it every time we go to the game, and we always have a good laugh from it. It's for Yankee fans and our superstitions.

I consider every child the greatest blessing in the world from God. We're expecting our second child later this year. If we have a boy, great. If we have a girl, great. Whatever my wife and I have, a second daughter or our first son, I will share my love of baseball and the New York Yankees with my children with all of my heart and soul. Lots of my friends have daughters, and they have passion for the games just like their dads. The apple doesn't fall far from the tree whether it's a son or a daughter. I know my children will have that same passion, too.

1964: THE YEAR THE CARDINALS CHASED THE PHILLIES . . . UNTIL THE PHILLIES CAUGHT THEM

Bob Curto

Bob Curto grew up in Scarsdale, New York, and graduated from Iona Prep. He now lives in Stanford, Connecticut. He is the associate publisher of magazines for Questex Media, a large publisher in the travel industry. He handles all of the northern hemisphere for Questex.

My first memory of baseball was the 1964 World Series. In Game 7, I was watching as my father and uncle got upset because the Cardinals beat the Yankees. At the time, it meant little to me . . . I was eight years old.

The next year, my dad took me to my first game at the Stadium. I was overwhelmed to walk down the runway into the Stadium and see the expanse of grass come into full view. The sheer size of the Stadium . . . the incredible green of the grass . . . the blue seats . . . the famous facade—all joined together to assault the senses of a nine-year-old boy.

We sat on the third base side. The first time Mickey Mantle came to bat, I sensed something different—the crowd reaction—the way he looked—the whole scene seemed somewhat surreal. Mickey launched one on an impossibly high arc that landed deep in the right field bleachers. From our seats, we had a perfect view of the trajectory the ball took as it left his bat. I was mesmerized by the fact that any human being could hit a ball *that far* and *that high*. As the crowd cheered, I stood on my seat and watched as this bigger-than-life figure made his way around the bases . . . head down, elbows bent.

> Baseball is so much more than a game. It is woven into the fabric of this great country and helps bind fathers and sons in a way no other sport can.

I determined Mickey Mantle was the greatest human being who ever lived . . . never mind the greatest ballplayer of all time. I was hooked! Remember, that was 1965, just after the Yankees won their last pennant before embarking on twelve long years of mediocrity. That didn't matter. I was indoctrinated into the fold and, to this day, live and die with the boys in pinstripes.

My sons, Ryan, Brandon, and Cameron, are carrying on this tradition. I took great pleasure in seeing the look of awe on their faces when I took them to their first games at the big ballpark. Baseball is so much more than a game. It is woven into the fabric of this great country and helps bind fathers and sons in a way no other sport can. Some of our best family times have come when we're cheering together, along with my wife, Martine, a converted Met fan, for our beloved Yankees.

In 1995, I worked for a major publishing company. Joe Torre was manager of the St. Louis Cardinals, and he was good friends with our senior vice president. At an awards dinner at the end of our sales meeting, Joe Torre, Jose Cardenal, Lou Brock, Red Schoendienst, and Bob Gibson appeared. This was quite a treat for all of us who were baseball fans. They were giving mementoes to some in the group, and, Joe Torre grabbed the mike from our VP and says, "We're not done yet. Would Bob Curto come to the stage?" I was totally shocked and found out later it had been set up by our VP who knew I was a baseball junkie. I go onto the stage . . . they all crowded around and gave ME things to sign for THEM! I told Bob Gibson I was upset with him, and he looked at me like I was crazy. I explained that since he had won Game 7 of the '64 World Series against the Yankees, I could *never* forgive him. We all laughed about that. Then Joe Torre asked if I were right- or left-handed. He gave me a bat they all had autographed and said,

"Stand over there because Bob Gibson is going to pitch to you."
Bob Gibson pitch to me!

Bob Gibson lobbed one in, Joe caught it, and I made believe I was actually going to swing. As the ball went by, I said, "Hey, Bob, if that was in a game, I would have taken it downtown." He glared back, with a smile on his face, and said, "If that was in a game, you wouldn't have gotten that pitch—you would have gotten one here," and he pointed to a spot just below his ear!

When the Yankees fired Buck Showalter and announced Joe Torre would be the manager, I was dismayed. One of our VPs heard me say what a bad decision that would turn out to be. A couple of hours later, my phone rang and this VP requested I come to his office immediately. I was a little nervous when I got to his office because he said, "Come in and close the door." Then, he turned to his speakerphone and said, "He's here." A voice said, "Is that you, Curto?" I recognized the voice and said, "Is that Joe Torre?" Joe replied, "No . . . it's Buck Showalter!" We had a good laugh, but I have to admit I felt a little embarrassed.

Later that year, Joe invited four of us to the Stadium where we went out onto the field for batting practice, got to go into the dugout and clubhouse and even into his office before the game. He gave my wife and me tickets to Games 2 and 6 of the 1996 World Series. He is a great, genuine person, *and I never missed Buck Showalter after all!*

> I recognized the voice and said, "Is that Joe Torre?" Joe replied, "No . . . it's Buck Showalter!"

I'm such a huge Yankee fan. I always have confidence the team will ultimately prevail . . . and, in fact, it's always a surprise when they don't. I guess our fans are spoiled by the embarrassment of riches the Yankees have created.

Glen, my brother-in-law, is a huge Mets fan, who absolutely hates the Yankees. This makes for a lot of good-natured fun between us. During the '96 World Series against the Braves, we made a bet—if the Yankees won, he would have to take me to a Yankee game of my choice in 1997, dress in full Yankee regalia from top to bottom and openly and sincerely root for the Yankees against whatever team they were playing. By contrast, if the Yanks lost, I would have to do the same for him with the Mets. The Yankees, of course, didn't let me down. They won a thrilling series against Atlanta in six games.

During the off-season, it was announced that, beginning in 1997, for the first time ever, there would be interleague play! Since I was able to pick out any game I wanted for Glen to pay off his debt, I thought it had to be the first Yankee-Met regular-season game! He was miserable as we sat in Yankee Stadium, dressed in Yankee hat, shirt, shorts, socks—even a Yankee keychain holding his car keys—with his beloved Mets out on the field. He had to root for the Yankees the whole game. What made it even funnier for me was the fact that the Mets WON the game 6–0 . . . and, he couldn't enjoy it at all. Immediately after the last out, he took off the hat, shirt and shorts—fortunately he had on another pair underneath the Yankee ones—threw them at me and walked out of the Stadium bare-chested.

That was the only time I remember laughing at the conclusion of a Yankee loss!

What's the definition of Gross Sports Ignorance? 144 Mets fans.

WHERE THE PAST IS PRESENT

Gary Barcia

Gary Barcia has been a Brooklyn resident his entire life. After graduating from LIU he taught elementary school for years. He now runs Yore Meat Market in Brooklyn.

My father was a great Yankee fan. He was born in 1908 in the Bronx, where he grew up with Yankee Stadium. When I came along in '52, the Yankees were on top of their game. As soon as I was old enough to walk, Dad would take me to one or two games a year, always a doubleheader.

Throughout the baseball season my father would tell baseball stories about the great Yankees, and each story included an ending with a new tale about **BABE RUTH***. As he grew older, my dad became prouder of the stories about the Babe and, with age, he knew that fewer people were living who saw the great Bambino play.

When he was eighty years old my wife and I gave him a plate that pictured the Babe at bat, silhouetted against the screaming fans at the Stadium. His number 3, the pinstripes, his large bat, the crowd, all trying to capture a moment in time that told a story about the Babe. My father loved the plate and hung it in the kitchen, where he spent most of his time after he retired.

My father's mind and memory began to slip a little by the time he became eighty-three or eighty-four. One summer day I went over

*BABE RUTH was the first player ever to hit 30 home runs in one season, the first to hit 40 in one season and the first to hit 50 in one season . . . and he accomplished those feats in the same season.

my parents' house to visit and found him in the kitchen standing in front of the plate.

"What are you doing Dad?" I asked him.

"You know, I might be one of the people in that crowd. I'm looking at the faces; I think I'm in there."

> . . . All I saw was Babe Ruth's picture on the big screen. I had to look away because my eyes filled with tears and I didn't want my wife and girls to see my face.

I laughed at the time. I honestly thought he was just kidding with me, but a couple of months later I found him in the kitchen again staring at the plate. "What are you looking at?" I asked, startling him. Again he told me how he was looking for himself in the crowd. This time I didn't laugh. I did not want to intrude on his belief that maybe he was at the Stadium that day. I found him two or three more times before he died, at the age of eighty-six, looking at the plate.

The day he passed away, which was the same week Mickey Mantle left us, I was at his house gathering some papers and clothes to take to the funeral parlor. I remembered the Babe Ruth plate. I wanted him buried with the plate. I know it was silly, and I guess it would have been a nice memory for me to have, but I also felt that of all his earthly possessions, this was his most cherished and he needed to have it.

Three years later, on May 17, 1998, I took my children to a Yankee game. Now there are no more "two for the price of one" days at the Stadium. They have been replaced with "giveaway" days. This was Beanie Baby Day, the last time my three daughters were all able to get their gift (My oldest girl turned 15 in June).

Pitching for the Yankees was David Wells, who is a Babe Ruth fanatic. He is a great collector of Ruth memorabilia. He wore the number 33 in honor of Babe's retired number, 3. He also went as far as to try to wear an original Babe Ruth cap while pitching at the Stadium.

The only seats available were upper deck, but we were happy just to be in the ballpark. As the game progressed, Wells was perfect. "Perfect" not being just a figure of speech: He was pitching a **PERFECT GAME***. Every inning, three up and three down. The crowd, the excitement, the heart pounding—all things that as a baseball fan, you only dream about or hear stories about. The amazing thing about this game was, it is my dream come true and my story to tell.

While David Wells was warming up to pitch the ninth and last inning, I glanced up at the large scoreboard at Yankee Stadium. There was some kind of advertisement being shown. I really don't know what the commercial was about because all I saw was Babe Ruth's picture on the big screen. I had to look away because my eyes filled with tears and I didn't want my wife and girls to see my face. At that time I knew my father was giving me back the plate he loved.

With two outs, the batter hit a soft fly ball to right field, Babe's position. I never saw the right fielder catch the ball because I looked toward the pitching mound and David Wells. I could see his number, 33, the pinstripes, and the crowd along the first base line. My eyes did not focus on the silhouette of David Wells, but on the faces in the crowd. I just knew that if I looked hard enough I would be able to see my father among those cheering fans.

I am not overly religious or superstitious, but sometimes in my life I just have to scratch my head and say, "Thanks Dad."

*In 1995 while pitching for the Expos, Pedro Martinez pitched nine perfect innings versus the Padres. In the 10th inning Bip Roberts, of San Diego, doubled. Martinez was the winning pitcher, but did not get credit for the **PERFECT GAME** or the no-hitter.

FANECDOTES

I lived and breathed and died with the Yankees—mostly died—because they were terrible from '65 through '70. They were just awful. I was a kid and every game meant so much to me. That's why I remember, on those rare occasions when something great, or exciting, happened. It's just so vivid in my memory. Here again, one game, **1966***, the Yankees were playing a double-header against the Orioles. In '66, the Yankees finished last! The Orioles ended up going on to win the World Series—so a big disparity in the teams. For the Yankees to even beat the Orioles in the game was the highlight of the season. I remember watching in the first game of the doubleheader, bottom of the ninth, Yankees are down by three runs, and Roy White was up. He was batting left. Remember Yankee Stadium had the short porch back then. He launched a fly ball to right field with the bases loaded and two outs. Frank Robinson was playing right field for the Orioles, and he goes back. The wall was only 3 or 4 feet high. Right fielders fell over into the seats all the time. Robinson goes back and times his jump. He and the ball disappear into the stands at the same time. No one knows if he caught the ball—if he didn't catch it—if the Yankees win—is the game over? No one knew. The umpire goes running out to right field and after about fifteen seconds or so, Robinson emerges from the stands with the ball in his glove. The umpire calls Roy White out, game over, Orioles win. Ralph Houk comes out of the dugout going berserk. Kicking dirt. Throwing a tantrum. How do you know he caught it? He could have picked it up off the ground.

Now, flash forward to the early 1980s, I was doing PR for the USA Network. We had a weekly show called *Sports Pro,* modeled after *Meet the Press.* We'd have one sports personality as the guest

---

**Sports Illustrated* rated New York City in <u>1966</u> as the worst time and place to be a sports fan. The Yankees, Knicks and Rangers finished last, the Mets escaped last place for the first time and the Giants were 1–12–1. The best time and place to be a sports fan?: Philadelphia, 1980.

---

and three journalists on the panel. The show was hosted by Larry Merchant. Many times they would talk about controversial subjects. I used to go to the shows and sit in on them when they would tape them a few days before they would air. I would sit in on them to see if there was any news value as a show. If there was, I would call the Associated Press and say so and so said such and such on *Sports Pro* to air Friday on USA Network—to get a little exposure for the show.

This one show I went to for taping—who's the guest? Frank Robinson. I'm thinking, "All right. I know it's him. It's been almost twenty years, but I'm going to find out once and for all if he caught that darn ball." Robinson was getting his makeup put on for the show. He comes out, walking to the set. I said to him, "Excuse me. I have to ask you one question. You're probably not going to remember this, but, in 1966, bases loaded, bottom of the ninth, Yankee Stadium"—and before I said anything else, he said to me, "You want to know if I caught that ball." I said, "Yeah. I really have to know." He said, "Yeah, I caught it." I said, "OK, that settles the record for me." I figured that after twenty years he probably didn't have reason to lie. I felt better. I slept that night because I thought, "Well, we didn't get robbed." Even twenty years later, I just had to know.

—<u>MARK BRAFF</u>, owner, Braff Communications

In my household, the Trinity was comprised of God, my father, the Yankees. It sounds like a joke, but it's pretty much the truth. My father made us a Yankees family.

After going to Yankee Stadium, then going to Shea, it was a lot like going to Macy's . . . then going to Wal-Mart. There's something majestic about Yankee Stadium. Shea Stadium just seems like a postmodern architectural nightmare. Their visuals. Also, I knew all the Yankee players. I listened to the game so going to the Mets was like visiting some very distant relative that you didn't really care about.

> In my household, the Trinity was comprised of God, my father, the Yankees.

I have very mixed emotions about the Yankees moving to a new stadium. I like Yankee Stadium, and I appreciate the fact that it's rather spartan compared to some of the more new-fangled ballparks. In the ten-year span I've been going to games there, the attendance has increased by more than 50 percent. It's gotten to be almost unmanageable, especially in the upper deck. The concourses are so narrow. It takes so long to get in and out of the Stadium and that's so frustrating. I'm not really looking forward to the new stadium because I think, especially where I sit, I'll be further back about 20 to 30 feet from the field. I love the way Yankee Stadium is so steep in terms of the upper deck relative to Shea Stadium, which is much more recessed. You're never going to get a foul ball in the upper deck of Shea Stadium compared to the way they come flying all over you at Yankee Stadium. I worry about the decrease in capacity. It's going to drive prices even more out of control. I think my days of attending ten to fifteen games a year are probably not long for the future.

> The question is, "How high can prices go?"

The question is, "How high can prices go?" I don't know. I do think that, from my own pocketbook, these tickets, that are getting to be above $50 a game, are definitely starting to wear on my wallet, leading me to think, "You know what. I've been to one hundred games at Yankee Stadium. The 101st isn't going to be that much different. Do I really need to go to ten games next year?"

If I owned the Yankees, the one thing I would do is find a way to keep the current stadium viable. I think there is some value to the cachet of Yankee Stadium, and I really wish they could have figured out a way to keep that ballpark rather than building a new one. I think the new one is just going to be a very different experience.

Comparing going to a Salt Lake Trapper game and going to a Yankee game—well, obviously you're going to see a much higher caliber of player at Yankee Stadium. The place has much more history in it. You're not as close to the field. You're spending, exponentially, more money. You just don't get the kind of intimacy that you get from a minor league ballpark. I do like the minor league parks. I've been to the Cyclone Stadium. I've been to Staten Island. I've been to a lot of Salt Lake games. My grandparents lived in Walla Walla, Washington, and I got to see Tony

Gwynn when he was in the rookie leagues there. I'd seen him play basketball in college. San Diego State was in the same conference as the University of Utah. He was an All-Conference point guard then. He still holds the San Diego State career record for assists. When asked why the record has stood for so long, Gwynn said, "Poor recruiting." He was drafted by the hometown Padres and San Diego Clippers on the exact same day. Now, the two drafts are months apart.

—JAY JAFFE, 56, Salt Lake City, founder of www.futilityinfielder.com, one of the oldest baseball blogs

I first remember watching them in 1955 on a small black and white TV my family had. Since my dad was a Yankee fan, that was the game that was on, and I, of course, followed suit rooting for the Yanks and the Mick. Most of our neighbors were from Brooklyn—we were living in St. Albans—and after the World Series ended, they brought over to the house "crying" towels for me. They knew how hard I would be taking the loss. Next year, I happily returned the favor after the Yanks beat the Dodgers. I was just thrilled to bring towels to each of their homes.

The only time I ever seriously cried after a sporting event was after the 1960 World Series. I was sitting in the basement of our home in Rosedale, watching the seventh game against the Pirates. I absolutely could not believe the Yankees lost to Pittsburgh. They had *slaughtered* the Pirates in the games they won—something like 15–3, 10–0. If only Casey had started Whitey in three games instead of two. The Pirates never touched him in the games he pitched. I was so upset after that game, I couldn't even eat supper that night.

My first experience at Yankee Stadium—I was twelve, and I was awestruck of how green the grass was and how beautiful the Stadium was. I also was lucky enough to be at Mickey Mantle Day. I remember him being driven around the field in a golf cart and remember that the people just did not want to stop cheering. The Mick was my first sports hero, and it was so disappointing to see him struggle those last few years he played.

Rooting for the Yankees is just a way of life for me. I have formed my dearest friendships with fellow Yankee fans. Being a Yankee fan is what binds me to so many others. I guess we fans have been spoiled the last decade but, to be honest, I don't get tired of the winning. It just seems natural that the Yankees should be winning. It seems like all is right in the world when that happens. The only thing I cannot figure out is how my son, Craig, came to be a "Mets" fan. Guess I did something wrong when he was growing up. Maybe it was the wrong baby formula. Who knows? What I do know, however, is that I will never stop being a Yankee fan.

—BOB EDELMAN, 55, Merrick, New York

> ... if somebody hit a home run, they'd be banging on the pipes to tell my father, "Ha, ha, we just hit a home run off you."

I was born during leap year, so I'm only fifteen. When I go to Yankee Stadium, and they're giving away things to anybody under the age of sixteen, the people there won't believe me. Even when I show them my driver's license, they won't give me anything.

Six families lived in a six-family house in Brooklyn. There were a couple of different type of fans there so whatever day the Dodgers played the Giants, or the Yankees played the Dodgers, in the World Series, if somebody hit a home run, they'd be banging on the pipes to tell my father, "Ha, ha, we just hit a home run off you." That was a big thing in that house there. We had everybody there—mostly Brooklyn, but my father was the rare one.

The old Yankee Stadium is not even the same hallowed grounds that Babe Ruth played on. When they rebuilt the Stadium in '74, they moved the home plate forward about 20 feet. They raised the turf up for drainage. All there was left was the shell. So they aren't really playing on the turf that Mantle or Babe Ruth played on. I would have loved to have seen them stay at the original Yankee Stadium, but what are you going to do—go back to Shea Stadium? Their stadium is getting old. We live in New York, supposedly the greatest city in the country, and it should have a new stadium.

My basement is a replica of Yankee Stadium. In right field, where I always went to catch baseballs, in my painting, you see my whole family and friends sitting there where the home run

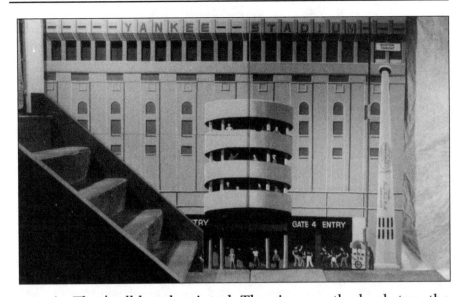

area is. That's all hand-painted. The signs on the backstop, the billboards, are from 1990. It goes from foul pole to foul pole. It's 4 feet high. It goes 8 feet and then around the wall a foot so it's basically 16 by 4. Everything you see: Monument Park, vendors in the stands, people in the stands, complete stats. We're playing Boston, we're winning—Don Mattingly is at bat. The stats that are on the scoreboard—let's say his average was .321 at the time are real stats. Mattingly gave me one of his bats for my room. I also got the same exact baseball glove from Franklin, which I sent down to the dugout and Don signed for me. The room I have is fabulous, but the one mistake I made is I painted the floor. The Yankees allowed me to measure the whole field so I had the whole field measured to scale—the pitching mound, home plate, everything. I took infield dirt, outfield dirt, and some of the grass—I took a baggie of each out with me. They're going to sell that dirt so I've got a fortune worth of dirt here. The colors are all matched exactly, and it's to scale. I went out there with a measureing wheel, and I've got great pictures of my wife and me out there with the wheel. I painted the concrete so when I sold the house, I couldn't take the floor. They still have the field there, but I took the backdrop, which was on billboard board. I rebolted it at the new house. I made the floor, this time, 3/4-inch plywood, 4-by-4 sheets, and put it down like a puzzle so I'm not losing another floor.

—RON FUSCO, 60, South Plainfield, New Jersey

This story is a recurring story that took place time and time again for many years. My father, born and raised in southern Italy, came to this country in the early '60s and is not exactly a sports fan. He doesn't care much for the game of baseball. But his three sons and nephews grew to love the game of baseball. Being the great father he is, on many a Sunday, he would take my brothers Joe and Nick and me and sometimes my mother, as well as cousins to Yankee Stadium. The hour-long journey that would start in Brooklyn and end at the House that Ruth Built, was always the same. My father would arrive at the ticket window and always request the proper amount of seats—with two conditions. One—that they were the best available, and two—that they were in the sun.

> The best part about the scene going on would be when there was some action going on. Dad would peek out from behind his paper and ask "hanno fatto uno punto?"

Being that my father was only making this trip to make his sons and nephews happy, he found it necessary to find some enjoyment for himself. As we would find our seats, the process would begin. He would take off his button-down shirt and place it over the back of his seat . . . open his duffel bag—at that time you could still bring them into the Stadium—pull out his paper and enjoy a late lunch in the sun—at the Stadium so all his sons and nephews could see their baseball heroes. The best part about the scene going on would be when there was some action going on. Dad would peek out from behind his paper and ask "hanno fatto uno punto?" (Did they make a point?) Then, he would return to his paper and radio program. Some people may find that a bit strange but, for my brothers, cousins and especially for myself, I find that to be awesome. Here is a man who took the time out of working two jobs, six to sometimes seven days a week to bring a bunch of kids to baseball Mecca.

Another story revolves around the family journeys. It was 1974 and was my first Yankee game, but it was at Shea. Yankee Stadium was under construction. Sometime after the game had passed, my brother and a friend decided to make their own tape-recorded talk show. I was one of the guests on the show, and the topic of discussion was my first Yankee game. Great! A well-rehearsed three-year-old being questioned about a baseball game, the goodies my father bought us, and then the hard stuff—play-by-play. So, in my three-year-old tongue, I proceed to break down "My Hero," Bobby Murcer's double that scored Jim Mason with the winning run. In an age where we have videos for everything—our children's birth to their college graduation—to have this small piece of audio tape with the cute little voice on it brings a big smile to my face.

It was the '98 ALCS, Game 1, Yankee Stadium—Yankees versus the Indians. I had seats in the right field bleachers, Section 39. Wow! I was still working for Bear Stearns, and one of my coworkers had three seats to the game. I didn't have my seats because my brother was taking his wife so I was out until Game 2. What luck! I was going to see both games and, best of all, Game 1 was going to be "on the arm" [for free] and in the bleachers. The game starts, and they begin with the roll call. That was great being part of it from its originating location—it was so loud. The funniest part of the roll call was when they finished with the fielders, and they start chanting for Wells. Dave stepped off the mound, looked back, and tipped his cap. Dynamite! Here is a guy, locked in on getting his job done, and he realized how important it was to acknowledge the fans. But the best is yet to come.

My friends and I came straight from work—still wearing our suits and ties. The bleachers don't let you get away with that. They start the chant, "Lose the ties, lose the ties." Being the smart guys we were, we made sure they all watched us take the ties off and place them in our pockets. Now the fun begins. They start their ritualistic chant, which picks up at the end of the cowbell song, "Cleveland sucks, Ramirez"—Manny was the right fielder for the Indians at the time—"Sucks, box seats suck, everybody sucks!" Hysterical. We couldn't stop laughing.

Now, the box seat fans take offense to this, not to mention Ramirez—the hell with him—and start retaliating. Of course, they see my friends and I about halfway up right against the rail, next to the ambulatory driveway that separates the box seats from the bleachers, and they start on us because we have our suits on. They start with, "Hey, nice suits, you must be big-shot brokers," and a lot more less desirable comments. We weren't going to take that. We start blasting back and bless those Bleacher Creatures. When they saw we were not the typical suits, they joined in and helped us verbally assault those clowns in the box seats. Now, all that action going on, **MANNY RAMIREZ*** getting completely trashed with a number of profane chants, what could make the night better? Oh yeah, the Yankees won. It was a great time, and I will never forget that night.

—ANTHONY FALCE

In 1979, long before he co-created *Seinfeld,* Larry David called me to go to a Yankees game. He said, "When you get there, don't buy tickets until I show up."

I got there, and the line was very short. I stood for a while, waiting, watching the line grow longer. When he showed, the line was a mile long. I was irate with him, but he said, "Don't worry. I can get right to the front of the line. I don't do it often, but I can act retarded."

Larry wasn't bald yet; he had curly hair that went straight out, a style comedian Freddy Roman referred to as the "Jew-fro." He was wearing round glasses and an old army jacket.

Suddenly he hunched over, changed his walk, and went to the front of the line. Right in front of the ticket booth, the next people to get their tickets were a quartet of couples who put the "yup" in yuppie. Larry lumbered up past this patch of happily chattering, yellow Lacoste sweater-wearers. One of them must have said something because Larry turned around and gave them this look, the strangest mix of stupidity and psychosis. They moved back and started talking among themselves, I guess hoping Larry would buy his tickets and not attack or drool on them.

Larry got the tickets, shot them one more look, and shambled toward the gate. I stood away from him until the last minute, when he slipped me my ticket and we entered the stadium.

—BRANDT VON HOFFMAN, comedian

*MANNY RAMIREZ grew up in the Washington Heights area of New York. His two sons are both named Manny Ramirez, Jr.

Chapter 2

Growin' Up a Yankee

12 Years Old Forever

IF ROGER EBERT WATCHED
THE BRONX IS BURNING,
HE'D CUT OFF BOTH HIS THUMBS!

Joe Petrecca

Joe Petrecca was born and raised in the Bronx and moved to Queens in 1981. Since 1987, he has lived in New Brunswick, New Jersey. In 2004 Petrecca discovered he had non-Hodgkin's lymphoma, the same disease that afflicted Roger Maris.

B eing born and raised in the Bronx, I was a Yankee fan. My dad was not a baseball fan at all. He worked a lot of weekends so we never had very much in the way of conversations about it. I only went to one baseball game with my father—a doubleheader against the Tigers, but he didn't know that—he thought he was taking me to one game. He got good box seats, and we sat out in the sun. He fell asleep in about the third inning of the first game and when he woke up, it was early in the second game. He couldn't believe it. He said, "How long is this game going on?" I had to tell him it was the second game of a doubleheader. I figured I had him there . . . I might as well squeeze two games out of him.

But, I was blessed with having an uncle, still around at ninety-two, who had two daughters and no son of his own. He loved the Yankees so he would take me to Yankee games. He really saved the day for me. I got to see a lot of games and some great ball players as a kid going with him to ball games in the '50s and '60s.

From the time I was six years old till I was fifteen, my uncle and I regularly went to one or two games a week. It would invariably be night games because he worked during the day as a produce guy in a supermarket. At that time, there weren't as many night games as there are now. He would pick me up at my house, and we would drive to the train station and then take the train. I don't know why, but he never wanted to take his car. We would hop on the train and go down to Yankee Stadium on the Woodlawn Line. We'd sit in the bleachers. He didn't spend a lot of money on these tickets—they were typically fifty-cent deals. I didn't mind sitting in the bleachers because I got to stay by the bullpen and watch the bullpen pitchers. Being in the bleachers, I was as close as you could get to Mickey Mantle and that was the whole idea. The infield didn't matter that much to me.

Fly balls—from the bleachers—every one of them looks like a home run. But, they would be pop-ups. In those days, the guys in the bullpen weren't the best pitchers, but some of them were very nice. Ryne Duren was a nice guy, who would talk to the kids. A lot of them would just ignore us. Some of them would take the time to acknowledge you. When you're seven, eight, nine years old, that's

> Fly balls—from the bleachers—every one of them looks like a home run.

great. I didn't autograph hound. Autographs didn't mean anything. Kids today hound players for autographs simply because of their value—for money—not because they idolize the players.

My Uncle Tony now has dementia. A few years ago, I gave him an autographed picture of Charlie Keller. I remembered Uncle Tom telling stories about Keller, about how good he was, how clutch a player he was. It was relatively inexpensive—$40 or something— so I bought one for him. Another time, I went to Yogi Berra's museum and bought him a picture of Yogi and Babe Ruth together, signed by Yogi. I gave him a signed autograph of Joe DiMaggio that I bought, too. He has them on the wall in his living room. Now, he's fairly nonverbal. He says "hello" and "God bless you." That kind of stuff. When I see him and try to talk about the Yankees, I don't know if he gets it or not. He looks at you with a sparkle in his eyes and he goes, "Yeah. Yeah." But, he doesn't say much back.

Every kid, growing up, us Yankee fans would idolize Mickey Mantle. He was like the all-American boy. He was the star player on our team. He was bigger than life—muscular—and he hit those monster home runs. He was the guy we all looked up to. We would get into the typical arguments about who was the best player. Was it Willie Mays? Was it Duke Snider? I was too young for that debate because I don't remember much of Duke Snider. Mickey Mantle was the guy, and he's the guy in New York— always has been. I remember when they booed the heck out of him every time he struck out. He would throw his helmet, and the crowd would boo. He really became an idol to a lot of other people later on, but, for me, as a kid, he was *the* guy. You'd wear No. 7. Standing at bat, you'd mimic the way he swung the bat—those practice swings. You'd stick your finger out on the bat like he did. He had an odd way of holding the bat where his index finger would point out while he was taking his batting swings. I don't know why he did that, but he would, and we would all imitate him when we would play ball. We'd do the exact same thing. He was the guy everybody wanted to be like.

> Mickey Mantle . . . bigger than life— muscular . . .He was the guy we all looked up to.

We imitated other players, too. We had them all down pat—all their idiosyncrasies. Clete Boyer, who just passed away, would get up at bat and had this strange way of batting where he would bend his back leg almost like he was sitting. His front leg would be stiff. We would do the Clete Boyer stance. . . . In fact, we would sit around on the steps in front of somebody's house and take a bat in our hand and we'd do somebody at bat. Yogi Berra would be the guy who would bat left-handed, and he would swing the bat back and forth like an old man as if he couldn't carry the bat—tired. We would do these things. . . . Hector Lopez had a very close stance and would lean forward and hold the bat high over his head, leaning almost like in a crouch over the plate. . . . Bobby Richardson had a strange way of taking practice swings. He would almost stiff-arm when he was taking a practice swing.

When he got to the plate, where he was looking at the mound, his hands would be parallel to the ground. He would tilt his head to the side as he was taking warm-up swings. . . . We would do these guys, and the rest of the kids sitting around would try to guess who it was we were imitating. It was a good time in the summer. . . . Roger Maris was a big guy in the '60s. We'd pull up our sleeves so you could see muscles—he had so many muscles. His biceps were so big they didn't fit in his shirt. You'd pull up your shirt. Roger had a way that when he was doing his practice swings left-handed, he would jerk the bat really hard as it got to the plate . . . We didn't do visiting players—I never really paid that much attention to batting stances of visiting players.

In 1978, I was an adult and was doing an investigation of Harry M. Stevens for the government. Stevens had the vending contract at Yankee Stadium. I was going in there looking at their payroll records and their employment records. While I was there one day, I just happened to park my car and went into the executive offices. This was right after the World Series in '78. Coming out was Ron Guidry with his little daughter. He was dressed regularly, and he's a very small guy. I hadn't realized how thin and frail he was. I met him and talked to him. He was very nice. I had taken some pictures at the parade after the World Series and told him I would send them to him, and he said he would sign them and send them back to me. I went into the Stadium, doing some stuff, and then I walked around in the bowels of the Stadium.

I said to myself, "There's nobody here. It's my one opportunity." So I walk out of the dugout and went out and stood on the pitcher's mound.

I stumbled upon the entrance to the Yankee dugout. I walked up the ramp, went into the dugout and sat there for a while. I looked around, and there wasn't anybody in the Stadium—not a soul. I said to myself, "There's nobody here. It's my one opportunity." So I walk out of the dugout and went out and stood on the pitcher's mound. I wanted to see what it feels like to be on the pitcher's mound at Yankee Stadium. Now, I'm in a suit and tie looking around. It was eerie and scary—in that empty Stadium. I knew I had to do it—I ran around the bases—first, second, third, and home. I said, "Now I know what it feels like to hit a home run at Yankee Stadium." I actually did that, as an adult, at twenty-eight years old! Don't tell anybody that.

While I had sat in the dugout, I was thinking about all the great guys who sat there before me—Joe DiMaggio, Babe Ruth, Mickey Mantle. I was really curious—looked in the bathroom there right off the side of the dugout. I always wondered what happened if guys had to go to the bathroom. They don't have to go far—it's right there. All those memories flood right through you. It's hard to explain. Why would you do a silly thing like that? I kept looking to see if Bob Shepard would say, "Young man, man, man. What are you doing, doing on the field?" You almost could hear his voice. But, no, fortunately, nobody saw me running around the bases and acting like a jerk at twenty-eight years old! I've taken people to the Yankee tours where you can go to the Stadium, and they show you the clubhouse and let you sit in the dugout, but, as a twenty-eight-year-old, that was the first time I was ever on the field. I got a real charge out of it. . . .

Unfortunately, I'm not one of those guys who still have their old Mickey Mantles. I have a couple, most of which I bought as an adult. As a kid, I had tons of them. The story I tell about my baseball cards is that I was a very, very good flipper. We used to flip baseball cards in the schoolyard on breaks. We'd flip heads or tails, and front cover and back cover. One guy would flip ten cards. I had a wooden box filled with baseball cards and had cards I was not willing to lose—usually my Yankee cards. The only time I would put them into competition is if the other fellow was also flipping Yankee cards. Then, I had other cards I was willing to lose. We tossed them like you would toss a Frisbee. You had to get them close to the wall. The ones closest to the wall won. If you leaned on the guy who got closest to the wall, you won. We used to flip them that way, as well. . . .

One day, before I was ten, a neighbor and I had an all-day competition of flipping cards. He had about 2,000 cards, and I had a few thousand cards. We flipped until I cleaned him out of all his cards, which took all day, from early in the morning until dinner. Then, while we were having dinner, the phone rang . . . it was my neighbor's mother on the phone calling my mother to tell her that her kid was crying, that he was inconsolable because he'd lost all his baseball cards. It was traumatic for me, as a kid, because my mom made me give him back his cards. I thought that was terribly, terribly unfair 'cause I had won them fair and square. My mom didn't want to hear any of that. I understand that it was the next-door neighbor and you don't want to be enemies with your neighbors, but having to give back those cards was a very, very hard thing for me to have to do. I only did it at "the point of a gun"—probably at the point of a wooden spoon!

> We flipped until I cleaned him out of all his cards, which took all day, from early in the morning until dinner.

For me, the baseball game is enough to entertain me. If I'm with someone who I've chosen to be with at the game, I want to spend the time in between pitches talking to that person either about the game or about whatever else I want to talk about. I don't need to hear the "Charge" sound after every pitch or music in between every pitch. It's a different approach today to what I used to do.

I watch a lot of ball games on TV. Sometimes if the game is not really good, I will switch and go to something else and then come back to the game. In the old days, I'd sit there for the whole nine innings or however many innings it took to watch the whole game. I can't do that anymore. Now I have choices . . . I can watch four games all at once. If nothing is happening on one game, you go to another game. When the Yankees are on the West Coast I still go to bed at night, at age fifty-eight, with the earplug in my ears listening to their games. When the first spring-training game comes on the radio, I make it my business to listen to it.

I think you can't get too attached to a player because in a year or two, he could be someplace else. We didn't have that issue when I was young. Guys were Yankees until the Yankees traded them. You grew up with the players, and you were loyal to them. You knew them very well. Now, the choices—I see it all around me—kids are not fans of the Yankees or the Mets. They live in New York, and they're fans of the **SEATTLE MARINERS***! They've got satellite dishes or buy the baseball package and are watching the ball games all across the country. When I was a kid growing up, there was only one game in town. You watched the Yankee and the Yankee games or you listened to them on the radio. I do remember listening to San Francisco Giant games on the radio. I'd never realized why they were on the radio until later until I realized there must have been a station in New York that carried those Giant games back to New York because of all the Giant fans who were still here. Other than that, it was one game in town, and you knew all the players and knew all about them. Nowadays, I guess it's a form of protection. You fall in love with Alex Rodriguez and next week or next year, he's going to be playing for somebody else. You can't have much allegiance. We've been fortunate in New York with the Yankees, at least, because Steinbrenner's money keeps a lot of the players here, especially the good ones. That's part of the reason why George has four million people come out to Yankee Stadium. He's got a loyal base because they've been with the Jorge Posadas and the Derek Jeters and the Paul O'Neills. Those guys were there year in and year out because Steinbrenner paid the money to keep them there. I have championship T-shirts that have the names of the players on the back. You look at the ones from 2004, there are four guys still on the team from 2004. If you're a kid, who are you rooting for here?

Yankee baseball has meant a lot to me. I can remember things in my life based on what was happening with the team in

*During the **SEATTLE MARINERS'** first year in 1977, the distance to the fences was measured in fathoms. A fathom is 6 feet. For instance, whereas one park might have a sign that denotes 360 feet, the Kingdome sign would have the number 60 . . .

comparison to my life. I can remember 2004 was a pretty big year for me. I had a lot of things happen to me in terms of my health. Two thousand four was a tough time between the Red Sox and me not doing well physically. I think that's what it means in the long run. You point to certain things in your life and you remember what you did in your life or what you were doing in your life based on remembrances you have of the Yankees.

There's no way I could work while the 2004 playoff games were going on. I had to take the day off to watch the game at home. At the time, I had a "lucky Yankee cap" I used to bring with me to the game. I had twenty-two straight wins in a row with that cap. I remember sitting watching a game with a friend wearing my lucky Yankee cap. I can remember those things—and, why do you remember them? Because the game brings it all back to you.

> . . . you remember what you did in your life or what you were doing in your life based on remembrances you have of the Yankees.

I drove by the
Buck Showalter Museum
of Progress today.
It is still not open.

THE WRITE GUY

Bill Andrews

Bill Andrews has been retired in Brockport, New York, since 1995. A former political science teacher at SUNY-Brockport, Andrews grew up in Greeley, Colorado, and graduated from Colorado A&M, which is now Colorado State University. Andrews, 77, received his graduate degree from Cornell.

When I was a sixteen-year-old high school student in Greeley, Colorado, I was an aspiring journalist. My mother, who is Norwegian, was returning to Norway for a visit and took me along. I wrote a series of articles about our trip. One of the articles I wrote was about Johnny Lindell, who was born in Greeley but moved away when he was about two years old. He was almost the Rookie of the Year in one of the war years when there wasn't a lot of competition for that title.

We spent a week in New York on our way to Norway. I decided I wanted to interview Johnny Lindell for one of my articles. I found out he lived in Riverside, a huge apartment development owned by Metropolitan Life Insurance. I took a bus out there. I got off the bus, and another man got off at the same time. I wanted to try to find Lindell so I asked this man if there was a rental office. He said there was not and asked me who I was looking for. I said, "Johnny Lindell." He said, "I know him, and you'd never find him even if they had a rental office because he's subletting." He took me to where Lindell's apartment was, on the east side of Manhattan, north of Midtown, but no one was home. I decided to hang around there hoping Lindell would show up. This guy left but an hour later came back to me and said, "You're in luck because when I got home, my wife was talking on the phone with Aaron Robinson's wife and Johnny Lindell and his wife were with the Robinsons." Lindell told him to have me come to Yankee Stadium at ten o'clock the next morning, and he would arrange for me to come in. I went out there and the gatekeeper called Lindell who came out and arranged for me to come in and to sit in the Yankee dugout during their batting practice.

Johnny Lindell would bring over various Yankee players for me to take their pictures with my little Brownie camera. I took pictures of Joe DiMaggio and Phil Rizzuto and Aaron Robinson and Yogi Berra and Tommy Heinrich. I still have all of those little black and white photos except for Rizzuto's, which I somehow lost. This was in July of 1947. When it was time for the game, Lindell arranged for me to have a seat behind home plate. He said to me, "I'll see if I can't hit a home run for you today." For decades after that, I had in my recollection that he hit two home runs and a single that day. A couple of years ago, I got to wondering if that was just a fantasy, so I went to the *New York Times* microfilm file and found a game on July 24 when he did hit two home runs and a single. I confirmed my fantasy that I did, in fact, have a home run hit for me in Yankee Stadium!

My mother was not into sports so I don't think it ever penetrated to her that it was that important. My friends back home believed me. When I was back there for my fiftieth high school reunion, one of my friends came up to me and said, "I still have that autograph you gave me of Joe DiMaggio." *I don't have an autograph of Joe DiMaggio.* I've got the picture I took of him, but I don't have an autograph. My friends were certainly more impressed than my mother was.

> Johnny Lindell would bring over various Yankee players for me to take their pictures with my little Brownie camera.

That series was the first time an African-American player played in Yankee Stadium. The day before was actually the first day. Two African-Americans had been brought up to the St. Louis Browns after Jackie Robinson had been brought up for the Dodgers. This was announced over the loudspeaker. It was a historic event. I understood that it was an important event, but I don't remember having special thoughts. I came from a town where there was only one or two African-American families.

> . . . these drivers were shouting at me, "Steve Brody. Steve Brody." Remember, he was the guy who jumped off Brooklyn Bridge?

My mother and I were visiting friends in New Jersey before leaving for Norway. I was supposed to take the subway down to the Fulton Street station. I got on the subway, but I wasn't paying attention, and I got off at the Fulton Street station in Brooklyn rather than Manhattan. I walked down to the river, thinking I was in Manhattan . . . but I looked across the river and I could see Manhattan. I asked some people how to get back to Manhattan. These Brooklynites didn't know. I saw the Brooklyn Bridge there so I decided to walk across that, but I didn't realize there was a pedestrian walkway in the middle of the bridge . . . so I was walking along on the curb, alongside the traffic lane—it was five o'clock during rush hour, and these drivers were shouting at me, "Steve Brody. Steve Brody." Remember, he was the guy who jumped off Brooklyn Bridge? So, these drivers are encouraging me to jump off the bridge! When I got to the other side, a policeman was there. He said, "What are you doing on Brooklyn Bridge? You have a camera. You could be taking pictures of the Brooklyn Navy Yard. You might be a communist. I'm going to take you in." He thought this sixteen-year-old hayseed from Greeley, Colorado, was a communist! But . . . I talked him out of it. He just told me to get back to New Jersey. I think my mother was more impressed by that part of the story.

My mother and I went on to Norway, where I stayed for six months so I wrote the article there and mailed it back to Greeley. By the time I got back to Greeley, that trip to New York and my article were "old hat."

OUR SON, PAUL, THOUGHT WE WERE TOO SNOOPY. AT LEAST THAT'S WHAT HE WROTE IN HIS DIARY

Paul Keck

Paul Keck, 46, grew up in Hawthorne, New York, and now lives in Briarcliff Manor. A graduate of SUNY–Purchase, he is a photographer with Tiffany and Company.

I was fifteen years old when I started a general sports diary in the off-season of 1977 after the Yankees won their first World Series in my lifetime. In November of '77 I was writing about football, basketball, whatever sports were running at that time. It was one of those cheap $1 stationery store diaries that has the little key lock on it. I started writing it as a personal diary. I always liked writing. I decided to write about the events in my life for a year. After doing that for a month or so, I got bored, for whatever reason, and ripped out the fifteen or so pages I had written. I decided to make it a sports diary because I loved sports. My friends and I played sports year-round, whatever happened to be the sport of the season. When I got through April of '78, being such a Yankee fan, the book turned almost entirely into a Yankees diary, with a smattering of other sports. I started writing during spring training.

The first entry had to do with some of the free agents the Yankees had picked up like Andy Messersmith, for example, and a bunch of others, like Catfish Hunter and Don Gullett. George Steinbrenner got in a real spending spree. Goose Gossage was the biggest acquisition for the '78 season.

The year started out reasonable for the Yankees, but by the middle of July, they had dropped fourteen games out of first place behind the Red Sox. At that point, I wrote in my diary something to the effect that "this season is over—the Yankees will be lucky if they finish in third place." There were a few months left in the season. Very fortunately—mostly because I loved the team so much, and I really cared what place they finished in—I decided, "You know what? I'll continue to write."

Within a month or so of making that statement, I saw the newspaper where they had printed the remaining schedule for both the Red Sox and the Yankees. The Red Sox were on a tear in first place with Jim Rice and Fred Lynn and Don Zimmer and were just blowing away everyone. Just for fun, I started to calculate the Red Sox schedule and show where they were playing the remaining two months. I said, "They'll win this game. They'll lose this game. They'll win this game." Then, I did the same thing for the Yankees based on their opposition and what I thought they would do for each individual game. I came out with this dead tie for the last day of the season . . . which is exactly what happened.

> The only people who would have known I was doing this would have been my parents and my brothers . . .

I don't know why I decided to do that. I guess I just loved baseball. I didn't tell anyone what I was doing. When I did the calculations and came up with the tie, it was a goof. I wasn't really thinking this was what was going to happen. It certainly did not look like that at all. When it came toward the end of the season, when they finally tied it up and went on to win the World Series I wrote in the diary a notation that I had made that calculation. I said, "Pretty good, huh!" I hadn't written it down in the diary when I did the calculation because I was thinking it was such a goof. I'm glad I did report it later on—wrote something about it—'cause I might not have remembered doing that.

For my last entry, I wrote in big block letters, "1978 New York Yankees—a season I will never forget!" I didn't even think about doing a diary the next year. It had just been a totally spontaneous thing. I hadn't thought about writing it for any kind of commercial purposes, and there wasn't any intention of publishing it at all. It was just for fun. There's a secondary reason, probably because it did take a lot of energy. I would not only listen to almost all the games on radio or watch them on TV, but the following day I would always go to the newspapers. It was a ritual of mine to go look at the box scores and what the players did and the team. I would fill in those as well as my recollections of the games. It was a bit of work, too, I'd staple in a lot of box scores and newspaper clippings. It was like a little work of art. The only people who would have known I was doing this would have been my parents and my brothers, who probably would have seen me scribbling each day into my diary. If I told anyone—I might have told a friend or two, but it was just my thing. I don't remember that anyone else really knew. The diary is in my apartment now.

> It's something that really speaks from my heart. It's about being a fan.

One of the diary entries was where on Opening Day, Reggie Jackson came up to bat. That day they gave out candy bars—they had come out with the Reggie Bar that year. Promptly, he hit a home run. Immediately, tens of thousands of Reggie Bars were showered down from the stands all over the field. They had to stop the game for about fifteen minutes. Players and many of the fans were out on the field helping to pick up these Reggie Bars and putting them in buckets so they could play again. That was the beginning of the season. You can imagine how it got red hot in August when the Yankees started to just pulverize the Red Sox and make a tremendous comeback.

There are a lot of great memories there. To me, it was divine providence that I wrote in the book. It's something that really speaks from my heart. It's about being a fan. I read parts of it over the last four or five years. I get goose bumps sometime when I'm reading through the pages. It's that meaningful to me. Each day I would make relatively short entries, mainly because of the size of the diary, which was very small, probably 3 1/2 by 5-inch size. I had to be very sparing with my words but also it forced me to pick out the best parts and keep my verbiage very interesting. It was written by a kid instead of an adult with a commercial motive. The theme to me has always been . . . about the whole book is about the comeback. I definitely can relate to that in my life. Everyone in their life has something to come back from. It was almost like something spiritual. This crazy, crazy team finally got it together . . . and did it!

My mom and dad appreciated my interest in the game of baseball. They knew I absolutely loved it whether I was playing it or watching it. I don't think anyone, including myself, really knew what was going until the dust had cleared off after that season and I was holding that diary in my hand and said, "Wow!" It's pretty unbelievable that somehow, by some inspiration, it's captured in pen and ink.

Do you know the difference between B*rry B*nds and government bonds? Government bonds mature.

IT WAS A BALL

I went to a school that was in the bowels of Brooklyn. Brooklyn Prep was within walking distance of Ebbets Field. Every day, going over to our cross-country practice in Prospect Park, I would have to walk past Ebbets Field. It was like whistling past the graveyard—because that was the enemy's territory there. I don't think any of my friends ever realized I was a Yankee fan. I kept that to myself—they were all rabid Brooklyn fans. I was spoiled in my youth because invariably, the Yankees were the World Series champs. They seemed to pull it out for the most part.

I remember standing outside Yankee Stadium at a time when you could get autographs from the players. I still have scorecards that go back to the early '50s. I have Eddie Lopat's signature. I have Marty Marion when he was player-manager for the St. Louis Browns. He'd had a great career with the Cardinals. I got him just as he was stepping into a cab, and he took the time, with the cab door open, to sign an autograph for me. I must have been eleven years old at the time. At that time, you were close to the players. They'd walk right past you. They'd park their cars across the way in a fenced-in private parking area. Then they would cross the street and enter the clubhouse area. You were able to talk to them . . . say hello to them . . . they'd shake your hand . . . you could get an autograph. It's a lot different today. There was a closeness there.

We used to pitch our baseball cards against brick walls. I have 1950 era and 1951 era cards. Unfortunately, I have a fifty-five-year-old scrapbook that they are *pasted* in. I do have a Mickey Mantle card, not the first year—it's the second year, but it's pasted beautifully in a book. I have Allie Reynolds. I've got Gene Woodling, all of those old cards—all pasted in there. They're worth everything to me and worthless to collectors.

> I have 1950 era and 1951 era cards. Unfortunately, I have a fifty-five-year-old scrapbook that they are *pasted* in.

I say to Red Sox fans, "You know—actually you got rid of the wrong team because you got rid of the Braves, and they went on to have a lot of success in Atlanta . . . and went to two World Series in Milwaukee along the way." That's always one of my comments to the Boston people. They don't like it.

—JOHN MALMFELT, 66, Greensboro, North Carolina

I was born and raised a bit more than a mile from "The Stadium." That's what we all called it back in 1952 . . . and what I still call it now during my annual pilgrimage once a year. No other explanation is needed. My kids are Yankee fans, too. The running joke in the house is that if they wanted to eat, they had to be Yankee fans!

My father was a Dodger fan, and it broke his heart when they moved to California. He just didn't get into baseball as much after that. He also loved Red Barber and *hated* Phil Rizzuto as announcers. When I went off to college at SUNY–Oswego, I asked him to do me a favor and buy me a Yankee cap and send it to me. It was 1970, and the Yankees weren't very good. But, they were . . . and always will be . . . my team. My father was a cab driver in Midtown, so I figured he could easily get a cap and mail it to me at "the land of horizontal snow."

> I went to Shea Stadium once—to see the Ice Capades, of all things. They laid out a temporary ice rink in the infield.

The bag came, and I was very excited. I tore it open and promptly dropped it to the ground when I saw the colors. He had sent me a Mets cap! I think he did it as a joke, but I was very upset. The half-opened bag, with the cap still inside, stayed on the floor of my dorm room until my roommate finally picked it up and threw it away when we moved out at the end of the semester. How could he send me a Mets cap of all things? Any true Yankee fan cannot also be a Mets fan at all.

I have been to one Mets game in my life. As a Cub Scout, my troop went to the old Polo Grounds. I think I might have been the only kid in the stands rooting for the Phillies! I went to Shea Stadium once—to see the Ice Capades, of all things. They laid out a temporary ice rink in the infield. My mother likes ice-skating and thought it was neat. I hated the idea that the Mets were going to get any of my ticket price for the event.

I wish I had all my old baseball cards, but . . . then, so do a lot of other guys my age.

—MARK DiGENNARO, a misplaced Bronx kid living in upstate New York

Our group of neighborhood kids won a contest sponsored by 7-Eleven convenience stores. The prize was a day at **YANKEE STADIUM*** in 1970—the old Stadium. The prize included a boxed lunch down the leftfield line in the stands with a pitching and catching demonstration put on by Rick Dempsey, the backup catcher, and Fritz Peterson. They actually were demonstrating how to throw different types of pitches. What an awesome thrill for all of us. As part of the prize, we also got a chance to walk along the warning track to centerfield and stand amongst the monuments. As a young kid, six years old, home plate seemed like a mile away. It was hard to imagine that someone could hit a ball that far.

We are a family of huge Yankee fans. My grandparents started it. Grandma was a huge Lou Gehrig fan, including being in the stands for his famous farewell address. The day Thurman died, August 2, 1978, my two older brothers and I were down the street at a friend's house sitting around a picnic table playing the board game Risk. His mother came out and told us the news. At first, we thought she was teasing us, we were the only Yankee fans within our group of friends. But it was quickly apparent that she was not kidding. My brothers and I ran home. When we heard the news on TV for ourselves, it was devastating. In those days, the only sports news on TV came during the major networks newscasts. When the news came on at 6:00 p.m. and we again heard this with our whole family, everyone was crying. That evening I cried myself to sleep. To us, Thurman was the man, Mr. Clutch. He always seemed to get the big hit at the right time, always played hurt and seemed to do whatever it took to get the job done. We admired his determination. We would often imitate his batting

---

*Thomas Edison sold the concrete to the Yankees that was used to build **YANKEE STADIUM**. Edison owned the huge Portland Cement Company. . . . Edison's middle name was Alva, named after the father of onetime Cleveland Indians owner, Alva Bradley.

style playing stick ball in the street. I get goose bumps just thinking about the day of his funeral and the game played that night. In a time when entertainment side of sports was not as exploited as it is today, the drama of that game was unbelievable. To have the Yankees take the field without anyone behind home plate was an emotional tribute to a great Yankee.

—JIM CACI, Brick, New Jersey

I was introduced to the Yanks by Grandma Anna, who lived in Ithaca, New York, where I spent my summers. In the afternoons, we would listen attentively to the gifted voice of Mel Allen broadcasting the games. I can still hear his reporting of yet another "Ballantine Blast"—the sponsoring brewery. His description of a homer was " . . . going, going, GONE!"

When I later attended Brooklyn Prep, literally within earshot of Ebbets Field, I found myself surrounded by Dodger followers. In those pre-air conditioning days, we could hear the roar of the crowd through the open windows in April and May. During my prep school days, **DON LARSEN*** would strike out Dale Mitchell to reach Yankee "perfection" in 1956 but, alas, the Yankees would also *finally* lose a series to Da Bums in 1955. Grandma brought me my one and only baseball glove—a Nippy Jones first-baseman's mitt—which I still have. It looks like a crushed lobster claw, but the smell of the leather takes me instantly back over half a century. She also took me to my only visit to Cooperstown. While there, she spotted Frankie Frisch, the Fordham Flash and member of the famous St. Louis Cardinals "Gashouse Gang." He signed his name for me across a postcard bearing a picture of his bronze plaque. Unlike the mitt, I lost the card in the ensuing years.

During those summers, I started a scrapbook—an old photo album with black pages. In those years, the New York *Daily News* and *Mirror* would be delivered upstate by overnight train. After everyone else had read the papers, I'd cut out the pictures of

> *In the Yankee locker room, on the day of **DON LARSEN**'s perfect game, Larsen was served divorce papers. . . .Years later Don Larsen threw out the first pitch the same day David Cone threw his perfect Yankee game. . . . Larsen and David Wells, another Yankee with a perfect game, graduated from the same high school in San Diego.

players and paste them in the album. A page was devoted to each team—sixteen in all, at that time. I also glued in baseball cards— Phil Rizzuto, Eddie Lopat, Allie Reynolds, Joe Page, Don Bollweg, Gene Woodling. Yes—even Mickey Mantle's card is there. Since this was during the Korean "Police Action," there are shots of Dr. Bobby Brown and Jerry Coleman in military garb. This scrapbook will be passed on to my son, Kevin, and then to his son, Ryan—both following in the Yankee tradition. Ryan, not even two, has already been to the Babe's Monument in the Stadium. Four generations of Yankee fans!

—JOHN MALMFELT, retired from AT&T

All the Yankee fans are bitching and moaning when the Yankees lose, but I say, "Look, just remember one thing, especially at my age—think of five years 1949, 1950, 1951, 1952, 1953 . . . you know what I'm referring to. Five years in a row—the World Series. You'll never see that again—never see any other team do that. Back then, all you had to do was win four post season games to win the World Series . . . now it's eleven.

In the old day . . . that was when baseball was baseball, but now it's all watered down. Now, you've got a couple of hundred ball players playing, who would be in the minor leagues or not even playing baseball back then. You've got players making $400,000—the minimum. You've got guys making over a million dollars who are **BATTING .250***.

One Sunday in '49, when I was eleven years old, this was a time when they were playing all those doubleheaders on Sunday. The Yankees were playing a doubleheader against the Philadelphia A's in Philadelphia—Shantz and Art Ditmar against Reynolds and Raschi. We didn't have a television then, but I just had to see that doubleheader. I had to. I decided to go down to Port Authority, hop on a bus, go to Shibe Park, and see the doubleheader. That's exactly what I did. I wasn't scared at all. Crime wasn't as prevalent as it is now.

My mother didn't know anything about it. Back then, a doubleheader didn't take that long so I got back home before dark. She probably thought I was out playing ball because that's all we

*The difference between a .250 and a .300 hitter is one hit per week.

did growing up in East Harlem—stickball and stoopball and boxball. We didn't have time for anything but sports. I never told her—there was no reason to. That was a case of "what she didn't know wouldn't hurt her!" I learned a long time ago that it's a lot easier to beg for forgiveness than it was to ask for permission.

I went down to Port Authority, got on a bus to Philadelphia, got off the bus, and took a cab to Shibe Park. I saw the double-header—the Yankees won both games. I was happy as a pig in doo-doo. I got back on the bus and went home. To this day, I still have the ticket stub. I was so excited to be at Shibe Park . . . it reminded me so much of Ebbets Field. Compared to Yankee Stadium it was a dump—it was different . . . to say the least. It was fun, and I enjoyed it.

—<u>VINNY ROMANO</u>, 69, retired policeman

> . . . we were always looking for the elusive Mickey Mantle card, which was as rare as hen's teeth . . . you could never get one.

When I was a kid, at the local corner candy store, we used to buy wax packs, which were also made by **TOPPS***. We'd buy these nickel wax packs, which came with five to ten cards in a pack. Being Yankee fans, we were always looking for the elusive Mickey Mantle card, which was as rare as hen's teeth . . . you could never get one. There would be *maybe* one guy within a radius of 20 miles who had one. You'd want to get an eye on it and see what it looked like. Now, with the Topps Company, they reissue these very rare cards, and I'm seeing them at work, which is very ironic to me.

When I was a kid, the way we treated those cards, was that they were something to put in a shoebox under your bed . . . to collect them . . . trade them with your friends . . . flip them. We'd attach them to the spokes of our bicycles with clothespins to make a motorcycle-like noise.

Today, it's become a business. They're more for collectors. I find that sad. They've taken away the innocence. The marketplace

---

*In the very first set of **TOPPS** baseball cards, the first card (#1) was Andy Pafko.

has a lot of these cards. I'm sure they're very valuable and are really coveted by the collectors, but it seems to have lost that certain innocence we had when were collecting them. . . .

My dad knew of a certain Yankee Stadium exit. I don't know how he found it. One summer, I was a young boy, about eight years old, I broke my leg and had a full leg cast. My father physically carried me into the Stadium because he felt sad about me being cooped up all summer. There I was with my leg sticking straight out, propped up on one of the seats. After the game, we waited by one of these "secret exits". It looked almost like one of those folding accordion doors, like a garage door on the side of the Stadium. After waiting a good forty-five minutes or so after the game, quite a few of the players would come out there. Bobby Richardson came out. Don Larsen came out, and I got his autograph. I was so in awe of the guy. He was such a big, huge guy compared to me, being a youngster eight years old. I just treasured that autograph forever.

There was such a connection between my father and me with baseball and the feelings and memories went deep. When he passed away, I really missed a lot. There is a lot of emptiness that was left when he passed away—that baseball connection. It's something that is unspoken, but there it was.

Dad's secret exit looked like an aluminum accordion door. It almost looked like a roll-up store kind of gate. It wasn't like a normal exit or entrance. When players today come into the ballpark, they go into the players' parking lot and they go into this main entrance. But, this was like a secret exit where they came shooting out of there when, maybe, they didn't want to get mobbed by the fans. . . .

Back in the late '80s, we started this group called FOUL, which was an acronym for "Fans Opposed to Useless Leadership." Being the creative guy in the group, that was my brainchild. What we were doing was protesting Steinbrenner's maniacal firings—twenty-two managers in twenty years. We felt he was taking the franchise down the tubes. After a while, Steinbrenner seemed to calm down a little bit. We like to think we had an effect on him 'cause we got some publicity out of it. We sold T-shirts. The oddest thing was having a bunch of us in the same section

> Met fans strike me as being mentally unbalanced . . . to be honest. The reason? Well, did you ever see a Met fan? They just seem a little bit odd.

wearing our FOUL T-shirts. We came out with a huge banner that said, FOUL TERRITORY. We tried to hang it over the side of the upper deck and some security guys came over and stopped us. We did attend Banner Day and paraded around the field with it. We thought that was an odd sight for everyone to see . . . nobody else knew what it meant. They no longer have Banner Day. I thought it was neat . . . I liked it. Everyone was allowed to come out and express their individual whinings or whatever. One time, when the Yankees played their games at Shea, people were shouting "Shea Stadium," and Graig Nettles hit a ball that went on the backstop net. It was teetering on the edge where we were sitting. Everyone was jumping up . . . that ball just kept teetering on the edge there and *finally* fell off. While everyone was jumping, I stayed down below and captured the ball. The funny part of the story is I treasured this ball. You know how rare it is to catch a baseball . . . and *my dog ate it*! I guess she just smelled the rawhide and thought it was her chew toy. She chewed the heck out of it. I was so mad at her. I always thought of Met fans as strange in general, and it was strange for the Yankees to be playing at Shea. It was like we were in somebody else's house. I guess it's going to be like that when we move to the new place, too.

Met fans strike me as being mentally unbalanced . . . to be honest. The reason? Well, did you ever see a Met fan? They just seem a little bit odd. They're mostly an odd bunch. . . .

We try to prevent it, but sometimes there are mistakes on the baseball cards. There is an extensive approval process that the card goes through. There are proofs sent. They're read, approved, and rechecked to make sure everything is all right. Occasionally, there are times when the printer will discover something that's an error and stop the presses, "Hold the presses! We have to fix this." It does happen, and they have to be remade, reprinted. These errors don't occur as often as you might think.

—JOHN DELL-SOTO, Topps baseball card designer

I wanted to write a book and call it *The Fans in The Stands* to tell exactly how we fans in the stands feel with these ball players. How things have changed. Back in the '50s when I was growing up, I was a Dodgers fan. They moved in '58. A lot of my relatives have all passed by now, but a lot of them stopped watching baseball when the Dodgers left—that's how beloved the Brooklyn Dodgers were. As a kid, I liked Mickey Mantle. We didn't have ESPN, so what was I to do? The only thing that came on was Channel 11 showing the Yankees . . . so I became a Yankee fan. That's how that happened.

I was about thirteen years old, and I would take one train right to the Bronx. At that period of time in New York, you could send your kids up to the Bronx, and I'd go every Sunday to watch the games—doubleheaders only! We would get general admission tickets for about $1.25. After a while we would go downstairs toward the field and find real good seats. At that time, there were ushers at the Stadium—they knew what we were doing. They wore goofy hats and jackets and they used to clean your seat off. By the end of the game we would want to be downstairs because we could exit the Stadium by going through the Yankee bullpen in right field or the visitors' in leftfield. You could walk right out on the field and go out to the three monuments that were originally in centerfield at the old Stadium. Sometimes we'd have a ball with us and on our way out, and we'd be playing catch. We'd have forty-five minutes or an hour when we could be out there playing around. You know what it was for a thirteen-year-old kid to have a catch on Yankee Stadium? We always ended up downstairs.

> You know what it was for a thirteen-year-old kid to have a catch on Yankee Stadium?

The ushers surrounded the infield so you couldn't get out there. As a kid, that was the greatest thing in the world. To walk out of the Stadium, especially if I had caught a baseball there, throwing that around with my friends—the best, absolutely the best.

It was cheap to go to the games. I paid 25 cents for a scorecard. My father would give me $2 to $3 to go to the game with. We'd get hero sandwiches. If you've never had Italian bread from Brooklyn, you've missed something.

When we were twelve, thirteen years old, a bunch of us would go to the games together—but only to the doubleheaders on Sunday so we got to see two games. I learned how to keep score. Every one of my scorecards was always kept the right way.

Batting practice was the best. We used to line up in the seats in the grandstand. Friends of mine stayed by the right field foul pole. The Yankees were always set up for left-handed power hitters—still are. A lot more home runs went to right field than leftfield. We used to catch balls there. I may have one hundred baseballs in my basement that I personally caught. Roger Maris hit a lot of shots in the grandstands. Yogi Berra was great because he was all over the place, so he was good. Johnny Blanchard was very good over there, so were the Tony Kubeks of the world. Mickey Mantle used to thunder them. He used to either go upper deck or the right center bleachers. There was also batting practice for the other teams. We used to rag on them.

All three of the ballparks were great. You were right on the field at Ebbets Field. Yankee Stadium was always a cathedral. The Polo Grounds were nice. Centerfield was 500 feet away. There was a Chesterfield cigarette sign out there. When someone hit a home run there would be a puff of smoke out of the sign. The Polo Grounds was the shape of a horseshoe. Ebbets Field was gorgeous.

—RON FUSCO, 59, Brooklyn

We couldn't get the Yankees on the radio so I had to rely on the local newspaper for baseball results, back in the '30s. I really got into following the Yanks when I got out of the Army in 1947. I saw my first Major League game at Yankee Stadium in 1951. I remember this because it was DiMaggio's last year, and I got to see him play. I lived about 200 miles from New York, and I went on a baseball excursion with the guys I worked with in North Adams, Massachusetts.

It as about a four-hour train ride each way, and the excursion package included a three-game set against the Boston Red Sox, a day game on Saturday, and a doubleheader on Sunday. It was not an important series as the Yankees had already clinched the pennant, but it was very exciting to me to be able to see a big-league game, especially against the Red Sox, whom my co-workers were all rooting for. I lived in Stamford, Vermont, which is just a small town near the New Hampshire border, and I was an anomaly—a Yankee fan in New England.

Besides the three ball games, the excursion package also included a night at the Hotel Piccadilly and tickets to the Jack Carson Show at Radio City Music Hall. Unbelievably, the entire package, including train fare, cost the princely sum of $20. It was the only time I ever got to see the great DiMaggio play. He retired after that season. In one of those games, Allie Reynolds came on in relief of Whitey Ford, who had started the game. I can't remember who won any of those games, but I remember that Reynolds threw much harder than Ford.

—JOE BUSHIKA, 80, Stamford, Vermont

In 1979, I was fifteen and going to summer school because I'd failed algebra. I had my paper route working at the *Daily News*—switched to them so I could have a morning route so I could play high school sports. It was August 2, and I had been studying all afternoon. My mom called me downstairs to tell me Thurman Munson had died in a plane crash. I was in shock. It was like a death in the family. I put the news on and watched the special report and knew right then it was real. The rest of the summer was just a bummer—the games were secondary. The next morning, when I saw the *Daily News* front page—that's when it really sunk in that it had really happened.

Two days later, I'm reading the stories in the *Daily News* about what had happened at the funeral. Two things stick out in my mind. As they came out of the church after the funeral, a little plane was flying overhead. Lou Piniella looked up at it and continued watching it poignantly, as if he knew the irony of a small plane flying overhead when Munson had died tragically in a plane crash. Second, as I watched the coverage on television—watching Billy Martin crying hysterically with Paul Blair holding him up. I will never, ever forget that. . . .

> My mom called me downstairs to tell me Thurman Munson had died in a plane crash. I was in shock.

My dad is from Brooklyn, and he grew up as a Dodgers fan. He was from the East New York section of Brooklyn. He was born in

1938, and growing up in the '40s, New York was still an Irish-German-Italian integrated community. He and his brothers would sneak into the old Brooklyn Bushwicks semi-pro park. They used to play there, when the Bushwicks weren't playing, until they'd get tossed out. My dad would play catch with me all the time. He took me to as many games as we could when he could get tickets. What really got me into being a Yankee fan were two things. First, those old Mike Wallace biographies in black and white. I watched the Babe Ruth program. My dad told me about Babe Ruth . . . him being an orphan and all the things he'd gone through in life and how he became the greatest player. My dad told me about all the players he grew up with. We would watch Old Timers Day together on television when Joe DiMaggio and Mickey Mantle and Casey Stengel would all come back.

> I loved Roy White because on some pretty mediocre Yankees teams, he always went above and beyond . . .

I remember reading my baseball cards like they were textbooks in school. I read everything about the players. The Topps cards in the early and mid-'70s, when you flipped them over, would have something personal about the player. Clay Kirby, who pitched for the Expos—his card said, "Clay Kirby's into racing cars." I'll never forget that . . . because I like cars, too. Roy White was my favorite Yankee growing up. He was from Wayne, New Jersey. I remember Bill White, Frank Messer, and Phil Rizzuto referring to him as "The Pride of Wayne, New Jersey." I think that info brings us closer to the ballplayers, especially the ones we love the most, when we know a little bit more about them—where they're from, what they're about, what they've done in their lives, where they've gone to school. If you know something about them, as people, it makes it even better to root for them.

I loved Roy White because on some pretty mediocre Yankees teams, he always went above and beyond what I thought was effort . . . he hustled out every play . . . ran out every ground ball. I thought he really personified the Yankees.

I saw Roy White two weeks ago. When we go to Yankee games, we always get our pregame meal at the Court Deli, where they always treat my dad and me like family, right on the corner up the block from Yankee Stadium, right across from the historic Bronx Criminal Court House, the great building you always see beyond Yankee Stadium in centerfield. . . . Another one of the things that got me to be a Yankee fan was as a child when I first saw the movie, *Pride of the Yankees*, with Gary Cooper playing Lou Gehrig. So, finally getting to see that building in person, seeing all the things about Yankee Stadium, which I'd always heard about, sent chills up my spine even though I was only thirteen at the time. . . .

Anyway, I saw him walk in and thought, "Hey, that's Roy White." He sat down a few tables from us, eating his meal and reading the paper. No one was noticing him. I wanted to go up to him and thank him for all the great memories, but I thought better of it. I didn't want to disturb him when he was eating. I'm sure I'll have other opportunities to do that. I never met him at all and, unfortunately, don't have his autograph. I've heard he's a very gracious, very nice man.

However, a few weeks later, my dad and I ran into Oscar Gamble and Mickey Rivers who played for the Yankees championship teams from 1976 to 1978 as they were coming through the turnstiles to attend a game. I recognized them right away. When I said: "Hi, Mickey!" Rivers came right over with a huge smile and shook my hand and my dad's too. I then said, "Hi Oscar!" and Oscar Gamble made a point of coming back over to me and my dad to shake both our hands. Oscar looked great and I told him that and he thanked me for the compliment. Both Oscar and Mickey seemed very happy and flattered that we had recognized them and made a point of saying hello. But, I was even happier that they said hello to my dad and me. Having seen them so many times on television and in person when I was a kid, it was like being thirteen years old all over again.

—MATT DONNELLY, Eagle Transport Services, New York

If you grew up in New York City in the '50s, you were pretty much destined to be a baseball fan. One New York City team or another was in the World Series most years. On those rare occasions that they weren't, it felt like an epiphany, because it was something that was foreign to you. Something was not quite right with the world. After all, impostors were playing in place of your team.

I got my love for the game from my father and brother. They were immigrants from Puerto Rico where baseball is king. If they spoke no English, it didn't matter during a baseball game. A game was a game, and you knew what was going on. In my household, my father and brother were New York Giant fans. I was the deviate—I was the Yankee fan. The one thing we did have in common was that we three hated the Brooklyn Dodgers.

> The one thing we did have in common was that we three hated the Brooklyn Dodgers.

It was a source of pride for us to see recognizable names in the box score—like Ruben Gomez, Jose Pagan, and the great **ORLANDO CEPEDA***, from our beloved homeland, and the Alou brothers and the great Juan Marichal, from the neighboring Dominican Republic. That was the motivating factor for their loyalty to the Giants. I recall being very young and going to the Polo Grounds and Ebbets Field and joining my brother and father booing the Dodgers. Baseball is important business in Puerto Rico, and to be able to see our own succeed and thrive in the big leagues reinforced our belief that we could indeed play this game at a high level.

I, on the other hand, followed the Yankees religiously. I had no choice. The Stadium was a half-hour walk from my doorstep, and when us kids could scrape together the 75 cents for bleacher seats, we could spend one magical afternoon in baseball heaven. Occasionally, we would be able to scrape together an extra 30 cents for the round-trip fare on the southbound 163rd Street bus at Simpson Street. Some of us had shoeshine boxes and would station ourselves outside the Spooner Theater on Southern Boulevard and wait for businessmen to come by and have their shoes shined for a dime. The tips were the big thing because that helped us get that much closer to the coveted 75 cents. The Yankees were

---

*ORLANDO CEPEDA used more bats than any player in Major League history. He believed each bat had exactly one hit in it. When Cepeda got a hit, he never used that bat again.

the kings of baseball then. As far as we were concerned, the dynasty would never end. None of us ever thought that Mickey Mantle would ever age and retire and that the Yankees' fertile farm system would dry up. It was blasphemous to think that the Yankees would not be in a World Series for years after 1964.

In the '50s, television was a fairly new advancement in home entertainment. If you wanted to enjoy the game, you had to listen to Mel Allen, Red Barber, and Phil Rizzuto on a radio, if you were not one of the lucky families to own one of those new-fangled televisions. As I think back, it was common for older people to believe televisions could cause a fire if you weren't careful. Everybody always knew someone who knew someone that had a fire caused by a television set.

Imagine my surprise when, as a very young child, I discovered that the president of the United States was a black man. I had not yet attended school, but I knew our president's name was Eisenhower. He looked rather like a distinguished looking, bald white man in the newspapers. I knew the very first time my father chanced a fire in our apartment and bought us a television set that baseball was the first thing turned on, and I could see my heroes for the very first time. We're sitting there, and it was time for the president to hit. I knew that he caught for the Yankees during the day and ran the country at night. I often thought how remarkable he must be to be able to play for the mighty Yankees and be the leader of the Free World. As he strode to the plate for the first time, in the very first live game I saw on TV, I remember thinking he did not look like he did in the papers. I could hear Bob Sheppard's voice announcing, "Now batting for the Yankees, the catcher, No. 32, Elston Howard."

—STEPHAN P. WOLFE, Bronx

The first baseball experience I remember was a Yankee-**CHISOX*** doubleheader dad took me to in 1950 when I was eight. Yogi Berra homered into the right-center bleachers, and I was a Yogi fan forever after. When I had the mumps during spring training of '52, he bought me a magazine with '51 MVP Yogi on

*In 1943 the **CHICAGO WHITE SOX** played forty-four doubleheaders. Last year they played one.

the cover. A few years ago, I purchased a collectible copy of that issue. In '51, I rooted for the Yanks against my dad's New York Giants in the Series. When the Bombers won, I felt guilty so I raked the leaves for my father.

I was such a Yogi fan that I sent him birthday cards for several years. I still have his autograph on a Charlie McGill drawing that was in the Bergen Record in 1955. McGill continues to do sports artwork in that paper to this day. Four to five years ago, I found out where Yogi lives in nearby Montclair, and I took the framed picture to show him how well it's held up. I thanked him for being "my guy" when I was growing up.

> I still carry in my wallet the ticket stubs of the last game my dad gave me tickets to.

To this day, I can rattle off Yogi's lifetime stats, especially his amazingly low strikeout career strikeout total of 414, which most of us kids back then learned from looking so often at our baseball cards! That's what we did. We enjoyed our cards, read them over and over. They weren't put away as "future investments." Even at only a nickel a pack, they were tough to come by. Buying the entire series at once was not an option. We had a hard time trying to see through the wrapper who might be in each pack. It was a crapshoot, and more often than not, we got doubles or triples of bench players rather than cards of our favorites.

Every afternoon and Friday nights, we followed the games on radio with Mel Allen and Jim Woods, and later Red Barber who never ceased being a Dodger broadcaster, as far as I was concerned. It was a real treat when my dad, when he worked late, would bring home the evening *Daily News* with the line score of the game "in progress," listing the pitcher-catcher batteries. Guaranteed to see Berra there!

I still carry in my wallet the ticket stubs of the last game my dad gave me tickets to. My son went with me so the baseball connection continues from generation to generation.

—JOHN GROH, Clifton, New Jersey, teacher for 40-plus years

Chapter 3

Put Me In, Coach

A Hard Way to Make an Easy Living

DOCTOR, DOCTOR, TELL ME THE NEWS ABOUT MANTLE AND THE MEMPHIS BOOZE

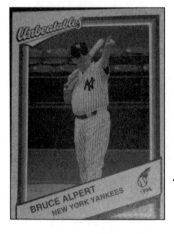

Dr. Bruce Alpert

Bruce Alpert is a professor of pediatric cardiology at the University of Tennessee in Memphis and has an endowed chair professorship there. He graduated from Albany Academy, the same school as Herman Melville. He then graduated from Dartmouth in the late '60s and has lived in Memphis for twenty-three years. He has a very extensive New York Yankees home library.

My dad was an attorney and worked for state government so he worked a lot of weekends. Mom and I would get on the Trailways at seven in the morning, get to the Port Authority about 9:45, walk or get a cab to Macy's, where she'd drag me around for a while shopping. Then, we'd take the subway up to the Stadium to see a Saturday afternoon game, come back, eat at a Chinese restaurant. My dad had done some legal work for the restaurant owner, so they got us in and out fast so we could get back on the Trailways at seven o'clock at the Port Authority and back up to Albany. By about 10:15, we were back home, having spent the "day in the city."

I still have an autographed Yogi Berra picture I got when I was about eight years old. I had appendicitis and developed a post-op infection and had to convalesce for a long time. Somehow my dad was able to get somebody to get Yogi to personalize a picture for me. I still have the envelope—with the two-cent stamp—that it took to mail the picture from the Stadium to my home.

Living in Memphis, most of the people here are Cardinals fans. My response to that is the only reason to worry about the National League is who the Yankees are going to play in October so I don't follow the National League much at all. There are a surprising number of Yankee fans all throughout the South, even though they should be Braves fans or St. Louis or Marlins or Devil Rays or whatever. They're Yankee fans because they migrated from the North, and they've lived in the South for a long time like me.

Back in 1991, I tried to get our children's hospital to do a fundraising autograph show because many other children's hospitals had gotten Mantle in the late '80s. They would make 50 to 60,000 dollars in profits for the hospital. That's a good fund-raising event. Our hospital waited a bit late and then underpublicized it, and it turned out not to be a very successful event. The people who came were Johnny Blanchard, Hank Bauer, Moose Skowron, Tommy Tresh, as well as Mantle. Plus, we had to pay Mantle fifty grand for the weekend. He signed 700 autographs per day, plus we had the mail-orders.

I had a full-size Chevy van at the time. Greer Johnson, Mantle's long-time assistant, and the show promoter were counting money in the back of my van—tens of thousands of dollars, and it was all cash. It was pretty amazing to watch.

I was warned about the Greer Johnson situation. She was very protective of him. I told the hospital personnel I would be picking these people up at the airport and would be spending the weekend there at the hospital helping them out and ferrying them back and forth. So, when I got them at the airport—back in those days you could still go to the gate when you'd meet somebody—we had him pull his cap down on his head, but it was like the Israelites going through the Red Sea—the whole terminal parted as Mickey walked by. We put him in my van, and he just sat in the back seat and Greer and I went to get the luggage.

I had been to Mickey's house a few years earlier in Dallas—'87. My wife had decided we would go visit him when we were there for a family event. She got his son, Billy, to let us into the house, and he gave us a tour around. I told Mickey on the way to the hotel that I'd had the privilege of seeing his collection and that his son Billy had let us into the house. He goes, "Billy? Billy Mantle? He's not nice to anybody!"

I went back later that afternoon and picked up the other players. Blanchard had just been discharged from the hospital for a heart rhythm problems and I taught him how to take his pulse and how to count it and what things to worry about. Then, once I got to know the other players, as well, I told them, since I'm a physician, I can get samples of medications delivered to my office, and, if they were on any medications that I could get, I would compact them down to smaller bottles and send some to them.

> "Billy? Billy Mantle? He's not nice to anybody!"

So, for a while, I was sending medicine to Blanchard, to Moose's wife, Hank Bauer's wife, Larsen's aunt and uncle, and kept them supplied in their medications because their insurance was real crummy, and they were on very, very modest pensions. It was very helpful to them. Some of the medicines I gave them literally saved them thousands of dollars per year. I've been able to help out that way. To thank me, they invite me to Old Timers Day or, every once in a while, they arrange for me to get a game-used something or other from one of the current players, which is neat. I have a personalized Mattingly game bat.

These guys are all very dedicated to each other. Mantle would not accept an invitation to do card shows unless some of his buddies were invited as well. He understood that, although he could command very large amounts of money, others were unable to do that. Their livelihood was, to a good deal, dependent upon getting card show commitments. Blanchard, Skowron, and Bauer came with Mickey almost all the time. Thank goodness, they could do that because otherwise they wouldn't have been able to make it on their retirement incomes. They primarily would talk to each other about their grandchildren and how their kids were doing—they were really very non-sophisticated, very dedicated to each other, your next-door neighbor kind of people.

When Mickey first asked me what I do for a living, I'd say, "I teach and do research and see patients at the medical school. I'm a professor and teacher." Mantle said, "Teacher? They need teachers at medical schools?" I said, "Well, yeah, that's how you get to be a doctor. You have somebody teaching you different courses. It's like college." Of course, he had never attended college, so it was a little bit different. There were matter-of-fact naive comments about different matters.

I got a picture from Mickey's original Holiday Inn in Joplin, Missouri. Along the walls, Mickey had lots of pictures of his teammates in game situations. Most of those have been confiscated by somebody and then resold. I had one where Bobby Richardson was greeting Mickey at the plate presumably after a home run, with Bobby on base. I asked Bobby if he would inscribe that with something about Mickey for me. He wrote four or five lines, "Mickey was the best teammate we ever had. He always supported the team and never let anybody go without. On the road, nobody ever went hungry. Nobody ever was alone. Mickey would always make sure that everybody was taken care of."

That was a neat concept. Thinking of today's stars—all they do is say, "leave me alone." Mickey would invite the rookies out to dinner with them. He never let any of the young guys pay for anything. Blanchard was telling stories how Mickey always paid once they started on the autograph circuit—once their feet hit the airplane terminal, either the promoter or Mickey always paid for everything. It was never a question of them having to pick up the tab for their meals.

During those times, Mickey was drinking. Getting back to the first day I met Greer . . . about four o'clock, when we first got to the hotel, Mickey asked when the bar opened. They told him it didn't open till 5:30, and they had a six o'clock television interview they were going to do. Mickey hands Moose forty bucks and says, "Go out and get us some vodka." Moose looks at me, and I said, "We'll find a place. Don't worry." The promoter had gotten a hotel near the airport with very nice sized rooms, but a pretty crummy neighborhood.

We went to a liquor store that had bars on the windows and looked pretty seedy. Moose looks at me and says, "Doc, this doesn't look real safe." I said, "Moose, you're right. This doesn't look safe at all, but I'm really glad you're going in, not me, 'cause Mickey gave you the money." He said, "Doc, I'm a seventy-year-old guy. You can't let me go in there by myself." I said, "Moose, I'll protect you. I'll get your back. Don't worry." He's shopping around, trying to make sure that he gets the right bargain on the bottle. I have to calculate for him—if you buy a 32-ounce bottle versus the 60-ounce bottle . . . He wanted to decide which of them would have the best booze for the buck. We got two bottles, and Mickey started to drink. Greer brings me over and says, "Listen. The way we mix Mickey's drinks are you take the glass and put the ice in, you fill the glass almost to the top with the tonic, and then very, very slowly, you pour the vodka in so it doesn't mix.

> The way we mix Mickey's drinks are you take the glass and put the ice in, you fill the glass almost to the top with the tonic, and then very, very slowly, you pour the vodka in so it doesn't mix.

That way, the first sip Mickey takes will be almost all vodka so he thinks you have mixed a real concentrated drink. In fact, there's not a whole lot of vodka in there at all." She was protecting him. The other guys would never allow anybody to bother him.

I made arrangements for them to go to a locally owned steak place and got them a private room. I dropped them off and they let them in the back door. I didn't stay with them because we had theater tickets. When I picked the guys up the next morning, Moose said, "Doc, that was the best place we ever went. We made reservations to go again tonight because nobody knew we were there. Everybody was discreet. Nobody asked for autographs." It was the best steak they had in a long time. They had a wonderful time there. That night when they went back, the waitress had bought a Yankee shirt and Yankee cap to wear and took care of them. Mickey gave her a $500 tip! She broke down crying on the floor hugging his knees while he was standing there, sobbing and thanking him. That was the most generous thing anybody had ever done for her in her whole life. Mickey was like, "You did a wonderful job, and we had a relaxing time." They never really get to be without outside pressure, and it was worth it to him to just be able to sit back and relax and not worry about the outside world coming in.

The players were a lot of fun to be with 'cause they have stories about the practical jokes they used to play on each other. They have amazing memories for certain key events. It was like, "Remember when I hit the two-and-two pitch into the right field corner, and we beat the so-and so's." It's like holy #*&@. . . you can remember it was a two-two pitch. I can't remember what I'm wearing today, but they can remember stuff from thirty years past.

Since then, I've gotten to know Blanchard and Larsen very well. Blanchard gives me tickets to Old Timers Day every year. Last year, we sat in the Whitey Ford suite or whatever it's called with a lot of the families from the '77–'78 Yankees. Just to sit back and listen and watch these people who haven't seen each other for a long time—they were teammates and friends, but their lives have gone off in different directions. For the most part, they haven't stayed in touch. They get caught up with each other and start telling stories about their playing days. That's like going to a fantasy camp.

> Mickey gave her a $500 tip! She broke down crying on the floor hugging his knees while he was standing there, sobbing and thanking him.

I went to Mantle's last fantasy camp in '94 before he became really ill. It was the "week of my life" because there you are with a bunch of "never-were's" playing baseball with a bunch of has-been's. Bob Costas was one of the campers with me that week. There were people who are bankers, doctors, lawyers, sanitation workers, but everybody is equal once you put on the uniform 'cause wherever they grew up, everybody worshipped

Mickey and that was why they paid their four grand to come back for a week—to watch and look and listen.

Costas was trying to do a television piece so he actually had much better access to Mickey. As a player, Costas looked good in the uniform but was not a particularly good fielder or hitter . . . but, he looked good out there! There were some people who were incredibly good athletes. Then, there were the rest of us who went through the motions and threw wild.

Costas was nice when you could see him and talk to him, but that was very rare. We almost never actually saw him because he was off interviewing Mickey or other people. He was working a fair amount that week and only stayed a couple of days.

> As a player, Costas looked good in the uniform but was not a particularly good fielder or hitter . . .

The best story from the week for me was in the Friday night game against the recently retired Yankees, there were six teams during that week in fantasy camp. Each team got six outs per inning and you played two innings so everybody was guaranteed at least one at-bat against the Yankee players. Out of my twelve-member team, I got the only hit. I have that on videotape. My hit was off Guidry. I remind him on a yearly basis—at least, I used to when I'd see him—"Man, I'm a lifetime .400 hitter off you. I was one for four in the fantasy game you pitched, and then in the Friday night game, I was one for one. I didn't see what was so tough about that hook you threw." He looked me straight in the eye and says, "The next time I see you, you're going down." They just love playing that kind of stuff with you. It's not like, "you're bothering me," it's that they really appreciate the fans 'cause that's what made their careers. . . .

My sixtieth birthday was coming up and our kids were trying to plan something. I didn't want to do what we did for my wife's fiftieth, which was go to a beach and sit there for a week. I said, "If we went to Maine, it's beautiful country. There's a lot of stuff to do. Beautiful drives. You can walk along the beach. It's not ridiculously hot, and you can have lobster at least twice a day." They talked about that but said it was really too boring. "We're not going to do that." About a week later, my second son, who is an attorney, called and said, "I've got to give away the surprise because we're having some trouble. We want to take you to Yankee Stadium—all eleven of us—together, including kids, their wives, et cetera." They had called Blanchard to ask if he could help get eleven tickets together. If you've ever tried to get medium-sized parties to Yankee games, it's not possible. You go on the Web site or you call Ticketmaster and you say you want eleven, they say that's not big enough. The team has tickets for parties of twenty or more. They'll offer to get two seats here and three there, etc. I called a good friend in New York to ask for some advice. He was able to contact somebody who was able to work it out so we got Row D, Seats 1 through 11—fabulous seats. It worked out unbelievably.

I have literally one-of-a-kind Mantle pictures that were obtained through Mantle's sister: his fifth-grade class portrait, his seventh-grade individual class picture, and the photographs that were used in his high school yearbooks—the informal shots. All of them came indirectly from his family.

Tommy Catal, from Cooperstown, who started the whole phenomenon of autograph card shows, had Mantle in '80 on Long Island at Hofstra. Mantle signed for about five bucks a signature and thought it was a lot of fun and wanted to do it again. About eight weeks later, they did it again . . . and the price went up to $10, where it stayed for a long time. Then, it went up a little bit more—a little bit more. Mantle was the first one who really pushed the envelope.

Then, other players, like **TED WILLIAMS***, got on the bandwagon. They felt like they could get more than that . . . and then everything escalated way out of anything like reality.

*TED WILLIAMS and his son John Henry are among only 161 people world-wide who await rebirth from a cryogenic state . . . 157 are stored in three U.S. facilities . . . In real life many are cold, but few are frozen.

One time Tommy went and visited Mickey's sister and was able to get a lot of the family stuff for his collection—he had a Mickey Mantle Museum in Cooperstown. It didn't have enough people visiting, or he didn't want to keep up all the maintenance on it, so he bought another building in Cooperstown and has most of the stuff in storage or at his house.

There's a guy in Jersey who's got clearly the best Mantle collection in the United States that we're aware of, but he never lets anybody in there because he's afraid somebody will break in and lift several million dollars worth of stuff.

Name the Orioles manager --win valuable prizes!

Derek Jeter invented electricity.

FREE AGENTS AREN'T FREE
PAY BALL!

Vince Gennaro

Vince Gennarro is the former president of the Pepsi Cola Fountain Division. He grew up in Wayne, New Jersey, 20 miles from Yankee Stadium, and now lives in Purchase, New York. Gennaro, 55, has an MBA from the University of Chicago and an undergraduate degree from Seton Hall. He also owned a professional women's basketball team, the St. Louis Streak of the WBL, which folded in 1981.

One time when I was at Pepsi, I was bidding for the Burger King business and so was Coke. I ended up going back to the Pepsico Board saying, "We're not going to win this. I can tell that they are married to Coca-Cola. They've been in there for ten years, and they're not going to change because they feel like making a switch is a huge operational undertaking, and they're saying, 'Why should we do it?'" Now, the goal is if Coke is going to win it, let's make them win it at a price that'll kill them, so we ended up bidding this thing up. Much later, the Burger King guy told me, "It was funny. When you guys gave us your final bid, we went to Coke and said, 'Look, we want to keep you, but, here's what it's going to take.'" Coke said, "We're not giving you that kind of funding. We're not giving you that low a price." The BK guy said, "I'm just telling you. I don't want to show you the Pepsi sheet, but I'm telling you, so don't say you weren't forewarned. You're going to lose the business." Coke told us, "Pepsi would never give you that price." They were right, in a sense, because the only reason we put that price up there is we figured where Coke would go to match before they would break. Sure enough, we cost Coke $40 million more to retain their business than they were paying before we were in the bidding. If Coke hadn't matched the offer, we would have had to "pay the piper." At that point, we were talking to Roger Enrico, who was our chairman. He said, "I agree with you, Vince, that we are, in all likelihood, still going to lose it, and I realize we're taking a risk, but, at that point, we're going to have to think of it as marketing spending and advertising spending to be in that chain. If we have to cut our advertising dollars on TV we will—we'll eat it." It's not a price we'd want to pay but we all agreed this was the right thing to do. Eventually Coke stepped up. Frankly, after they signed the Coke deal, Burger King showed them what our offer was 'cause they said, "Congratulations, you got this money out of us, but did Pepsi really put that up?" They showed it to them, and they said, "Son of a gun. I can't believe it. It's so out of character for Pepsi to do that." I just found all this out a couple of years ago, and the negotiations were in '99.

I tell the story because it's analogous to what is going on with the bidding in baseball. The Red Sox or Cubs could have played the A-Rod game up for everything it was worth. Despite the fact I'm a Yankee fan, I think they could have taken the Yankees to the cleaners on this. They could have made the Yankees ante up. Of course, A-Rod becomes the winner in the deal. But, if the Red Sox can hamstring the Yankees so that they have to pay A-Rod so much they feel like they've got so much tied up in this guy, they can't also do this and this and this. The Red Sox would help themselves in the long run—they had to look at this as an opportunity, even if you don't win the player. Of course, now that A-Rod has signed again with the Yankees, it's a moot point.

In the '70s, when I was in business school, I did some research for a paper. I researched on "How much was Catfish Hunter worth to the Yankees?" Steinbrenner had signed him for five years at $3.75 million, which sounded off-the-charts back then. I put this statistical model together and figured it out. I took it in to the Players' Association and discussed it with them. That was a gutsy thing for a guy my age to do. I always felt like I had a destiny of maybe being in the game some day, and being in and around the game. I thought I had something to contribute to it.

I had met with Dick Moss, who I think was Marvin Miller's No. 2 at the time. A couple of years later, I'm out of business school working as an economic consultant in Chicago. I decide to take this concept of "how much is a player worth" and really try to make more of it. I create a series of models where I estimate the value of a win to each team. It was based on their attendance. I didn't have the amount of data you have today on TV contracts and the like. With this formula I had, I could plug in a player to the Orioles, and if he improved the Orioles by four wins, I could tell you how much the Orioles could afford to pay him, if they went by the book. Back then, this was unheard of. *The Sporting News* wrote it up. They write an article in March of '79. Nolan Ryan sees the article. I get a phone call from Dick Moss, who, by this time, is Nolan Ryan's agent. I spend two or three hours with Dick in his Columbus Circle office in the spring of '79 talking about the system. He said to me, "Vince, this is fascinating, but I gotta tell you. I really don't think baseball is ready for this. I cannot imagine sitting down across the table from **BUZZY BAVASI***"—at the time Nolan was with the Angels—"and really having this work for me." He said he thought it was very interesting stuff. I went off and decided to go buy a women's pro basketball team right after that so it was a funny tack that I took.

I don't have an issue with free agency. I think it's fine. It's a way of life, and we're all adjusted to it. One of the negatives is that it creates a transient ball player. Brooks Robinson has the record—his twenty-three years with the Orioles. But, you don't see that anymore. You don't even see ten years with a team. Players like Craig Biggio and Chipper Jones are really the exceptions today.

The Yankees have always made the biggest splash. They've always been at the front of the free-agent line in terms of who

*The late **BUZZY BAVASI**, when G.M. of the Dodgers, once offered his pitchers $25 if they would run a mile. Don Drysdale said he would do it right after Jesse Owens won twenty games. . . . Drysdale once said that his most important pitch was his second knockdown pitch. "That way the batter knew the first one wasn't an accident."

they've gotten. If the Yankees have wanted a player over the years, there haven't been very many that if they really wanted him that they haven't gotten. What the Yankees have done very well, they've exploited their financial resources. They've exploited being in the biggest market. Now you add to the biggest market, the YES Network and the financial prowess that gives them. Basically, the Yankees—and you can say this about the Red Sox, too—whole entire business model is built around winning. You can't say that about the Pirates or the Royals. If the Pirates or the Royals win, they're a little better off, and if they lose, they're not so good off. The Yankees really are built to win. If they don't win, frankly, it's catastrophic. People say, "Well, people are gonna always come to Yankee Stadium." You know what, you turn in a couple of 84-win seasons in a row, and you're going to see an exodus out of the Stadium. I estimated that if the Yankees were a mid-80s win team or low-80s win team for two years, they probably draw 8,000 fans less than they draw per game today. That's what my models say, and I absolutely believe that, too. People forget that the Yankees, like most teams, their crowds, their success are predicated on being a winning team.

> You know what, you turn in a couple of 84-win seasons in a row, and you're going to see an exodus out of the Stadium.

Relatively, gate success is less important today given the media revenue. The average price of a Red Sox ticket is over $46 and the average Yankee ticket is over $28. That's when you do an average of the whole house. As the Yankees move into their new ballpark, the word is that the average ticket price will be in the mid-fifties. As much as broadcast revenues are a critical part—I think the Yankees get 60 million from YES, but they own 35 percent of YES so you could add 35 percent of the profits of YES and 35 percent of the value of the Yes network into that, but still when you start adding four million times $50 a head, you're talking about two hundred million in ticket revenue. In the new Stadium, ticket revenues will become more than half of all Yankee revenues.

It used to be that the baseball business was built around the fan. You go back to large stadiums with modest ticket prices, and it was all about getting the Average Joe into the ballpark. If you look at the wave of new stadiums, including the two that are coming here to New York, both of which are going to be significantly downsized . . . The Mets Stadium is going to be 10,000 less seats, and the Yankee Stadium 5 to 6,000 less seats.

> It's crazy. I do think there's a vulnerability to an economic downturn that didn't used to exist.

Now the baseball business is being geared to corporations as buyers, whether it's client entertainment or whether it's a perk for your employees or whatever. They're so much more with luxury suites and high-priced tickets, dependent on businesses. They're much more vulnerable than ever in the past to an economic downtown.

The Yankees' best seats for day of game—they probably don't have very many of those left—are four hundred bucks—this is face value—I think they're $300 in advance or for season ticket-holders. But, in those seats where you see a Rudy Giuliani or a Mike Bloomberg, that's what those seats cost the day of game—they actually have a $400 seat. Those are not individuals. Those are business people of some kind or hedge fund traders or something. It's crazy. I do think there's a vulnerability to an economic downturn that didn't used to exist. Really, it was pretty impervious to that, but I think those days are over. And, if the tax laws change, that is an issue. There are some clear benefits so that's another factor if that should happen. Game day price for field championship level seats—first five rows of Sections 1 to 68 are $400—the advance price is $300.

A lot of people believe that the Yankees have achieved what they've achieved on an uneven playing field. Clearly, winning breeds in a faction that's opposed because we have a bit of an underdog mentality in this country and some people don't like to see the same guys winning all the time.

YANKEES FANS' SUMMER COTTAGE BY THE LAKE: EXHIBITION STADIUM

Dan Mangone

Dan Mangone recently retired from East-man Kodak after thirty-two years. He now works with young people with disabilities at the Greece Central School District in Upstate New York.

It started in Toronto at old Exhibition Stadium. I was a big fan of Reggie Jackson. Rod Carew wasn't really one of my favorite players. There was a boy standing outside—first in line at Exhibition Stadium. He was wearing a California jersey and had an Angel hat on, and had a poster that said, ROD CAREW IS THE BEST. I said, "You really like Rod Carew, don't you?" He said, "He's my favorite ball player. I have everything that's ever been printed on him." I said, "You really do?" He said, "Almost."

Many people don't know that Rod Carew was raised in the Bronx but was born unexpectedly on a train in Panama. An American doctor named Rodney Cline, who was a passenger on that train, helped with the birth. Rod Carew's full name is Rodney Cline Carew.

We go into the Stadium. It's before the game. The players are working out in the outfield. Rod is running back and forth. This little boy is standing there with his poster. Rod's not looking around. He's just doing his exercises. Reggie is running around, looking at everybody. I notice that this boy just keeps standing there. Rod was running back and forth. I yelled, "Mr. Carew, I think there's a young man here who would like to see you." Rod stopped . . . he looked at the boy standing there . . . he saw the poster and the California Angels hat and jersey. He said to the little boy, "Go behind the dugout." The little boy ran over behind the dugout. Rod finished his workout in the outfield, came in, went over by the dugout, had his picture taken with the boy, signed a ball for him, and talked with him for a while.

I walked over. I said, "Wow, that's pretty classy. That's really nice. Rod, the year you're elected to the Hall of Fame, I'll be there. You're just a real good ballplayer and a real neat person." He throws me a ball. I go to catch it . . . and I dropped my camera onto the ground . . . I drop the ball onto the ground. If you jump over the fence to retrieve anything, they throw you out of the Stadium, but I knew I had to get this ball. I jump over the fence, pick up the ball, and said to myself, "I've got to get this signed somehow." I run behind the dugout, and just as I get there, the usher said, "No more autographs. Everybody has to go back to their seats." Rod is standing right there in front of me, and he motions for me to come down to him. I said to the usher, "Rod Carew wants me to come down to see him." I went down there, and he autographed the ball!

> If you jump over the fence to retrieve anything, they throw you out of the Stadium, but I knew I had to get this ball.

That started the whole thing. That year I sent him a Christmas card and we established the friendship. The year he retired from baseball, he sent me a Christmas card with a picture of him, his wife and his three daughters. His one daughter has passed on. She developed acute leukemia. Over the years, whenever California was up at Toronto, I would go up to see him. We'd exchange greetings. I sent him photographic paper because he had a darkroom in his basement. He used to use that color paper to make prints. It was a real nice relationship we had over the years. Last year, he came to Rochester, New York, because Rochester now is the affiliate of the Twins, and he's a scout for them. It was Hall of Fame induction weekend so they brought Rod into town as a promo. Everybody bought a ticket to this luncheon with Rod Carew. I walked up to him and said, "Rod, do you remember me, Dan Mangone? He said, "Oh, my God, how have you been? It's been a long time." He got up to give his speech and said, "People like the Mangones who travel all over to watch us play are the kind of sports fans we need in this game." We used to go to games in Cleveland and Toronto to watch him play. Then, he came and sat at the table where my wife, Judy, and I were sitting and had lunch with us. Then he went up to podium and talked to everybody. It was one of the highlights of my life. Imagine Rod Carew sitting at our table. There were 500 people there, and he sat at our table. I never dreamed that my favorite ballplayer would be a non-Yankee.

> I never dreamed that my favorite ballplayer would be a non-Yankee.

I established friendship with Reggie Jackson through a model car I made for him. Ken Kaiser, an umpire who lives in my hometown of Greece, used to have a sports dinner every November. He'd bring in different baseball players that he had a working relationship with or a friendship. The first dinner he had, he brought in Billy Martin, plus he had some professional wrestlers. They didn't really blend, but it was a dinner, and the money he gathered he gave to the St. Joseph's Villa Children's Orphanage Home here in Rochester.

In '85, Reggie Jackson was coming to Kaiser's dinner. That same year, I went to Toronto. Reggie was down by the dugout. I went over and started talking to him, "I understand you're coming to Rochester, coming to Ken Kaiser's dinner. I understand you are into classic cars, and your first car was a '55 Chevy. I'd like to know the color of it and the interior and things like that." He told me the color was a burgundy, two-door and was the very first car he had. I said, "When you come to Ken Kaiser's dinner in November, I want to give you this model car I'm going to make for you. I want it to look somewhat like the car you had." I had from April to November to get this car made for Reggie.

When we were in the lobby of the Westin Hotel, Mr. Jackson, Reggie's dad was there. I was talking to him telling him I was making Reggie a car. He misunderstood me. He thought I was going to give Reggie a '55 Chevy to add to his collection. Reggie walked by, and he said, "Reggie, Reggie, this man's going to give you a '55 Chevy when you go to Rochester to Ken Kaiser's dinner." Reggie said, "No, Dad. He's going to make me a model of my first car. He's not going to give me a car." His dad said, "Oh, oh, I'm sorry." Mr. Jackson was a very personable, a very nice man. He was smaller than Reggie. Reggie was quite big compared to his dad. Reggie's dad was a very well spoken, very nice man.

I made the car over the months. I painted it the color he had told me—a purple reddish color metallic. I had it specially made, and I had it put in a spray can so I could actually make it the exact same color. I did all the complete details. It took me four months to complete this car and get it right the way I wanted to.

I liked Reggie because of his charisma and his just being Reggie. The three home runs—that's unbelievable—**MR. OCTOBER*!** When he came to Rochester, and I got to meet him in person, one-on-one, and I gave him the little model car I made for him, I saw a different side to him. When he was with his dad up in Toronto in the lobby, I saw a loving, caring guy with his dad. He was really a different guy and persona than was presented to the public most of the time. He was in the lobby of the Westin Hotel one night. I was there with my eleven-year-old nephew. Reggie was walking around the lobby with a lady friend. I said to Cory, "That's Reggie over there. If you want an autograph, why don't you go ask him?" He walked up to him and said, "Excuse me, Mr. Jackson, could I have your autograph?" Even though he was with a girlfriend, he accommodated my nephew very nicely. He's got a variety of autographs—when he's rushed, when he's not rushed, and when he cares about the autographs. I saw a side to Reggie,

---

*In **REGGIE JACKSON**'s last ten October games, he was 7 for 44 with one home run and 14 strikeouts. . . . Only 3 of Mr. October's 18 October home runs put his team in the lead.

---

especially around his dad. He just loved his dad. A lot of people didn't get a chance to see that.

November came. I went to the dinner. I took my son and we went up to the front. They had a private seating in the basement that only invited guests were before the dinner. I walked up to one of the security guards and said, "My name is Dan Mangone. I made this car for Reggie Jackson. I told him about it up in Toronto. I told him I was going to present it to him when he came to Ken Kaiser's dinner." He said, "OK. Come down." We went downstairs into the private room. It was like a child in a chocolate shop. There was Billy Martin. There was George Brett. There was Sparky Anderson. There was Harold Baines, Reggie, Lou Piniella—it was unbelievable. Here we are, just shoulder-to-shoulder with these people, and I walk up to Reggie and said, "I have the car here for you." I presented the car to him. He took it out, and he was very impressed. He said, "Thank you. That was very thoughtful of you." . . .

> I go to the receptionist and said, "I've got a dozen cannolis for Phil Rizzuto, which I brought from Rochester."

I had a black and white picture of Phil Rizzuto leaping up in the air to catch a ball. This fellow at Kodak gave it to me. I told him I wanted to put it in the Yankee Room. I wanted to get it signed. We were going up to a Yankee game in Toronto at Exhibition Stadium, before they even moved to the SkyDome. It was in late September. Reggie was there. I got a dozen cannolis here from an Italian bakery and put them in a nice box. I took them to Toronto and went to the press entrance there at the Stadium with my little bag I had with the picture in it. I go to the receptionist and said, "I've got a dozen cannolis for Phil Rizzuto, which I brought from Rochester." She said, "Leave them here, and I'll see that he gets them." I said, "Could I give them to him myself in person? I brought them all the way from Rochester in a nice box." With the security guard standing right there, she said, "That sounds like a nice idea. Wait right here." I waited about twenty minutes, and he came back and said, "Come with me. We're going to take you up to the press dining room." My heart was pounding—skipping a beat. We got through the bowels of Exhibition Stadium and get to a freight elevator. We go to the very top and walk through the hall and go into the dining room. All the press are in there, and Phil is sitting at a table. I walk over and say, "I'm Dan Mangone, from Rochester, New York, and I've got some cannolis for you. They're the best I ever had." I present him with the cannolis. He said, "Well, I've got to have some coffee." I look around and walk over to the coffee pot, which was on a server at the back—like I worked there. I get him coffee. He said, "Wow!" I said, "I've got something I'd like to show you." I open my bag and pull out this picture. He goes, "Holy Cow! Where did you get that?" It was of him making a catch. He signed it, "To Dan Mangone. Best wishes, Phil Rizzuto." Then he mentioned me on the broadcast that night, "My friend from Rochester, New York, who brought me cannolis, Dan Mangone." My buddies back in Rochester heard him say that on the air. That was one of the highlights of my career—meeting Phil and giving him cannolis and then having him sign that picture. . . .

My favorite player ever to play the game is Babe Ruth. I have an autograph that my next-door neighbor got back in the '40s. Babe Ruth came to the sanitarium where she worked and went to the men's dormitory. Then, someone said, "Are you going to visit the women?" He went over to visit the ladies, and she had an autograph book. He signed it, "Sincerely, Babe Ruth." I have that autograph. It's in a beautiful frame mounted with a picture of him and his Hall of Fame card. That's my prized possession.

Bud Selig was never on "The $100,000 Pyramid" because he doesn't have a clue.

CLONES ARE PEOPLE TWO

Mickey Mantle Fortin

Mickey Mantle Fortin moved from Waterbury, Connecticut, to Florida in 1990. Fortin's restaurant, owned by his father, was a Waterbury landmark for years. Now in the insurance business, Fortin, 54, is moving from Holiday, Florida, to Tennessee, claiming that Florida is "Paradise Lost."

My mom and dad were great Yankee fans. It was the 1952 World Series, and the Yankees were playing the Brooklyn Dodgers. It was the eighth inning and the score was 2–1. This young slugger was coming up. My father made a vow to the baseball "gods" that if this guy hit a home run, and won the World Series, he would name his soon-to-be-born baby after this baseball player. Mickey Mantle hit that home run to win the game. Six months later, when I was born, on June 10, 1953, my dad and my mother fought for about five days. They let women stay in the hospital a lot longer back then. I was named "Baby Doe," baby John Doe because my mother and my father were going round and round. My father said, "His name is going to be Mickey Mantle Fortin. My mother said, "We can't give him that name." She wanted to name me Michael. Mickey wasn't known as a Christian name, a Catholic name. My father was getting all kinds of repercussions from different priests. You couldn't find a St. Mickey anywhere, back in those days. The nurses kept seeing this baby with no name, and they were wondering what the heck is going on. They were told that these parents were fighting and couldn't decide on a name. My father finally found a priest and said to him, "Look, if you won't baptize my son, I'm going to go to the next church. If you won't baptize him with the name Mickey, I'll find somebody somewhere who will baptize this baby, Mickey Mantle." My father, stubborn as he was, got his way. I have all kinds of pictures—me at nine and ten months old, with Yankee pajamas and logos and the name MICKEY MANTLE right on my chest.

I got to meet Mickey Mantle many times. My father was friends with him for over twenty-two years. I was captain of my baseball team in grammar school. When I went to high school, Kennedy High School, I tried out for the baseball team. My dad came home from work and said, "Did you make the team? How did you do?" I said to him, "I didn't make the team. As a matter of fact, the coach told me to come back in a couple of years." My father said, "Did he see you throw?" I said, "No, we didn't even get to catch or do anything." He said, "Did he see you hit?" I said, "Nope. I didn't even pick up a bat." My father became so angry that the next week he went out and bought a house in Naugatuck, Connecticut, on Good Friday with only six weeks left in the school year. He pulled me out and I went to Naugatuck High School. There was a gentleman from Naugatuck, where I was brought up, a famous pitcher for the Yankees, Frank "Spec" Shea, who they used to call "The Naugatuck Nugget." He won two World Series games in his rookie year. He also won an All-Star game. Spec Shea would go to the New York Sports Writers Dinner, and, a lot of times, he would invite my dad to go with him to that annual bash and also to Old Timers Day. My dad got to meet Mickey Mantle.

> "His name is going to be Mickey Mantle Fortin. My mother said, "We can't give him that name."

My family owned a restaurant in Connecticut for thirty years, Fortin's Restaurant. My dad had gone to New York a couple of times and had visited a real fancy restaurant, Toots Shor's. That was the type of restaurant where all the athletes and movie stars would hang out. They'd come to the restaurant and Toots would get his picture taken with them sitting at a table or standing together. Then, he would post these pictures in the foyer or all around the restaurant to show signatures of famous people. My father started that with his restaurant. At the end when he finally sold it, he had over 250 different pictures of famous people that had come to our restaurant—from baseball players to guys like Glen Campbell, Tony Bennett. He had several Yankee players, Mickey Mantle, Joe DiMaggio.

Mickey Mantle and my father both died on the same date. My father died on August 13, 1984. Mickey Mantle dies on August 13, 1995. They both died of liver cancer. My dad owned a restaurant, so he was a drinker. There were so many people always coming in and buying him drinks. He did his fair share of drinking. Every year, from January 1 until Easter, my father wouldn't touch a drink, not a drop.

When I first met Mickey Mantle, live and in person, and did more than just shake hands, I was twenty-three. I met him at a popular restaurant in Southington. My father had picked Mickey up at the airport on numerous occasions and chauffeured him to speaking occasions. He'd played golf with him. To be honest with you, in those days, when I was in my late teens and early twenties, I was very intimidated by these people, and I didn't want to be around them. It just didn't turn me on. The first time I went to this dinner with my dad, Mickey Mantle was the guest speaker. I walked up to him and said, "Hey, Mick. I'm Clarence Fortin's son. I'm really glad to finally meet you. I'll bet you I'm the first kid in this country that's named after you." You've got to remember, in 1952

> I remember going out to centerfield on occasions, when I was young, and crying out there thinking, "Why couldn't I just have a regular name? Why are people making fun of me? I'm just a kid trying to play baseball."

Mickey Mantle was just a second-year player. Mickey Mantle looked at me and said, "Do you know how many kids in this #&@% country are named after me? I don't really give a &#^@.

Don't bother me with that." He was sitting at the head dais. Those bar shaker glasses—the glass part—that they make mixed drinks in. . . . He had one of those in front of him. The guy who owned the restaurant is good friends with my father. My father was president of the Connecticut Restaurant Association for five years. He said, "Do you see that big tall glass that looks like water in front of Mickey Mantle?" My father said, "Yeah." He said, "Well, for your information, that thing is nothing but straight vodka." Nice. I actually have the picture of Mickey Mantle and me standing together with his arm around me. His eyes look like two *#^@ holes in the snow.

Growing up with the name Mickey Mantle was like carrying a cross. When I was growing up, Mickey Mantle was still playing. He was still a big star. It wasn't like he had come and gone. When I went to play baseball, if I made an error, or, if I struck out, I was teased by a lot of these kids, like, "Oh, what's the matter, Mickey Mantle?" Even the parents were sometimes really cruel in their ridicule trying to get me rattled. I remember going out to centerfield on occasions, when I was young, and crying out there thinking, "Why couldn't I just have a regular name? Why are people making fun of me? I'm just a kid trying to play baseball." And, I did wear No. 7, and I did play centerfield.

Today, at this point, I'm glad to have the name. It's made me who I am. The funny part is that my dad obviously wanted me to be a baseball player or he wouldn't have given me the name of Mickey Mantle. Then, my father bought this house and transferred me from one school to another because he wanted me to play for this coach who was one of the most famous coaches in Connecticut, Ray Legenza. He's famous for his drill-sergeant technique of coaching and turning young boys into men.

When I transferred to Naugatuck High School, my freshman year, I made the freshman baseball team. Ray Legenza pulled my father over to the side and said, "Look Clarence, I know that you named your son Mickey Mantle, and I know that you moved to Naugatuck because you have high expectations of him playing baseball at our school, but I'm going to be honest with you. I know a ballplayer when I see one. Your kid's never gonna make it as a ballplayer." I was in my sophomore year then. The coach was just being honest with my father and trying to let him down easy—thinking he had all these expectations for his kid, but, realistically, "I've evaluated his talent, and I don't think his talent is that he's going to be a baseball star or whatever you wanted." Mr. Legenza had a knack of taking people when they were freshmen in high school and developing them for four years. I had teammates who got signed right out of high school.

> "... Mickey Mantle might have been one of the greatest baseball players, but, as far as a man and a human being, he's a jerk."

All I know is that every time there's anything mentioned about baseball and about baseball history, Mickey Mantle's name always seems to come up so it's a constant reminder to me. I have a collection of baseball cards, and I've got a '56 Mickey Mantle MVP Triple Crown card. I've got a 1960 Mickey Mantle card. I've got a bunch of balls signed by Mickey Mantle. I don't know what made him so great because when he insulted me that day at that restaurant, I walked over to my father, with tears in my eyes, and I said to him, "You know what, Dad, Mickey Mantle might have been one of the greatest baseball players, but, as far as a man and a human being, he's a jerk." That was exactly what I said.

I made All-New England my last year in school. Here we were at the awards banquet. My coach who said I never would make it as a ballplayer is presenting the batting champion trophy to me. He said, "This year's trophy goes to a kid that really doesn't deserve this, but he did have the highest average on the team so I have no other choice but to award it to him." That's how he gave me my batting championship trophy.

PLAYIN' FAVORITES

Growing up, my favorite player was Clete Boyer. One of the reasons was that I was an infielder and a third baseman and really revered his defense. I'd rather watch a shortstop or a third baseman diving for a ball and coming up making the play than a 450-foot home run. To me, that's baseball. That's what I love about it. I just fell in love with Clete. He was one of my heroes despite being a fairly light-hitting third baseman. He did have a couple of good years with the Braves.

For my fiftieth birthday, my daughter, who was fifteen at the time, went to the mall here in town and met Clete, who was there doing a ball signing. She bought a ball and had him sign it for me. I thought that was really special that on my fiftieth birthday she did that. She's really become quite a baseball fan herself and is very much following in my love of the game.

I grew up a Yankee fan. I was born in '51. In the Maris-Mantle year, I was ten years old, but I was an early fan. I went to my first Yankee game, and I kept the stub—May 17, 1957. I'd been planning for May 17, 2007, for years. As soon as the 2007 Yankee schedule came out, I said I was going to a Yankee game. My daughter and I flew to Chicago when the Yankees were playing the White Sox at U.S. Cellular Park on May 17. I'm sitting here at my desk now looking at two ticket stubs—May 17, '57, and May 17, '07—so I've been to Yankee games fifty years apart.

The next day, we went to **WRIGLEY*** because it just so happened that was the first day of the Cubs–White Sox interleague game. That was my daughter's first time at Wrigley and the first time at the White Sox park. She was shocked at the crowd. People had no interest in the baseball game. I'm not talking just the women—we were sitting in about the fifth row of the upper deck, and people were talking about mortgage rates. The baseball

*P. K. **WRIGLEY** and Milton Hershey were bitter business rivals. When Wrigley bought the Chicago Cubs, Hershey tried to buy the Philadelphia Phillies . . . and sell chocolate gum. Hershey failed in both efforts.

game was an absolute afterthought. One of my friends who lives in Chicago said they wrote in the Chicago paper that if they turn the seats around and faced them the opposite direction, they wouldn't sell any less tickets to the game, which I thought was a funny way to look at it.

—<u>VINCE GENNARO</u>, baseball consultant

> . . . if they turn the seats around and faced them the opposite direction, they wouldn't sell any less tickets to the game . . .

Mickey Mantle had a great smile. He owned the town. He owned the place. He could go anywhere. I had a big fight with Mickey Mantle. It was about two years before he passed away. I had about eight things I wanted signed. If you could picture this, Mantle was sitting in the middle of the table. To his left was his bodyguard. To his right, they said it was his daughter—I think it was his girlfriend. The bodyguard sees me there and tells me, "You're not to ask him to sign a bat for you." I said, "Oh no." I knew he wouldn't sign bats for anybody, even though he did for me in '84.

I got up there. I had my godson with me who's maybe a year old. I had my nephew Philip maybe six years old. I said, "Mickey, this is the bat I played with as a kid. Can you sign this bat?" He jumped up right in front of me, got in my face and said, "Why should I sign a bat for you and not for anybody else?" I said, "You should sign bats. It doesn't matter what you sign for $75 an autograph." Fifty feet behind us there was a man selling a Mickey Mantle autographed bat for 1,200 bucks. I said, "See, because you don't sign bats, see what he's doing." Then, Mantle really got nasty. I turned my hat around like Earl Weaver and said, "For what I'm paying you, you should sign my %@^$#." My nephew, Philip, who is a cop today, said, "But, Uncle Ron, that's Mickey Mantle." I said, "I don't give a &#^@ who he is." I said to Mantle, "Let me tell you something. If your stuff wasn't worth so much money, I'd throw you out of my basement room. I loved you and I idolized you as a kid, but, as a man I wouldn't %@*& on you if you were on fire." This occurred in a big building and it echoes when you're loud. I was so mad, I don't remember what Mickey said to me during all this, but after I turned my hat, we went nose-to-nose. He knew better than to hit me fearing a lawsuit, which I would never have done anyway. I'd had eight items signed by him so that was about $600. I've got twenty-two items signed by Mickey Mantle, total.

The assistant was saying, "Well, he's coming out with his own set of bats in a couple of months so he doesn't want to sign any bats." In '84, I went to a show in Brooklyn. For ten bucks, he signed a baseball bat for me, a Mickey Mantle bat. All of a sudden, those guys started to see *money!* What can I say?

When he died, a local newspaper called me up because they knew about my room. I was sad about him passing away. A month or two before, he had an interview with Bob Costas. He apologized to fans for being an *@&$ at card shows. Well, I felt like he apologized to me. He said right out that he was no good. He apologized, and I took his apology personally. When they interviewed me, I spoke up for him highly . . . and I always will.

I went to Monmouth Race Track with my kids. **DAVE WINFIELD*** was there. That was after the Opening Day and just before he got traded to California. He was there for batting instruction with the kids for an hour. There were about fifteen kids there he did baseball things with. He remembered every kid's name. That man is a pleasure to go see at an autograph show. He'll talk to you. He had a good time. He didn't have no bad attitude like a lot of guys do at card shows. He was a pleasure. And, Rickey Henderson, believe it or not, is a dynamite guy at a card show, who will talk to you.

—RON FUSCO, ex-Marine, electrical contractor

Mel Stottlemyre was my favorite Yankee. Because of the fact that he had just come up that summer of '64, when I started following the team, I just gravitated to him as my favorite player. I used to follow him very closely. I remember that home run—an inside-

---

*In 1973 **DAVE WINFIELD**, from the University of Minnesota, was drafted in the 4th round by the San Diego Padres, in the 16th round by the Minnesota Vikings, by the Utah Stars in the 4th round, and the Atlanta Hawks in the 5th round.

the-park grand slam by a pitcher! I was at a place called Memorial Pool with my transistor radio, which was attached to my ear in those days. I must have had it surgically removed at some point. I heard that on the radio that day—an inside-the-park grand slam. Also, there was a game where he went five for five. *He went five for five* and pitched a two-hit shut out.

Just a few years ago, I was walking between meetings in Manhattan. I walked past the Grand Hyatt Hotel. A lot of the out-of-town teams stay there when they come in to play the Yankees and the Mets. Stottlemyre and his team were boarding their team bus to go to Shea Stadium. I recognized him so I went over to him and told him, "You're my favorite player." When I was a kid I couldn't wait to see him pitch every fourth day. He seemed to appreciate it. He probably thought I was a nut.

> There is a baseball Web site called baseball-reference.com. This is like an online version of the Macmillan Encyclopedia. It's fantastic.

I met him one time. My youngest son had this blown-up poster from the front page of the *New York Post* when the Yankees won the World Series in 1996 against the Braves. He started collecting autographs of players from that team on the poster. It was 2006, and I had read that there was a ten-year reunion of the '96 Yankees to be held in one of the hotels in New Jersey and it included an autograph session. My son could not go—school or whatever, so I told him I would take it for him. I'd never been to one of these things where you pay and get in line for an autograph. I went to this show and saw Mel Stottlemyre walking in the corridor. They wouldn't let them sign in the corridor, but I walked over to him and had the opportunity to tell him again that he was always my favorite player when I was a kid and felt bad that he always pitched for such lousy Yankee teams.

There is a baseball Web site called baseball-reference.com. This is like an online version of the Macmillan Encyclopedia. It's fantastic. You can look up anybody any time. You can buy a very inexpensive sponsorship of your favorite player. I told him I had sponsored his Mel Stottlemyre page. You get to put a little blurb on it. I put my blurb of some Mel Stottlemyre tidbits. I mentioned the inside-the-park grand slam, the five-for-five game. I told him this as quickly as I could get it out because he kept walking. I have to say that he looked at me like I was probably out of my mind. When I walked away, I thought, "Boy, did I just make a jerk out of myself." He wasn't mean or anything. He was very polite. I could tell he was thinking, "This guy's a lunatic."

—MARK BRAFF, Glen Rock, N. J.

The most overrated Yankee recently would be Kyle Farnsworth—he comes to mind right away. Kyle Farnsworth can throw it 100 miles per hour *and can't get anybody out.* I think it's in his head. I go to so many games with my father. Every time we go to the game, we get there as soon as they open the doors. One of the great joys of baseball is watching batting practice, watching the guys clown around on the field, shagging flies, playing pepper, throwing the ball around—acting like kids. That's the real beauty of baseball—the pregame preparation. Kyle Farnsworth was always in leftfield all by himself—not talking to anyone—no one goes near him. He is shagging flies, tossing them back in, and when BP is completed, he jogs in all by himself—I never saw him fraternizing with anyone on the team or anyone else. That's odd. One of the great joys of being on a team is the camaraderie. Whether you're on any sports team, or even when you work in a company, the camaraderie you share with your co-workers or your teammates is priceless. To see him going through the motions like he's not even enjoying himself—there's got to be some issues there, and it's a shame.

Well, there is more to this story now. After having seen Kyle Farnsworth for a better part of the season keep to himself during batting practice at home games my dad and I went to, one day everything changed for the better. One late afternoon, my dad and I were down in the leftfield corner seats and Kyle Farnsworth was in his usual position shagging flies and tossing them back toward the infield during Yankee batting practice. Then, a young boy calls out, "Hey, Kyle, can I have a ball please . . . Please, Kyle, please!" I say to the kid, "Don't even bother with Farnsworth, he never even looks at anyone!" Well, Kyle Farnsworth heard me say that and gave me a very serious look of disbelief. The next ball that Kyle caught, he made a point of looking at me, walking over to the young boy who asked for the ball, autographed it for him, handed it to him, looked back at me, shook his head, and proceeded to sign more autographs. Boy, did I feel bad.

However, the next Yankee game my dad and I went to, we saw Kyle Farnsworth again during batting practice. When he saw us, he made a point of jogging over to us and said, "Hi, I'm Kyle! How are you doing?" He proceeded to shake my hand and my dad's hand. Kyle proceeded to sign lots of autographs and even took a few pictures with some kids. He tossed a lot of baseballs into the stands as well. Johnny Damon then came over and started clowning around with Kyle, and they appeared to be having a good time with the fans. At every subsequent game my dad and I went to, if Kyle would see us during batting practice, he would acknowledge us with a wave. I now consider myself a fan of Kyle Farnsworth.

—MATTHEW DONNELLY, 43, New York

I ran into a Red Sox fan yesterday. Then, I backed up and ran into him again.

Chapter 4

On the Road Again

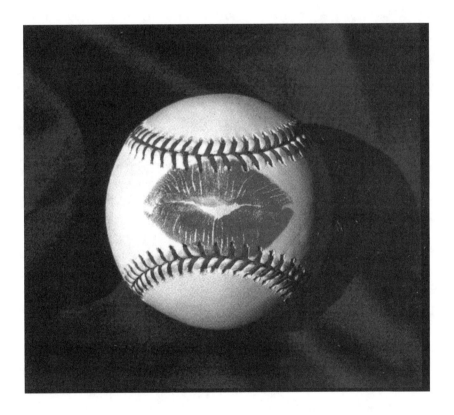

Today We Ride

THE MAN AHEAD OF ME KEPT SAYIN' "WHERE WE GOIN'?" I SAID, "I DON'T KNOW ... YOU'RE THE ONE DRIVIN' THE BUS."

Chuck Frantz

Frantz, 53, owns a trophy shop in Northampton, Pennsylvania, the town where he grew up and still lives today. Northampton is five miles north of Allentown. Frantz heads up the largest Yankee fan club in the country.

I'm fifty-three years old now, and I've grown up with the atmosphere of sitting there in the old Yankee Stadium. The old beams that were in the Stadium were really something. It was always electrifying when you went into Yankee Stadium for me, as a little boy, to see Mickey Mantle and all those guys play. It's something that's been with me since I was born.

Right now, I have formed this Yankee fan club, which is the largest one in the country. Our first meeting started with thirty-four people. Five years later, we're up to 340 members in our club. It's amazing how quickly it spread and how big it got. We meet once a month. Within the past five years we've been together, we've raised over $25,000 for local charities in our area. Besides rooting for our Yankees, we're trying to make an effect in Lehigh Valley here by helping out organizations like Dreams Come True, which is for terminally ill kids, for the American Cancer Society, and Alzheimer's.

The trivia question that really gets a lot of our members is when you ask them "How many retired Yankee numbers are there?" The Yankees have the double 8 with Yogi and **BILL DICKEY***.

*When **BILL DICKEY** managed the Yankees, his brother George was a catcher for the White Sox.

People get confused that two number eights were retired. That's usually one that gets a lot of people. There are fifteen jerseys retired for fourteen numbers.

We pick a road trip to see the Yankees on a weekend. We've been to Chicago, Cleveland, Baltimore, Toronto twice, Boston, Washington and Pittsburgh. We also go on trips to see the farm teams. We go up to Scranton and also to Trenton, which is about an hour and fifteen minutes from where we are to both places. Those are the Yankees top-two farm teams. We really do have fun. We do raffles on the bus. We raffle Yankee memorabilia. We play "Guess the Attendance" for the game where we'll send a sheet around, and people have to guess the attendance at the games.

> The Yankees have the double 8 with Yogi and Bill Dickey. People get confused that two number eights were retired.

Toronto was very good to us. Cleveland was a little boisterous to us. I could rate them almost as bad as the Red Sox fans. One time in Boston, we were walking from the game back to our train to get back to our hotel, and some Red Sox fans—about three or four guys with a few beers in them—were walking by me and my wife. They purposely banged into me looking for a fight because we were Yankee fans. Other than that, Washington was good to us, Baltimore is always good to us. Chicago was very nice. I was very surprised in Chicago because you would think it would be like New York because it's so big, but it's very clean, and the people were very friendly, not only in the city but also the park.

What we do is when we go on these weekend trips, we always spend a day—one day—always Saturday, sightseeing in that city. We'll go to the Friday night game and then Sunday's game, but on Saturday, all we do is sightsee in that city—go around and look at things there. When we got into South Bend, we visited the Notre Dame campus and the College Football Hall of Fame, which is also in South Bend. We got to see all that stuff when we went to Chicago. The Notre Dame campus was really neat because we were getting a tour from a student who was from our area. As we were walking toward the football field, the marching band came right by us—they were practicing, and they end up playing their fight song while we were right in front of them. It sent shivers down hearing the **NOTRE DAME FIGHT SONG***. I'm a big college football fan, but I don't have any particular team. I'll tell you what when you're on the campus and see the Golden Dome, and then the marching band walks by, and they play that fight song—Oh my God, it was outstanding. It put tears in my eyes. The campus is so beautiful, it's a great, great campus.

From Notre Dame, we went into Chicago, which was about a ninety-minute drive. Chicago's a great town. A lot of our fans said they'd love to go back there. There's so much there we couldn't see. We took the boat down the rivers. It was a great town, and the people were so friendly to us.

It was the same at Boston. Don't get me wrong. The fans were rude . . . Fenway Park is beautiful. I'm a nostalgia nut. It was just the fans. You sit in the stands and, when they see the Yankee stuff on you, they go nuts.

The first time our group was going to go out to Chicago to see the Yankees-Cubs game, I called early, and they assured me I was going to have tickets. When it came time for me to pay for the tickets, they said to me, "We don't have tickets for you." I said, "What do you mean? You told me you were going to put tickets away." What happened was, they did what Boston does now and the Mets, they didn't sell group tickets to anybody because they took those tickets and sold them to brokers for more money. That's what they did—they took those and gave them to brokers

*The "**NOTRE DAME VICTORY MARCH**" has won multiple polls as the greatest college fight song ever. It was written in 1908 by two alums, John and Mike Shea. John Shea, who wrote the words, lettered in baseball at Notre Dame before taking his volley cheer on high in 1965 in Holyoke, Massachusetts. . . . . In the late '60s, almost one-third of all junior high and high schools in the United States used some version of the "Notre Dame Victory March" as their school song.

and they ended up selling the tickets we would have had. That was really sad because I had to tell all our people—and everybody was pumped about going to Wrigley to see the Yankees out there, and I had to tell them we couldn't go.

I've been running buses to Yankee Stadium for thirty-some years. I put in for four dates this year and the only date they gave me was September 1. Tickets are very hard to get. What happened was they told me that the date that I have, September 1, was the only day available. This was back in March when we tried to order tickets and put my dates in. I made a stink with them because here I was, after all these years of doing Yankee trips. Every year, I bring buses down there. They told me that every Friday, Saturday, and Sunday from the first of May to the end of August were sold out and I couldn't get any tickets. In their eyes, we're just a number. With us being the largest Yankee fan club in the country, you'd think we would have some pull, but they don't even know that we exist. They don't give us anything. I can't even get a pocket schedule out of them. I request pocket schedules, and they won't give them to me. If I ask for anything else, and tell them we're the largest Yankee fan club, and I want to do this or that, they don't acknowledge us. I'll get acknowledgements from Scranton and Trenton but not the New York Yankees.

> They don't give us anything. I can't even get a pocket schedule out of them.

They allotted us tickets for September 1, when I started making a stink about it, and I called back because our first bus filled up so fast asking for another set of tickets, and they gave them to me. I had two sets and I sold them out real quick. I called back and they gave us another set—three sets total. I was surprised but now we've got three buses going down on that day.

We've never taken more than one bus when we go to out-of-town games. This year for the Pittsburgh trip, we'll end up getting two buses for that because there's been so much interest already before I even got the tickets. Everybody in our group knows how nice of a city Pittsburgh is. From here, if you go with two tickets for the games and your hotel and your bus, the cost for two people may be around $600 for the weekend. . . .

> If Mickey Mantle had been on that junk, he probably could have hit 800 home runs . . .

I had **NBC*** *Nightly News* come to my house and set up a portable studio in my basement to do an interview with me on steroids when the steroid thing broke a couple of years ago. They were doing a segment with Tom Brokaw and were here for five hours. They interviewed me for forty-five minutes. Their producer said to me, "You're going to be the spokesperson for Major League Baseball, all the baseball fans in America." She said this to me right when she sat me down. I was shaking like a leaf 'cause I'm thinking, "Oh, my God." She wouldn't say anything until they were ready to start.

This woman just drilled me on steroids and everything you could think about it, "Do you think it's right?" "What about the kids?" "Who do you blame?" "Do you think it's fair that these guys should have asterisks before their name?" "Do you think they're guilty of taking steroids?" "What do you think about high school kids or college students? What would you tell them?" She kept firing questions at me one after the other. I was nervous a couple of times. I said, "I'm sorry." She said, "Don't worry about it. This is going to be taped and we're going to edit it."

If Mickey Mantle had been on that junk, he probably could have hit 800 home runs, he might have been close to that, or way over that, especially at Yankee Stadium with the short porches. Whenever I hear about it, I turn the TV because I'm so sick of it. Major League Baseball is probably the biggest blame for it for letting it get the

*****NBC** Sports president Dick Ebersol recently paid $50,000 at a charity auction to have Carly Simon tell him the name of the subject person in her song, "You're So Vain." Only Simon, Ebersol, and that person know the identity, rumored to be Warren Beatty, James Taylor, or Mick Jagger.

way it is today. They had the chance to nail these people, and they let them go. They're just as guilty as the players. The reason they didn't do anything was that baseball ratings were down, people weren't coming back because of the strikes, and they figured they were going to let it go and let these guys hit all these home runs. That'll bring the people back. Well, it brought them back, but now they've got the steroid stink, and it's out of hand.

On one trip, there were some guys who went down on our bus but didn't go into the game. They stayed at the bars outside of Yankee Stadium and began drinking. It came time to leave, and these guys weren't back. We waited and waited, and they weren't coming back . . . we took off. From New York to where we are is about a two-hour ride. What they did was they took a subway to try to go into the Port Authority and get a bus back to Lehigh Valley and they couldn't. It was too late so they had to stay in New York for the whole night, and I'm sure that cost them an arm and a leg. . . .

Minor league baseball—going to Scranton and to Trenton—is really neat. You're right on top of everything. You get treated a lot better as far as public relations. They tend to you a little bit more than the big Yankees do. There's more entertainment for you, especially in Trenton, where they really go all out. Between every inning, they have something for everybody—the children, the people, they play bingo, they have great food and it's cheap. It's a nice atmosphere, plus, you see the young prospects who are coming up that will eventually be Yankees players.

When the Yankees weren't that good—and this is no lie—the Yankees always used to call me and try and push tickets on me. Now, they don't even bother calling. You don't get anything. I get calendars for Christmas from the Toronto Blue Jays, from the Baltimore Orioles, from the Chicago White Sox—everybody sends me calendars for bringing a bus to their game. The Phillies—you wouldn't believe what the Phillies sent me because I ran a bus trip there—send me all kinds of stuff thanking me for coming. What do I get out of the Yankees? Nothing. The Yankees just look at you as a number. For me complaining and bitching and moaning, there are six more behind me waiting for tickets. And, that's the attitude they have. Their attitude is so terrible they couldn't care less about us. They couldn't care about our fan club being the largest in the country—but, it's just a number. I'm a number. They don't care about me. That's the attitude they have. I'm hoping that the day comes when they're going to come back and say, "Please come back. We want your business." I'm going to say, "Remember back in 2008 when I wanted tickets and you said you couldn't give me any, well, there you go." That's why I'm really upset.

Those people there at the Stadium are so arrogant, not only the ticket people but anyone you talk to in their front office, they're very short with you. They're very arrogant. It ticks me off. They're the richest organization. They rip you off the most. That's how you're treated.

Name two Yankees with over 2,000 hits.

Don Mattingly and Steve Howe

BEER:
MORE THAN JUST A BREAKFAST DRINK

Duane Czajka

Czajka grew up in Buffalo and moved to suburban Rochester in 1962. Czajka, 67, is retired as an elementary school vice principal, after thirty-five years of service. He walks five miles a day and plays tennis every other day.

I had never seen TV before. There was a bar on the corner. There was a sign in the window, WORLD SERIES CAN BE SEEN HERE. This was the 1947 World Series. I was seven years old. It was a warm day, and the door into the bar was open, so I sat on the stoop outside the bar and watched the games. That's how the Yankees became my team because they were the ones I saw in that 1947 World Series. I don't remember any players' names. I don't even remember swinging a bat at that time—just playing catch around the neighborhood.

I probably didn't even know what "World Series" was. My father used to go to bars around town in Buffalo. He was a welder. On Saturdays, he would take me for a drink we called birch beer. I used to watch *Rin Tin Tin* on the tube and ***HOWDY DOODY*** and *Hopalong Cassidy* with William Boyd. There was only one TV station in Buffalo at that time.

I was thirteen years old and attended a parochial grammar school. One Saturday night, the second or third week in June 1953, my father told me, "You've got to go to bed early tonight. We're going

> ***HOWDY DOODY** had forty-eight freckles . . . one for each state in the Union at the time. His sister's name was Heidi and his brother was named Double. The host, Buffalo Bob, later owned a liquor store in New Rochelle.

to a ball game tomorrow." We used to go see the local Triple-A team, the Bisons, so I asked, "Why go to bed early?" He said, "We're going to Cleveland tomorrow." My dad hung out in a local tavern. These taverns used to run what they called "excursions." We got on the train in Buffalo about 8:30 Sunday morning to go to Cleveland. This was an all-male bastion—all blue-collar fathers with their sons. The fathers were drinking beer and eating ham sandwiches—the young lads were drinking their soda pop and waiting for the ball game to start. When we got on the train, I said to my father, "We're not staying overnight, are we?" He said, "No. Why?" I said, "Well, there are baggage cars connected to the train." He said, "Well, don't worry about that." We get to Cleveland. The fellow who owned the tavern says to me, "Go over to the baggage car." He opened the door to the baggage car and this guy hands me two cases of beer in cans—one for each hand. He says, "Carry those into the Stadium." That was no problem in those days. I carried two cases of beer into that stadium that day—at thirteen years old. Cleveland, in those days, and some other cities, apparently, served 3.2 beer, which was beer that was like water. Some of these fans had their tongues hanging out when they saw this regular beer coming in. I wasn't worried about this at all—after all, I was with my father. There weren't any regulations then. My thing was the excitement of seeing the games—it was a doubleheader.

> ... I carried two cases of beer into that stadium that day—at thirteen years old.

The Yankees were on a sixteen-game winning streak coming into **CLEVELAND*** for this doubleheader. I saw Reynolds and Raschi. As far as I can do with the statistics, it probably is one of the top five crowds that ever watched a baseball game. There

> *In 1916 the **CLEVELAND** Indians experimented with putting player numbers on the uniform sleeves. ... In 1929 the Indians became the first Major League team to put numbers on the backs of the jerseys ... first only because the Yankees were rained out on Opening Day.

were 80,000-plus. The Yankees swept them that day. That was my very first big-league game.

I just thought I was in heaven. You look around and see all these people. You see the team you've been watching on black and white TV. I had never seen the pinstriped uniforms before. I couldn't believe there was a yellow-golden hue on the background on the uniform—I did not know that until that day. I thought the background on the uniform was pure white.

I did not see any empty seats that day. I remember heading for the station about seven o'clock. St. Clair Avenue is the main drag. There was no traffic on St. Clair when the crowd was leaving the stadium because it was a mass of people walking down St. Clair Avenue. Many of them had come from New York state or from other cities on the train. I don't remember getting any hard times from the crowd at all. I talked to my father about it before he died and he didn't remember anything hard about it.

The car we used was a Pullman. Of course, the beds weren't down, but we had the seats. We had adults carrying in beer and the youngsters carried in stuff also. We had volumes of beer going in there. People paced themselves pretty well, but there was probably one-third who had to be assisted onto the train.

My first trip to Yankee Stadium was in 1957—a present for my high school graduation. Unfortunately, I haven't been back since. My son lives in New York in Queens and hopefully some day I'm going to get back there. I should go [soon] before they open the new stadium. Everybody says, "You go to Yankee Stadium, and the two things you've got to do is 'get in' and 'get out.'" I think that's a mistake.

> I couldn't believe there was a yellow-golden hue on the background on the uniform—I did not know that until that day. I thought the background on the uniform was pure white.

SO SAY YOU ONE, SO SAY YOU ALL

In 1996, Howard Stern had a commercial that said they could guarantee a World Series ticket in Atlanta and airfare for $600 a person—going down and coming back on the same day. Howard Stern's brother was in the travel business, and I think he organized this trip. I told my wife, "I really want to go. And, I'd like to take my fourteen-year-old son, Kenny." She said, "OK." She's a big Yankee fan too, so I asked her if she wanted to go, but she said, "No, I really don't want to."

> It was unbelievable. We are on the bus and have this police escort. The tickets had us up in the middle of God's country . . .

It was the fourth game we went to. About 150 of us crazy fans go to Newark Airport. I spent the $1,200, and the plane is delayed for an hour. It happened to be a Kiwi charter. Kiwi had gone out of business a couple of months earlier. We all get on the plane and are in the air for about an hour . . . and, we smell smoke! We have to fly back for an emergency landing at the Newark Airport. We saw the ambulances and fire engines out on the tarmac while we were landing. The decision is: when they fix the plane, should I continue on? I know what my wife would say with my fourteen-year-old son there—"There's no way." I'm there thinking about it . . . and twenty-five people do decide not to go, so, they found us a smaller plane. My only worry was that I wanted to fly down and still get to watch the game in its entirety, and they guaranteed we would do that.

We finally took off around 4:30. The tower, understanding our predicament, allowed us to take off in front of all the other planes. Then we are told we can fly at a higher altitude for speed. So, we landed in Atlanta around seven o'clock. On the tarmac, they are giving us our game tickets, and we get a police escort to the game.

It was unbelievable. We are on the bus and have this police escort. The tickets had us up in the middle of God's country—up in the upper deck. We didn't care. We were having a ball. The

Yankees were losing the game . . . until Leyritz hit the three-run home run to tie the game.

We left the ballpark around midnight, screaming and singing "New York, New York," there in the middle of Atlanta, on the way to the airport. We just had the most fantastic time. It was a great experience for my son. He'll never forget it, of course, and I won't. We got home around five o'clock in the morning. My son insisted on going to school the next day so he could show everybody his ticket—to prove that he was actually in Atlanta the night before for the World Series game!

When we got to Atlanta, I called home and left my wife a message, "Don't worry. The plane didn't crash! I'll talk to you about it when I get home." She was mad—she would never have let me take my son on down—I knew that, but I did it.

—JOEL SEILER, 56, Brooklyn

My first memories of being passionate about the Yankees was as a seven-year-old in 1961 watching Mantle and Maris. Like most kids, my favorite was Mantle. Both my bat and my baseball glove were an autographed Mantle version. I always dreamed about someday going to Yankee Stadium. But growing up in a small town in Montana, only 60 miles from the Canadian border, a trip to New York City was more than this hick from the sticks could handle. In 1978, the year before I got married, I was able to go to a Yankee series in Seattle with my best Yankee friend, Larry Schlepp. We were lucky to see Ron Guidry pitch during his magical season. It was one of the greatest experiences of my life, but, in those years, Seattle was still just an expansion team. The rivalry between the Yankees and Mariners had still not been established and the crowds were small and unenthusiastic. The possibility of going to Yanke Stadium seemed like a remote possibility at best.

After marrying in 1979, I continued my love affair with the Yankees and I was determined to pass on my passion to my little girl and boy. Some of our earliest pictures are of our babies in their Yankee hats and pinstriped Yankee pajamas. I wanted to instill a love for the game, so both my wife and I became involved in the local Little League program. We both coached and I was the commissioner of the league for twenty-three years. All our efforts paid off as both kids grew to love the game of baseball.

In 1996, Jeter's first year and the start of the great World Series run by the Yankees, my son began to develop his own deep love for the Yankees. At an age where fathers and sons start to grow apart, we developed a deep bond over the Yankees. We would be glued to the television watching the one or two games a month that we could get in this remote area. So, our main source of following the Yankee progress was through the box scores in the local paper. New York City never seemed farther away.

In 2003, at the age of forty-nine, my wife surprised me and my seventeen-year-old son with a trip to **YANKEE STADIUM***. Christmas Eve night, we were shocked to find out she had helped arrange a trip to the Big City for the following summer for myself, my son, and my old friend, Larry. The next seven months were spent excitedly making all the arrangements.

That first day at Yankee Stadium is something that will live with me the rest of my life. We spent twelve hours at the Stadium that day. We got there in the morning and walked around the Stadium and then bought tickets to the stadium tour. We sat in the press box, in the dugout—stealing some dirt from the warning track—walked completely around the field to Monument Park. We all touched the same spot on the Babe's forehead that Clemens touched before each start. It couldn't get any better.

From there, we went to stand by the barricades next to Parking Lot No. 14 to watch players come to the ballpark. This is where we met the real fanatics. The ballplayers are like gods or rock stars. I'm a conservative Montana accountant screaming "Soriano," "Giambi," "Derek," and "Joe Torre" at the top of my

***YANKEE STADIUM** never earned National Landmark Status because of "problems with its integrity." Landmark status would have protected Yankee Stadium from demolition after the 2008 season. Major renovations from 1974 to 1975 drastically changed the Stadium from the 1923 original and ruined its historic significance.

lungs. Super Yankee fans, like "Baseball Henry," let us know what car every player drove and everything we needed to know about our beloved Yankees.

Between innings, my son Justin, Larry, and myself got goose bumps for the third time in the game, when the theme from *Rocky* blared over the **P.A.*** system along with scenes from the famous movie playing on the huge TV screen. Matsui's walk-off homer in the bottom of the ninth sent an electricity through the crowd that I will never forget. We stayed through three verses of "New York, New York" and hung around with thousands of people while all the players left the Stadium. A full day living out my dream . . . I will hold that day close to my heart as long as I live.

—<u>JIM MEIER</u>, Conrad, Montana

*The public address announcer for the Houston Colt '45s (later the Astros) in their 1962 inaugural season was Dan Rather . . . the <u>P.A.</u> announcer for the Brooklyn Dodgers in 1936 and 1937 was John Forsythe, later a TV and movie star.

Bug off,
Cleveland!

There's a "win chill" factor at Shea Stadium.

The Yankees once had a bullpen car (Toyota) that fans threw trash at constantly. The trash attracted rats that ate through the engine cables. The car was scrapped in favor of a golf cart.

In Babe Ruth's first major league game in 1914, he was removed in the seventh inning for a pinch hitter.

When Lou Piniella played minor league baseball in Aberdeen, S.D. in 1964, the team's batboy was Cal Ripken, Jr.

John Elway, Deion Sanders and Billy Cannon, Jr. were signed by George Steinbrenner and given $100,000 bonuses. All three quit baseball for the NFL.

The Yomiuri Giants are sometimes called "The New York Yankees of Japan." They have won the most pennants and have the deepest fan base in Yakyu (Japanese Baseball). . . . The Nippon Ham Fighters give free tickets to foreigners on "Yankees Day."

When Joe Girardi played for the Cubs, he caught a ceremonial first pitch from Mike Ditka. Girardi had a football curled behind his back. After catching Ditka's pitch, Girardi fired the football at Ditka which Iron Mike caught easily.

When Roger Maris hit his 61st home run, there were 44,000 empty seats at Yankee Stadium. The attendance was 23,154.

Chapter 5

Ah, a Female Yankee Fan . . . One of Life's Most Misunderstood Creatures

No Man Is Worthy

THE BABIES SHE HAD WITH BUCKY DENT WERE BEAUTIFUL . . . AND IMAGINARY!

Christi Counihan

Christi Counihan, born and raised in Oklahoma, is a longtime Yankee fan, following her father's passion for the Yanks. She loved them even before Bucky Dent came into the picture, but that did it for sure! Christi, a pharmaceutical rep, an Oklahoma University alum, a big Sooner fan, is married to Tom and has one son, Ian.

My favorite Yankee—Bucky Dent. Favorite memory— 1978—the home run. I was a junior in high school in Oklahoma. After school, I walked in the door, and turned the game on. It was that one-game playoff. It was an afternoon game, and I think it's so sad they don't do afternoon games any more. That inning had just started when I got home, got a Coke, and sat down.

I had Bucky Dent's poster on my bedroom wall. Dad raised me as a Yankee fan. Back then, you only got one game a week on Saturdays. Whenever the Yankees were on TV, the game was always on at the house, and my dad was watching them. I got into the habit of watching them with him. That whole group—Reggie Jackson, Chris Chambliss, and Thurman Munson and all those guys was the time I really got into the Yankees. When Bucky Dent rolled around, and he was *so hot*, that just sealed the deal on it for me.

I got home from school that day, knew the game was on, went in and sat down in front of the TV. Bucky Dent would have been the second or third batter I saw. For him, this little nondescript utility infielder, to get out there and hit that home run over the Green

Monster, I was going crazy in the house. Mark, my older brother, was looking at me, thinking I was some sort of crazed lunatic over the whole thing. My dad was at work. Mom was on her way home from work—her car had broken down that day, and she was stuck somewhere waiting for dad to come and get her. I was the only one who was truly engaged in the game on the television that afternoon.

How could you not get into Bucky Dent? You wouldn't understand that—I was sixteen years old, and he was soooo cute. Here's this guy who's playing a little shortstop occasionally. I guess he played a little bit of everything, but shortstop mainly. They put his picture on the screen when he came up to bat. He was so cute, so I guess that was a rite of passage for girls who grew up in my era who were into baseball. I have a good friend who grew up in St. Louis as a Cardinals fan, and she even had Bucky Dent's poster on her bedroom wall. He was the Derek Jeter for girls back then. I guess if you are a big baseball and Yankee fan now, at that age, Derek's probably the one you would have on your wall . . . but, Bucky was the one then.

> How could you not get into Bucky Dent? You wouldn't understand that— I was sixteen years old, and he was soooo cute.

I don't remember where we would have gotten that Bucky Dent poster. It may even have come out of a magazine. When that movie, *The Slugger's Wife*, came out, with Bucky co-starring, I sat and watched it just to see him, 'cause he was so cute. That was such a fun year.

That was when I first realized the deep animosity between the Yankees and the Red Sox. It had just been another game up to that point, and that was when that whole thing took hold, and I realized there was no love lost between those two teams. We have friends in our neighborhood now who are big-time Red Sox fans—their dogs are named Fenway and Big Papi. They grew up in Boston, and we go round and round.

I went to Yankee Stadium for the first time this year. It was euphoric! I had heard so much about it. It's got such an incredible history. I was just giddy! I was in New York for training on a new job, and we had meetings all day. We had a required dinner, which ended at 6:15. The Yankees were in town playing the Mariners, and the first pitch had gone at 6:05. I convinced my boss and one of the other girls that we needed to get a taxi and go into town. It was about a forty-five-minute drive. The taxi alone cost me $80—one way. Then, we had $60 for a ticket. The three of us went in and sat on the third base side about midway out in the outfield on the loge deck. I kept thinking, "I can't believe I'm here! I can't believe I'm here." When we walked in, it was bottom of the third. The others in my group wanted to go buy souvenirs. I was like, "You guys go ahead and buy souvenirs . . . I'm going in to see the game." I went to find our seats, and I passed the main box office area ticket gates where you come in right there behind home plate. I'm heading back down the third base side and glanced down the first entryway into the actual seats—the tunnel area. The first thing I saw was the big "NY" behind home plate. I just got chills. It was unbelievable.

> It really made me sad to think of all the history . . . and it will be turned into a parking lot.

Actually being there in Yankee Stadium, to me was just incredible. It was the atmosphere that was so amazing to me—just the feel of being at Yankee Stadium. You can look and see where they're building the new one. It really made me sad to think of all the history—all of the incredible baseball that has gone on here for so many years . . . and it will be turned into a parking lot. When you walk in, you can almost feel it. Anybody who is a true baseball fan, especially a Yankee fan, couldn't go in there without getting a lump in your throat. It was really incredible.

It's amazing how many Yankee fans there are in Oklahoma. I had seen the Yankees play before. I went to Texas and saw them play the Rangers—not even close to the same feeling as being in Yankee Stadium, but it still was fun to go watch them. At The

Ballpark in Arlington, there were close to as many Yankee fans as there were Ranger fans, which was amazing to me. I had my Yankee hat on and everywhere I looked, there were people in Yankee T-shirts and Yankee hats.

We went to church with Bobby Murcer a while back. When our youth group would go on a mission trip every summer to Honduras, we'd have a silent auction to raise money for the trip. In 2000, he donated two baseballs, one of them was signed by the entire Yankee team and one of them was signed by Yogi. My husband, Tom, and my son, Ian, were so sweet. They were like, "There's a Yankee baseball over there. We've got to buy it." Tom, who isn't a Yankee fan—he's a Mets fan, if you can believe that—says he's a Mets fan because they're *not* the Yankees! Tom and I bumped heads during the Subway Series.

Bobby and Kay Murcer are both so nice. Tom and Ian wanted to buy that ball. I said, "We can't afford that baseball. It's going to be out of our price range." It was! It went for over a thousand dollars. To me, it was cool, just to be able to sit there and look at it . . . and see those names, thinking, "All these guys have touched this baseball. How cool is that?"

I'm trying to raise our son, Ian, to be a Yankee fan. He was completely on board with Dad and me for a long time and now he's reached the rebellious teenage years where sometimes he'll cheer for them and sometimes he'll cheer for the other team. Like, when they played the Mets, he was cheering for the Mets. I think it's just to see if it annoys me.

When Dad was growing up, they could get the Yankee games and the Cardinals games on the radio. Because of the Yankee tie with the Oklahoma guys, Mickey Mantle, Bobby Murcer, Allie Reynolds, that was why he fell into line with the Yankees. Then, that's just been handed down. My brothers, Mark and Jay, didn't get it—but we still pray for them.

I have the XM radio so I can listen to the Yankee games almost every day. I don't sit and devote 100 percent of my attention to the radio every day, but it allows me to keep up and know what's going on. Also, if I've got something else going on, the display gives me the score and the inning so I can cruise through the room and, at any point, look and it will tell me exactly what is going on.

We've been to the Mickey Mantle Restaurant in downtown Oklahoma City only once. It's a very nice restaurant, right across the street from where his statue is in front of the baseball park. It's got some really cool memorabilia hanging around on the walls. I enjoyed walking around and looking at the photographs and the items on display. It's a nice restaurant, and I would recommend it. It's not the type of restaurant where you would rush downtown, park, grab a bite to eat, and go to a game. It's more a restaurant to have a nice steak or meal that you would linger over. I don't know who owns it—whether there's a connection with his family or if someone bought the use of his name.

Come to the Mets side
. . . We have cookies!

IS THE POPE A YANKEE FAN?
DOES A BEAR GO TO YANKEE STADIUM?

Vicki Csakany

Vicki Csakany was born and raised in the Bronx. The longtime United Airlines employee has lived in South Florida the last nine years . . . where not being able to see Yankee games on TV is forcing her to move back up North.

My aunts, uncles, and cousins are Yankee fans. My father was not—he was a Giants fan. My mother and brother were indifferent. Growing up, I knew three things for sure . . . I was Italian, Roman Catholic, and a Yankee fan. Win or lose, they were my team. I adored my father but even that wouldn't sway me, so we had this rivalry. My first trip to a ball game was to the Polo Grounds—I was not impressed. When the Yankees won, Dad would say they were "lucky." When they lost, they were "bums." In 1961, dad and I had a great time with little side bets about Maris' at-bats. When the Giants left New York, dad didn't switch allegiance. He was a National League fan and that was that. I don't think it would have been as much fun if we were both rooting for the Yankees.

When I became a teenager, I was still a Yankee fan and mad for Mickey Mantle. I was just the right age—I'm now sixty-six. My friend, Ellen, and I went to the Stadium as often as we could. We caught on pretty quickly that when spring came, we "lost" our guys. All they talked about was baseball. Their knowledge went far beyond just the Yankees. So, Ellen and I got the *Daily News* every day and started memorizing stats for all the top players in both leagues. We waited for the right time and when a baseball discussion began, we jumped in and spouted all kinds

> When the Yankees won, Dad would say they were "lucky." When they lost, they were "bums."

of statistics. The guys were quite impressed. One of our major accomplishments was learning how to fill in a scorecard.

> . . . when Bucky Dent hit the home run over the Green Monster . . . I just stood in the doorway and smiled— OK, I gloated.

In 1964, I landed my dream job with United Airlines. In reservations, we worked days, nights, weekends, and holidays. In 1965, Ellen's dad got tickets to Mickey Mantle Day, Saturday, September 18, 1965. I was scheduled to work. There was no contest. I called in sick and played hooky to go to the game. We had pretty good seats, and it was a perfect day. I still have the program and ticket stubs so I can tell you we were in Section 11, Row C. The real irony is that the envelope the tickets came in, which I also have, has United Airlines advertisements on the back. I was never busted for it, so all was well.

In 1975, United moved from Manhattan to northern New Jersey. Our office was combined with the Boston reservations office. There was much teasing back and forth about who had the "accent." In 1978, things really heated up. We were watching the Yankees-Red Sox playoff game on TV in our cafeteria. I was off duty but just couldn't leave. The Sox fans were all over me because they were winning. I finally left and put the game on in the car. I was at the stop sign leaving the complex when Bucky Dent hit the home run over the Green Monster. I made the quickest U-turn and went right back to the cafeteria. I didn't have to say anything. I just stood in the doorway and smiled—OK, I gloated. It was a truly wonderful moment.

I got married later in life. I met my husband, Nick, in 1991. We went to visit his brother and family upstate. We all went to Cooperstown to the Baseball Hall of Fame. I couldn't maintain a serious demeanor. I acted like a little kid in a candy store. They understood, though, because they are all Yankee fans. I knew it was a good match.

I've been telling people for years that it is an irrefutable fact that God is a Yankee fan. He just cannot let them win EVERY year—it just wouldn't be fair! The good news is that we're moving back up North this year, and I will have the YES Network. Oh, in the summer of 2002, I finally got up the nerve to do something I've wanted to do for a long time—I got the Yankee logo tattooed on my left arm just above my wrist. Imagine a sixty-year-old lady getting a tattoo? People may have thought I was crazy . . . but I love it.

> *If a woman has to choose between catching a fly ball and saving an infant's life, she will choose to save the infant's life without even considering if there are men on base.*
>
> —Dave Barry

There are some who say you can marry a Red Sox fan, yet still go on to lead a normal and productive life.

IF YOU WANT BREAKFAST IN BED, SLEEP IN THE KITCHEN

I am probably a bit of an unusual Yankee fan in that I go back to a time when very few women were interested in baseball. I became a Yankee fan in 1960. I have been teaching my thirty-year-old son the finer points of the game these past few years and have been telling him that the Yankees' mystique, popularity, and fans of today are not the way it used to be.

I remember talking about the Yankees when I was in school and not having a single other person interested in the Yankees or baseball. One would think I would have been popular with the boys; hell, no. The boys just stared at me when I was quoting ERA, RBI, and BAs of the players—looking like deer in the headlights. I became a Yankee fan in a most interesting way. My younger brother, then ten years old, and myself, then thirteen years old, were home from school because we had the mumps. My brother, being the "baby," insisted that we watch the Yankee game and won the "coin toss" by whining endlessly to my mother. So, we watched baseball much to my chagrin. It may as well been calculus to me. I had no clue what the heck was going on. I was really disinterested in the whole thing. It made no sense to me.

> I remember talking about the Yankees when I was in school and not having a single other person interested in the Yankees or baseball.

I was bored silly until the Yankees brought in a relief pitcher named Ryne Duren. If no one else other than me remembers Ryne, I wouldn't be surprised because when I tell this story, many exclaim, "who is Ryne Duren?" or stare that familiar stare at me the way the boys did when I was in junior high school. Mr. Duren wowed my then thirteen-year-old female mind by throwing his eight warm-up pitches, most of which sailed over Yogi's head and most of them hit the backstop or the screen behind home plate making a loud and unforgettable BOOM. I would guess that if the

JUGS Gun had been around then, Ryne would have been clocked at throwing in excess of 100 mph. I was absolutely speechless because Ryne was wearing thick glasses looking like the bottoms of Coke bottles. My eyes widened, and I remember vividly thinking, "this poor man is blind," and wondered where his seeing-eye dog was. This absolutely riveted my total attention to this game of "calculus," but I was absolutely transfixed and mesmerized.

When the first batter came up, stood in the batter's box and the first pitch soared over his head, my mouth was agape. I couldn't believe my eyes. The next pitch was so close to the batter's head, I ducked into a pillow as he fell to the ground like someone shot him. Little by little, I peeked out from the pillow, expecting blood on the field or worse yet the batter's head rolling around at home plate minus his body. But, to my shock, amazement, and wide-eyed innocence, the batter dusted himself off and remained up at bat. I said incredulously to my brother, "Oh, my God, baseball players have to be the bravest people on earth." My brother laughed at me but, from that point on, he and I squabbled over the TV with me wanting to watch baseball.

I arranged my social life around games after that day. I listened to the radio broadcasts, too, on my brand new Emerson radio—it being the first transistor radio to be available that my godfather had given me as a Christmas present. I didn't want to go to the junior high school prom because it was held on a Friday night. *What, me miss a TV broadcast?* But my mother insisted I go to the prom. Needless to say, I didn't need a curfew for I couldn't wait to get home. The voices of Jerry Coleman, Red Barber, Mel Allen, and Phil Rizzuto were the play-by-play announcers at that time. How about that? I wrote Jerry Coleman a letter and he answered me on Yankee stationery.

I was watching, and I have the back page of the *Daily News* the day Roger hit No. 61, and I am delighted the asterisk was removed. I remember Bobby Richardson's 14 RBI postseason. I can remember with a poignant sadness the day Thurman died. I am still awed by Jim Abbott's no-hitter and the heart and soul that young man displayed in overcoming his handicap and making history proving to us all that anything is possible when you have an awesome spirit and are wearing a Yankee uniform.

For the last forty-four years, I have heard people complain that the "Yankees win too much." Get a grip, people, winning is the object of any sport. As I continue to study this wonderful game, being a Yankee fan has only gotten better with time. The Yankee captains of my era, Thurman, Donnie Baseball, and Derek epitomize the class of the most successful professional sports franchise in world history. So what if we want to know who Pedro's daddy is? It was exciting and Pedro acted more in accordance with what the game is about: FUN. Yankee fans are a tough bunch of people, but then again isn't that what the Yankees have always epitomized? Never give up, never give in, never count them out, and win, win, win.

—RENE A. MASIELLO, freelance writer

> If the Yankees won the World Series, their uncle left a quart of milk on their front porch.

My parents loved the New York Yankees. They had an elderly uncle, who loved the Brooklyn Dodgers. Every year, my parents and their uncle had a standing bet. If the Yankees won the World Series, their uncle left a quart of milk on their front porch. If the Dodgers won, their uncle would win a quart of beer. Every year, their uncle faithfully left them a quart of milk. In 1955, his turn for a quart of beer arrived. Unfortunately, he died the night before the Dodgers won.

Several years ago, our daughter was dating Michael Coleman—No. 13. One night, my husband felt Michael had stayed too late. He asked Michael to leave. I still can't believe any beloved Yankee was in our home . . . and asked to leave it.

—LEDA WOZNICK CARMODY

I'd heard about SABR (Society for American Baseball Research) for a while. I wanted to do it, but, at the time, I was a student so I was like, "I don't know if I have $40 to spend." It seems a lot when you're not actually making money. I went to the regional meeting in New York and it was amazing. Then, the next year, I went to the convention in Seattle. I keep getting more and more involved. It's right up my alley. The weird thing about SABR is I get to talk about the game in the context of everything—the context of history and the present. Usually when you have a sports conversation, it's about what's going on now. Someone just quotes what they read in the *Post* or what they saw on ESPN or whatever. When I went to the national SABR convention in St. Louis, I ran into fans of all teams, so I did see a ton of Yankee fans.

The neatest thing about the SABR annual meeting was meeting all these people who know way more than I do. They had a trivia contest there and half the questions you just sit there and go, "Wow." You're just like "Who is this guy?" You're just amazed that people know this stuff.

—TARA KRIEGER, 25, Barnard '04, Wayne, New Jersey.

Five years ago in July, I went up to Fenway Park to see the Yankees play the Red Sox. I had tickets to the Saturday game but wanted to catch the Friday game in a Boston bar to get the local effect! After the game was over, since we were at a bar right across from Fenway, my boyfriend and I decided to walk around Fenway and see if we could find the Yankees. Sure enough, we found them getting onto the bus. Of course, I was frantic and waving to anyone and everyone. Well, Luis Sojo caught my eye and started waving back—this was just around the time when he started to coach third base. Through the window of the bus, he was asking me for my phone number—he held up his cell and gestured for my number. Since my boyfriend was ogling over David Wells, I said, "What the hell." So, I made each number with my fingers and, sure enough, he called me!!! My boyfriend didn't believe me and had to get on the phone to see for himself. About a week later, when they were back in New York, Sojo called and asked me to go out with some of my friends. We went into Secaucus to a local bar, had dinner and drinks like we were old buddies! I felt like a celebrity! At least to my friends, I was! After that, we kept in touch and randomly talked like we were pals. He even called about a month later and offered me a few tickets right behind home plate, where the family members sat. I've been to TONS of games but have NEVER been that close. Later, he gave me tickets where I sat next to Gary Sheffield's parents and son and Matsui's family. After that game, Sojo took my friends and me bowling with him and one of the announcers he's friendly with. I have never been so excited in my life! I'm trying to work my way to meeting Jeter and A-Rod, but this will do for now. It's awesome how friendly Sojo is and how very accommodating. I even got to try on his 2000 World Series ring. But, I have never bothered to ask for an autograph.

—DANIELLE COLASURDO

Steve Balboni hated sitting on the bench. How do you think the bench felt?

Reggie Jackson is one of the greatest ball players of all time. I think I'm quoting him correctly on that.

Chapter 6

A Yankee Reader

For Yankee Readers

EBBETS FIELD: WHERE THE YANKEES PRACTICED FOR THEIR REALLY IMPORTANT GAMES

Robert Mayer

Robert Mayer, 69, was born in New York City and graduated from CCNY and Columbia with a degree in journalism. He now lives the good life in Santa Fe, New Mexico, where he wrote one of the best, unsung, baseball books of all-time. First published in 1993, it was called Baseball in Men's Lives. *It was reissued in an updated edition in 2003 as* Notes of a Baseball Dreamer.

Growing up in New York City in the late '40s and '50s, I wasn't a Yankee fan. I became a baseball fan right at the end of the '46 season when the Dodgers were playing the St. Louis Cardinals in a three-game playoff, and they lost two out of three. I've always been for the underdog, and that was my beginning I guess. I became a Dodger fan.

All the other kids on the block were Yankee fans 'cause we lived about a mile from Yankee Stadium. The first Major League game I ever went to was when the Dodgers and Yankees played a three-game exhibition series on a Friday, Saturday and Sunday— right before the start of the season. I went to Yankee Stadium to see the exhibition game, and the first baseman for my Dodgers was Jackie Robinson. This was his first year because they'd had Eddie Stanky at second base. That was a major event. Always being for the underdog—that's one thing that solidified me as a Dodgers fan.

All my friends, Jackie, Bobby, and David, were all Yankee fans, which was what you're supposed to be in the Bronx. In those days, the Yankees always won. They won in '47, beating the Dodgers in the World Series. In '48 was the one aberration—the

Boston Braves played Cleveland. From '49 to '53, the Yankees won five straight World Series, which has never been done. So, I hated them. To me, rooting for the Yankees was like rooting for General Motors—the big corporation. They never lost. Yankee players always, when they trotted around after a home run, to me in my prejudiced mind, looked like they had a broomstick up their butts. Whereas the Dodgers were scrappers and scramblers and were always there just close enough to lose.

On the streets, being a Dodger fan among the Yankees, made it a lot less boring than if we were all Yankee fans. What would there be to talk about? This gave us arguments in the streets. The typical arguments were fairly well known at the time—"who was the best centerfielder?" This was the only time there were three Major League teams in the same city. That ended in '58 when the Dodgers and Giants left. We'd argue

> Yankee players always, when they trotted around after a home run . . . looked like they had a broomstick up their butts.

about who was the best centerfielder—Mickey Mantle, Willie Mays or Duke Snider. Of course, they're all in the Hall of Fame now. At the time, I would stick up for Snider, of course, being a Dodger fan. In retrospect, I would have to say I would give the nod to Willie Mays, with Mantle second and Snider third. But, they were all incredible. The other big argument was who was the better shortstop—Pee Wee Reese or Phil Rizzuto? They were both good. I always maintained that Pee Wee Reese was. I wanted to become the next Pee Wee Reese when I went on to be a ballplayer. Years and years later, I had great satisfaction when Pee Wee Reese was voted into the Hall of Fame and Rizzuto three years later so I had satisfaction from that. We would have these arguments, all in fun—we wouldn't get mad at each other.

My absolutely first introduction to baseball—I'll never forget this—it was the middle of August in 1946, when I was seven years old. I would hide under the covers and pretend to be asleep with a portable radio listening to the Dodger games if they were out on the road in a late-starting game. One night they were in St. Louis, and it was the bottom of the ninth with two men out. They had just brought up a kid, a catcher, named Gil Hodges. He struck out. That's my first baseball memory. Gil Hodges later switched to first base because of Roy Campanella—and he's also in the Hall of Fame.

> I could sooner die than root for the Yankees. I cannot root for the Yankees.

Then when I went to that Yankee-Dodger game, we sat next to the bullpen, which was in the bleachers and it cost 50 cents. Carl Erskine was one of the best Dodger pitchers then. He was warming up in the bullpen, and I took a whole bunch of pictures over the rail with my old Brownie Hawkeye camera.

I could sooner die than root for the Yankees. I cannot root for the Yankees. It's congenital. So, for four years, I just ignored baseball. I ignored the sports section until they formed the New York Mets, which I considered a combination of Giant and Dodger uniforms. I was assigned to do a feature story on the very first game, and the first sentence was, "The lost souls of the baseball world found a home yesterday."

The Yankees didn't count . . . to a Dodger/Giant fan.

In my childhood, fiction was dominated by the immortal John R. Tunis, the clackety-clackety-clack of spikes in *The Kid from Tompkinsville* and *World Series* was—since we ourselves played all our games in black high-top sneakers—like music from a foreign land. It was echoed in my childhood only by the clackety-clack of the trolley cars as they switched rails on the way to Fordham Road and the Grand Concourse, the Times Square of The Bronx. In the nonfiction section of the library, I read every book available about how to play baseball. I studied as scrupulously as a brash young scientist at work. I knew the game. By the time I was eight years old, I knew that on a hit to right field, the shortstop had to cover second base, while on a hit to leftfield, he had to go out for the relay. I knew that with a runner stealing and a left-hander at bat, he had to cover second. I knew that to sacrifice a runner, you squared around and caught the ball on the bat while laying down the bunt. And that bunting for a base hit was another matter entirely; hour after hour in the small front parlor of our apartment, where I slept, I stood with a bat in my hands and practiced dropping the bat on an imaginary ball, laying the ball down the third base line even as I broke toward first. I knew, therefore, nearly everything important about life. The only thing I didn't know was how to stop being afraid of the dark.

When I was six years old, my brother took me one Saturday afternoon to see my very first movie, at the old Surrey Theater on Mount Eden Avenue—14 cents for kids. The attraction was an animated Walt Disney film called *Make Mine Music.* It featured, as I recall, *The Little Engine That Could,* a bunch of penguins freezing their butts off on ice floes, and assorted other inspirations and amusements. Unbeknownst to me, however, there was also a second feature, which my brother wanted to see. It was *The Phantom of the Opera,* with Lon Chaney. As we watched the film, I took particular note of the Phantom's acid-eaten face. I did not venture into a dark movie theater again for two more years. I did not go to bed with the light off in my room for three.

"How can you be a baseball player if you're afraid of the dark?" my frustrated mother asked, trying a bit of psychology. "What's that got to do with anything?" "How will you play night games?" "There's lights."

The trouble was, even if the naked light bulb was burning on the ceiling of your room, when you closed your eyes to go to sleep, darkness inevitably descended. To rid myself of the monsters that immediately filled my brain, I began to chant, that summer of 1947, first summer of my fandom, the same refrain, over and over in my brain: *The Dodgers are gonna win the pennant! The Dodgers are gonna win the pennant!* Since I had never in my life seen a sheep, counting Jackie Robinson's and Pee Wee Reese's scoring runs was far superior to the

> "How can you be a baseball player if you're afraid of the dark?"

traditional escape. The problem was, the Dodgers actually did win the pennant that year, so when October turned to November, and then to winter, the mantra of the Dodgers winning lost some of its soporific effect. Which gave new meaning to the perennial Brooklyn refrain, "Wait till next year."

If the Dodgers did win the pennant that year, 1947, they maintained their traditional role as heartbreakers by losing the World Series to the hated Yankees. It was during that series that I learned an important lesson, however: While Dodger fans could run like hell, Yankee fans could fly.

> While Dodger fans could run like hell, Yankee fans could fly.

It was the fourth game of the series, played at Ebbets Field. The Yankees led, two games to one. Now, in Game 4, Bill Bevens of the Yankees was still pitching a no-hitter with two out in the ninth inning. To be no-hit in the World Series—that would be too much even for a Dodger fan to bear. I was listening in our two-story house, in our apartment that covered the entire first floor, when two men reached base on walks, and Cookie Lavagetto came up to pinch-hit. The Yankees were ahead, 2–1. Lavagetto swung. The ball sailed deep into right field—all this coming over a yellow plastic radio in the moderately hoarse voice of Red Barber, the voice of the Bums, the original "Music Man" of my youth. The ball hit the wall high over the right fielder's head. Two Dodgers raced around the bases and scored. The no-hitter was broken, the Dodgers had won the game and evened the series, all with that one swing, the most dramatic hit in history up to that time, and, for Dodger fans, for all-time to come. (We do not mention 1951.)

This little-known substitute player, Cookie Lavagetto, who would never play another season, had found instant immortality—this player who, until then, might have been to the vast uncaring public, or to my parents, some arcane vegetable, like a zucchini or a squash. *You don't get any dessert till you finish your lavagetto.*

Light-headed with joy, I raced out the door and down the three front steps to rub it in to my neighbor and best friend Jackie

Brownstein, who lived two doors away and was two years older and was a Yankee fan, antagonist in all my childhood arguments, William Buckley to my Bill Moyers. To my eternal astonishment, Jackie, who lived on the second floor, and thus had to churn his solid body down a whole flight of stairs, Jackie, who should have been brooding in solitude about the sudden turnabout, about the terrible loss, as I would have been doing had our roles been reversed. Jackie was waiting for me in the street before I got there waiting to chatter excitedly about the unbelievable ending. As if he knew his Yankees would triumph anyway. As they did. As in those days—they always did. But how had he gotten into the street so fast? How had he beaten me, for I had raced for the door in a flash? There could be only one explanation. He had leapt without fear from his upstairs parlor window. Yankee fans, it seemed, could fly.

This observation has held up fairly well throughout my life. In the byways of my mind, Dodger fans and Giant fans and now Mets fans tend to ride the buses or hitch with their thumbs, hoboes drinking beer at synaptic gaps. While Yankee fans drink Chivas Regal and fly first class, no matter how well, or how badly their team is doing. They need the wider seats for their menial bottoms. They do not suffer, they do not quit eating, when the Bronx Bombers lose. They are not now, nor have they ever been, either skinny or marinks.

A day or two after Lavagetto's hit came Gionfriddo's catch. With two men on base and the Dodgers leading 8–5, Joe DiMaggio belted a long drive into left-centerfield. A Dodger scrubbini named Al Gionfriddo, filling in at leftfield, raced far back to the wall and caught the ball as it passed over the low fence into the leftfield bullpen. Television had not yet reached Townsend Avenue in 1947, so this, too, I heard on the radio. A picture of the catch appeared in the next day's newspapers, and has been reprinted many times since. It shows Gionfriddo with his arm bent at his waist, over the bullpen fence, the ball in his glove. I studied the picture that day and have studied it many times since and still can't figure out if this was the follow-through of a traditional leaping catch or if indeed he caught the ball in that curious position. It remains one of the abiding mysteries of life, along with the origin of the universe and how anyone can eat boiled okra.

> Times Square . . . thick with traffic, with noisy people in the streets, as the electric lights on the Times Tower spelled out the Yankee victory.

Despite the immortal heroics of Lavagetto and Gionfriddo, however, the Dodgers lost this Subway Series, this first World Series in which I was an active participant. On the seventh day, God rested. He ceased his miracles; he let the Philistines win. When the afternoon of the seventh came, I was riding downtown with my parents in the family car, going I know not where. I heard the tragic ending on the car radio. Minutes later, we passed through Times Square, which was thick with traffic, with noisy people in the streets, as the electric lights on the Times Tower spelled out the Yankee victory. People were shouting and cheering and throwing confetti, and I, feeling sick to my stomach, could not imagine what it was they were celebrating. Didn't they understand that the Dodgers had lost?

The next day, my friend Jackie's father, Harry Brownstein, who was a policeman and a Yankee fan and had heavy jowls, came by our house and handed me a small white card. It was rimmed all around in black. In tiny letters in the center, surrounded by white space, were the words BROOKLYN DODGERS.

I didn't get the joke. I asked my mother what the card meant. She said it was the kind of card people gave out when someone had died: a black border with the dead person's name in the middle.

I didn't think it was very funny. I still don't.

OUTSIDE OF A DOG, A BOOK IS MAN'S BEST FRIEND. INSIDE OF A DOG, IT'S TOO DARK TO READ.

Jim Bouton

In 1970, former Yankee ace, Jim Bouton, wrote Ball Four, *one of the most enjoyable sports books ever. While it was embraced by baseball fans, it was scorned by the baseball establishment. Typical of the latter was Leo Durocher. After blasting the book and Bouton for several minutes on a national interview, the announcer—for some reason— asked Durocher if he had actually read the book. Durocher admitted that he had not and had no intention of doing so.*

In 2003, Bouton wrote a wonderful book, Foul Ball, *about his attempts to save an aging minor-league ballpark in Pittsfield, Massachusetts—not far from his residence.*

I went away to play baseball at the age of nineteen and came back after my first season of professional ball in the minor leagues and told my family and friends what a crazy and fun experience it was and they all said the same thing . . . you ought to keep notes and write a book some day.

The owners didn't like *Ball Four*. I realize now it had nothing to do with locker room secrets. It had to do with the fact that *Ball Four* was the first book to tell people how difficult it was to make a living in baseball. This was before free agency, and the owners had the players locked up. Had us tied to whatever team we were signed, and we had to stay with that team for the rest of our career unless they traded us. We had no say in the trades. So we had to sign whatever contract they gave us. They took advantage of it, and they would pay $10,000 or $15,000 to guys who played in the Major Leagues three to four years who were good ballplayers.

The year I was 21–7, my salary was $10,500. I talked about this in *Ball Four* and showed how the owners took advantage of the players. The owners and the commissioner were afraid that a judge would read this book, or a jury, or an arbitrator, or a congressman or something, and baseball might lose their antitrust exemption. The irony is that's exactly what happened in 1975 at the famous Andy Messersmith arbitration hearing in New York. I was the only former player called to testify against the owners. I read passages from *Ball Four,* which was accepted as legal evidence because it was based on contemporaneous notes.

The owners didn't like *Ball Four.*

So the owners were afraid of the economic impact that *Ball Four* might have on their game. The players had a different reaction. They believed the baseball commissioner when he said this was bad for baseball. But if they had read the book, they would have realized that it told the players' view of the game.

We had a very restrictive contract and we were not getting our fair value in the marketplace. That was pretty clear. The owners were stealing our money and they said they needed to do that in order to maintain competitive balance. That was a lie, because once there was competitive balance in 1975, when ballplayers became free agents, there was actually more competitive balance. The Yankees were winning the pennant just about every year under the old system, and under the new system of free agency, there were more teams winning pennants. So they were wrong about the reason they were tying us to teams.

Some sportswriters were jealous of the access that I had to meetings and other private goings-on that they didn't have access to. A lot of sportswriters were selling the "milk and cookies" image and they felt that's what they ought to do, and here was somebody coming along telling everybody, in effect, that that was all nonsense. So it sort of put a lie to their work. These guys . . . it was their life's work. Sort of painting pastel colors every year, so they were angry at me and jealous.

More kids during my day were signed directly out of high school and right off the farm. They would sign at eighteen and play minor-league baseball so they really weren't exposed to that much. Even though they traveled around the country, in most cases they were not inquisitive people. They didn't go out and look around the town. They didn't travel. They didn't explore. They didn't sight-see. They basically stayed in their room or

> Some sportswriters were jealous of the access that I had to meetings and other private goings-on . . .

went down to the pool hall or whatever. They hung together and were isolated in a sense. Some of the guys weren't that bright.

There were other guys who had been to **COLLEGE*** and had been away, and some had been in the service and they were much further ahead of the kids who had just signed out of high school. You had more of a mixture of guys when I played ball. Today, most of the players have been to college for at least one or two years, and some for three and four years. The players today are much smarter, as a general rule, than we were.

Part of what made *Ball Four* a successful book is that the time was ripe for it. It was a time in which the nation was questioning itself. In the early '60s we sort of had our eyes closed. By the end of the '60s we realized that Vietnam was a mistake and that our leaders had misled us and a lot of people were lying about our role in the world. We were starting to question things—question the old order—and that's when *Ball Four* came out. It was a period of great awareness . . . emerging self-awareness.

Ballplayers didn't read it because it was 400 pages and there was nothing to color in. Most guys didn't read books when I played ball. Somebody would read a book on the bus, and he would get a

*Of the 750 players on Major League rosters recently, only seventeen were **COLLEGE** graduates.

nickname as "Professor" or something like that. You were a genius if you got caught reading a book. Most guys didn't even like to read the newspapers. Joe Schultz, my manager in Seattle, when I asked him if he wanted to read the first part of the newspaper, said, "No, I don't read that section."

There's something about standing on the mound with a ball in your hand and the challenge of seeing if you can throw it 60 feet, 6 inches into this little square space and keep this other guy from hitting it. There's something challenging and fun about that. I'm sure it's the same for the batter. A baseball game is really a series of challenges. It's 120 challenges by each pitcher, 'cause that's how many pitches you throw . . . so you're putting yourself on the line 120 different moments. When you add them up for both teams, that 240 different moments of potential drama in a game. You hardly have that in any other sport.

> I didn't write *Ball Four* as a crusade.

I didn't write Ball Four as a crusade. I wasn't thinking of doing something that might catch flack. I wanted to write all this stuff down so I could share it with people and have the memories myself. If I hadn't written that stuff down, I would have never been able to recall it. I can just crack open the book any time I want and read whatever's on that page and it brings back these wonderful memories.

BITS AND BITES:
BEGGED, BORROWED AND STOLEN

In 1949 the Oakland Oaks were an ideal team to follow. They had finished first in the league in 1948, managed by the legendary Casey Stengel, who, based on his success in Oakland, had just been elevated to the prime position of manager of the New York Yankees. Although the team was rebuilding during much of the 1949 season under the management of Charlie Dressen, they still finished second in the league. Besides, their second baseman was a young brash kid by the name of Billy Martin. An all-around athlete and ballyhooed local football legend from the University of California–Berkeley, Jackie Jensen was playing his rookie baseball season in the outfield. All through the 1949 season, I caught as many Oaks' games as possible. I particularly remember thrilling regularly to the Sunday doubleheader games, the first game on the twin bill lasting the usual nine innings, followed by the shorter, seven-inning second game.

Since we did not subscribe to a daily or even weekly newspaper, my only source of sports information was the radio. I heard the announcers discussing batting averages and earned run averages, but I had no real idea how these were figured until one day in the local St. Helena newsstand-magazine store, I stumbled onto a baseball yearbook or almanac for the 1949 season. I do not remember the exact title of the little paperback volume, although I clearly remember its cover was mostly a colorful green. Within it I found a summary of the 1949 Major League season, including many tables of statistics for the

> I memorized many of the statistics for the Yankee lineup and the next year began following the team through radio news reports . . .

year, and information about how the statistics were figured. The book became my sports bible for the next year. The Oakland Oaks and their rivals in the Pacific Coast League paled in comparison to the details about the Major League teams in this yearbook. I fell in love with the American League champions of that season—the New York Yankees. I memorized many of the statistics for the Yankee lineup and the next year began following the team through radio news reports as well as through the national "Game of the Day" radio broadcasts, which I became addicted to over the next several years. Although I occasionally still listened to an Oakland Oaks' broadcast, these minor-league games no longer carried as much importance now that I had discovered the big leagues. . . .

I knew better than to use a regular ball for my lawn baseball games. Even with my meager hitting ability, those big living-room and study windows were far too close to allow for play with a real ball. My mother, short on tolerance for games in general, would never have allowed more than one broken window before banning lawn baseball forever.

My solution to the ball dilemma was certainly environmentally original. Howell Mountain, like much of northern California, produces oak trees in abundance. Many grew on our nearly two-acre property. Every year these trees hatched numerous small growths, the often nearly round appendages we called oak balls, generally somewhat smaller than real baseballs but close enough in size for my fantasies and not hard enough to damage the looming house windows.

As the season developed, however, the balls on the trees would dry out and turn dark brown and black, losing their hard qualities and becoming very light and rather feathery, often easily breaking in two with a particularly hard swing of the bat. When the oak balls became extremely light, a windy day would make it difficult for a ball to get beyond the imaginary pitcher's mound. Although such balls might not last beyond a couple of innings, I always had a ready supply near at hand since I could knock them at will from the surrounding trees with a rake or a hoe. By fall, many of the balls would actually have fallen from the trees and lay around on the ground within easy reach.

Playing lawn baseball alone with oak balls meant that I was always up at the plate and that there were no fielders and no pitcher. Everything, except the swing of the bat and the succeeding hits, was imaginary! The game went like this. I would pretend, sequentially, to be every hitter in the Yankee or opposition lineup. I would throw the oak ball into the air, swing the bat as the ball came down, and hit the ball out into the field, pretending that the ball would fall in for a hit, be caught, or be fielded, or, when Mickey Mantle or Yogi Berra or another power hitter was up, be lofted over the pretend fences. I would keep track mentally of what men were on what base, how many outs there were, and how many runs had scored. As the person in charge of the game, I could manipulate events in such a way that the Yankee rallies could go on for many minutes, with the opposition fielders making all sorts of errors, dropping balls, overthrowing bases, and the like, while the Yankee lineup often batted twice around in an inning.

The one drawback to my game was that each time I hit the oak ball, I would need to go retrieve it before the game could continue. On the other hand, those trips across the lawn provided ample opportunity for me to manufacture lots of colorful commentary in my head as to what was going on, similar to the radio broadcasts I was listening to with great regularity.

> ... while I could make my Yankee team score ten runs or more in an inning without so much as a pang of conscience.

My favorite opposition team was the Brooklyn Dodgers, based, no doubt, on the many World Series games of the time that pitted the two teams against each other, rather than on the reality that the two teams never met during regular-season play since they were in different leagues. It was amazing how often my fantasy pitchers, great ones like Allie Reynolds or Vic Raschi, or, after he came up, Whitey Ford, used to set down those Dodger batters in one-two-three order, while I could make my Yankee team score ten runs or more in an inning without so much as a pang of conscience. The Yankees were a great team during those years, but never greater than when playing on my front lawn!

—DELMER DAVIS, Angwin, California,
native who turned into a Cubs fanatic

Donald Fehr's ego applied for statehood today. If approved it will be the nation's third largest.

Hey! I know a guy who has a baseball not autographed by Pete Rose.

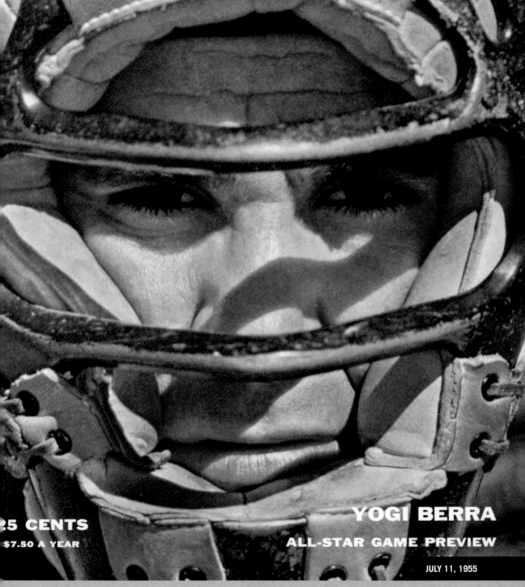

JULY 11, 1955

SPORTS
ILLUSTRATED

25 CENTS
$7.50 A YEAR

YOGI BERRA
ALL-STAR GAME PREVIEW

JULY 11, 1955

This section contains every Yankees *Sports Illustrated* cover.

APRIL 23, 1956

SPORTS

I L

25 CENTS
$7.50 A YEAR

BILLY MARTIN
SPARKPLUG
OF
THE NEW YORK YANKEES

APRIL 23, 1956

WEEKLY

JUNE 18, 1956

SPORTS

ILL

25 CENTS
7.50 A YEAR

MICKEY MANTLE

THE YEAR OF
THE SLUGGER

JUNE 18, 1956

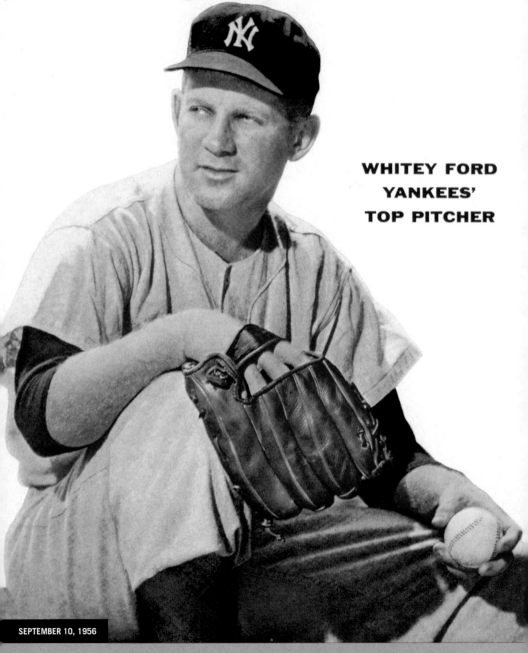

SPORTS ILLUSTRATED

SEPTEMBER 10, 1956

a Time Inc. weekly publication

25 CENTS
$7.50 A YEAR

WHITEY FORD
YANKEES'
TOP PITCHER

SEPTEMBER 10, 1956

SPORTS ILLUSTRATED

OCTOBER 1, 1956

a Time Inc. weekly publication

25 CENTS
$7.50 A YEAR

WORLD SERIES

MICKEY MANTLE
HOPE OF THE YANKEES

- THE COCKY NATIONAL LEAGUE

- SCOUTING REPORTS ON THE TEAMS

- YANKEE POWER IN COLOR

- DOWN THE STRETCH WITH STENGEL

- PLUS ALL REGULAR FEATURES

OCTOBER 1, 1956

MARCH 4, 1957

a Time Inc. weekly publicat.

25 CENTS
$7.50 A YEAR

SPORTS
ILLUSTRATED

1957
SPRING TRAINING

THE REAL MICKEY MANTL
BY GERALD HOLLAND

SPORTS ILLUSTRATED

JULY 22, 1957

a Time Inc. weekly publication

25 CENTS
$7.50 A YEAR

THE YANKEES

5 big questions
answered for
the first time

HANK BAUER

JULY 22, 1957

SPORTS ILLUSTRATED

MARCH 3, 1958

America's National Sports Week

25 CENTS
$7.50 A YEAR

1958
SPRING TRAINING
ARE THE BRAVES
ON TOP TO STAY?

MARCH 3, 1958

MARCH 17, 1958

America's National Sports Weekly

25 CENTS
$7.50 A YEAR

SPORTS ILLUSTRATED

An Exciting New Series

BIG LEAGUE SECRETS

*Told by five major league stars
in words and drawings*

Part I: SAL MAGLIE on PITCHING

MARCH 17, 1958

SPORTS ILLUSTRATED

MAY 5, 1958

America's National Sports Week[ly]

25 CENTS
$7.50 A YEAR

★

BIG LEAGUE
SECRETS—4

GIL McDOUGALD ON
PLAYING THE INFIELD

also

HORACE STONEHAM
A LONELY LINK
TO BASEBALL'S PAST

MAY 5, 1958

SPORTS
ILLUSTRATED

MARCH 2, 1959

America's National Sports Weekly

25 CENTS
$7.50 A YEAR

In this issue
A NEW VIEW OF YOGI BERRA

**SPRING
TRAINING
1959**

MARCH 2, 1959

SPORTS ILLUSTRATED

MAY 4, 1959

America's National Sports Wee

25 CENTS
$7.50 A YEAR

THE PITCHING CRISIS

BOB TURLEY
AND HIS $500,000 ARM

Sports Illustrated

WORLD
SERIES
PREVIEW

OBER 2, 1961   25 CENTS

MARIS
OF THE YANKEES

OCTOBER 2, 1961

Sports Illustrated
JULY 2, 1962
25 CENTS
Mickey Mantle
INDISPENSAB
YANKEE
JULY 2, 1962

Sports Illustrated

SEPTEMBER 30, 1963   25 CENTS

THE SERIES: A VOTE FOR THE LEFT

SEPTEMBER 30, 1963

Sports Illustrated

MARCH 2, 1964   30 CENTS

GOREN 3: DOUBLE MORE OFT

MARCH 2, 1964

Sports Illustrated

JUNE 21, 1965 · 35 CENTS

NEW YORK YANKEES
END OF AN ERA

MICKEY MANTLE

JUNE 21, 1965

Sports Illustrated

ALI SAYS N

MAY 8, 1967   40 CENTS

THE TANGLED AMERICAN LEAGUE

White Sox Star Ken Berry slides to avoid Mickey Mantle's tag

MAY 8, 1967

Sports Illustrated

AUGUST 21, 1972   60 CENTS

DAMN YANKEES AGAIN

SPARKY LYLE AND LITTLE SPARK

AUGUST 21, 1972

Sports Illustrated

JULY 2, 1973   60 CENTS

PRIDE OF THE NEW YANKEES

Bobby Murcer and Ron Blomberg

JULY 2, 1973

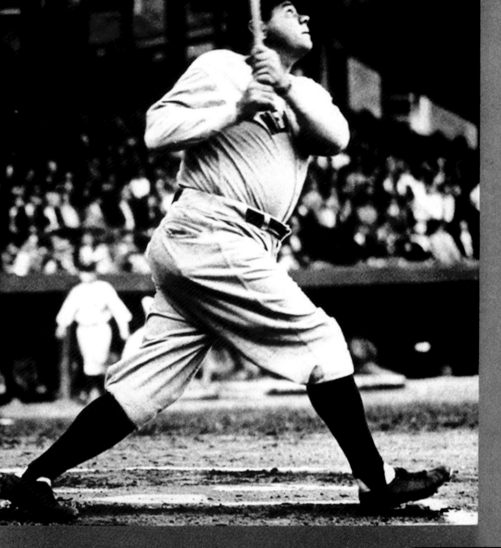

Sports Illustrated

MARCH 18, 1974   **60 CENTS**

BABE RUTH
THE LEGEND COMES TO LIFE

MARCH 18, 1974

Sports Illustrated

MAY 31, 1976   ONE DOLLAR

HEAD-ON COLLISION
IN THE EAST

Speeding Yanks Run Into
the Sputtering Red Sox

MAY 31, 1976

Sports Illustrated

MAY 2, 1977   ONE DOLLAR

CAN
EGGIE JACKSON
FIND LOVE
ND HAPPINESS
IN NEW YORK?

MAY 2, 1977

Sports Illustrated

OCTOBER 24, 1977 · ONE DOLLAR

THE WORLD SERIES

OCTOBER 24, 1977

Sports Illustrated

JULY 31, 1978   ONE DOL

DOUBLE,
DOUBLE
TOIL AND
TROUBLE

Billy Martin

JULY 31, 1978

HOCKEY 1978-79

Sports Illustrated

OCTOBER 23, 1978 $1.2

THE
WORLD
SERIES

LACY
34

OCTOBER 23, 1978

Sports Illustrated

AUGUST 4, 1980 $1.50

GOING,
GOING,
GONE!

Reggie on a Rampage

AUGUST 4, 1980

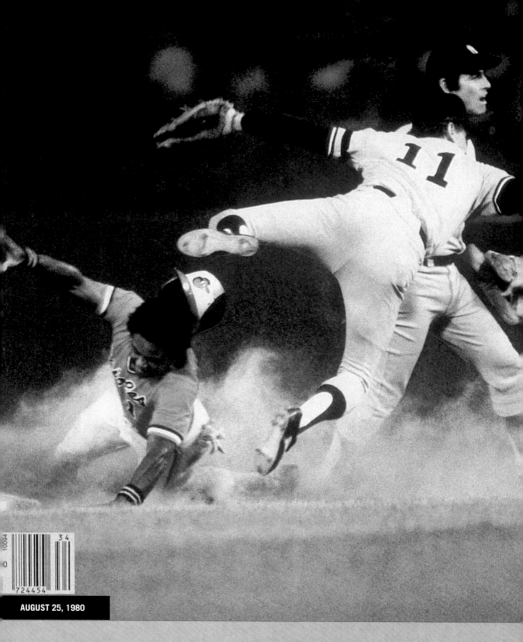

Sports Illustrated

AUGUST 25, 1980 $1.

BALTIMORE BATTLES BACK

Sports Illustrated

JANUARY 5, 1981 $1.50

THE MAN

WHO HIT THE JACKPOT

Dave Winfield of the Yankees

JANUARY 5, 1981

01

Sports Illustrated

OCTOBER 26, 1981 $1.50

SWINGING INTO THE SERIES

Yankee Slugger
Graig Nettles

OCTOBER 26, 1981

0 10094

Sports Illustrated

NOVEMBER 2, 1981 $1.50

THE WORLD SERIES

NL

NY

NEW YORK

LOPES
15

NOVEMBER 2, 1981

SPECIAL BASEBALL ISSUE

Sports Illustrated

APRIL 2, 1984

YOGI' BACK

...And Other Glad Tidings Of Spring

Cal Ripken Jr: Born To Be A Super

Are The Umps Too For Their Britches

Plus Complete Scouting Reports

Yankee Manager
Yogi Berra:
What Did He Say,
When Did He Say It
And What Does It Mean?

Sports Illustrated

IL 16, 1984 $1.95

GRAIG AND THE GOOSE

Graig Nettles

Rich Gossage

Two Ex-Yanks Find Sanity And Sanctuary In San Diego

APRIL 16, 1984

Sports Illustrated

MARCH 25, 1985 $1.95

THE NC
WHO CAN BEAT GEORG

WELCOME HOME!

Peter Ueberroth
Reinstates Willie Mays
And Mickey Mantle

MARCH 25, 1985

Sports Illustrated

MAY 6, 1985 $1.95

BILLY'S BACK!

BILLY MARTIN:
Yankee Manager
For The
Fourth Time

18
24454

MAY 6, 1985

Sports Illustrated

JULY 28, 1986

THE BRONX BURNER

Leadoff Man Extraordinaire Rickey Henderson

13, 1987 $2.25

Sports Illustrated

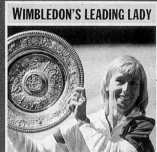

NEW YORK
HE METS ARE FEUDING

NEW YORK
THE YANKS ARE FLYING

RRYL STRAWBERRY

DON MATTINGLY

JULY 13, 1987

Sports Illustrated

Whatever Happened to the Yankees?

Thirty years after the magical season Mantle and Maris, New York has hit rock bottom

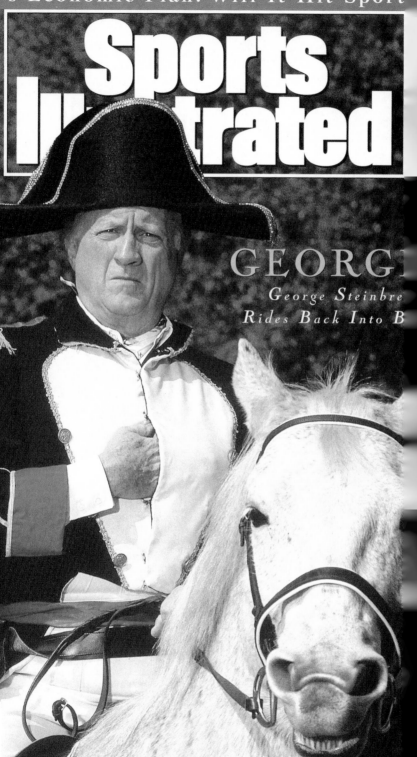

Sports Illustrated

GEORGE

George Steinbre
Rides Back Into B

MARC

MAY 3, 1993 • $2.95

Sports Illustrated

Where Have You Gone, Joe DiMaggio?

**IN ITS SEARCH
FOR HEROES,
A NATION TURNS
ITS LONELY EYES
TO SPORTS OTHER
THAN BASEBALL**

0 724454 6

18

MAY 3, 1993

Sports Illustrated

APRIL 18, 1994 · $2.95 (CAN. $3.95)

'I WAS KILLING MYSELF'

My Life as
An Alcoholic
By Mickey Mantle

APRIL 18, 1994

Sports Illustrated

AUGUST 21, 1995

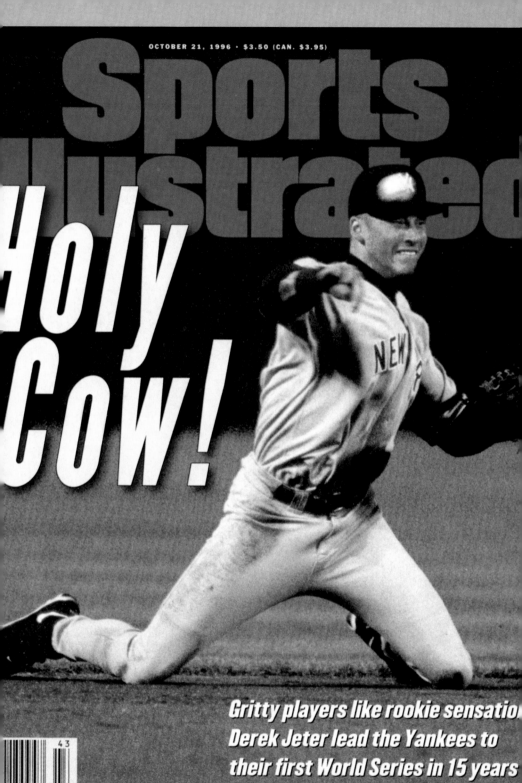

OCTOBER 21, 1996 · $3.50 (CAN. $3.95)

Sports Illustrated

Holy Cow!

Gritty players like rookie sensation Derek Jeter lead the Yankees to their first World Series in 15 years

OCTOBER 21, 1996

```
10094  43  7
```

NOVEMBER 4, 1996 • $3.50 (CAN. $3.95)

Sports Illustrated

A FALL CLASSIC

····················

*World Series
heroes
Joe Girardi
and
John Wetteland
celebrate the
Yankees'
return to
glory*

NOVEMBER 4, 1996

0 70989 10094

FEBRUARY 24, 1997 • $3.50 (CAN. $3.95)

Sports Illustrated

EK JETER
ALEX RODRIGUEZ
D UP THE FINEST
UP OF
RTSTOPS
CE
LD WAR II

SHORT STORY

FEBRUARY 24, 1997

Sports Illustrated

THE CHICAGO CU
NEW KING OF K's

NO STOPPIN' SH

Speed Power Heat

THE YANKEES HAVE IT ALL
Derek Jeter, Tino Martinez, Mariano Rivera

MAY 18, 1998

Sports
Illustrated

e
Babe

athlete
gripped the
ion the
Babe Ruth
in 1927

Sex, Religion
And the NFL
**The curious
case of
Curtis Enis**

Kickin' Bass
**Is big-bucks
fishing the
next NASCAR?**

24, 1998
i.com

AUGUST 24, 1998

Sports Illustrated

998 YANKEES

Perfect Fit

NOVEMBER 2, 1998

Sports Illustrated

1975?
1924?
1936?
1969?
1955?
1998?
1980?
1958?
1973?
1978?
1966?
1946?
1908?
1982?
1919?
1953?
1930?
1961?
1927?
1968?
1941?
1974?

What's the Best Sports Year Ever?

8, 1998–JANUARY 4, 1999
com • Display until 1/7/99

DECEMBER 26, 1998

Sports Illustrated

Chin Music

**The Yankees get
Roger Clemens and
strike fear through the
rest of baseball**

MARCH 1, 1999
www.cnnsi.com

MARCH 1, 1999

A FINALS
ball: Grand Slams Galore

Sports Illustrated

Good
Field
Good
Hit
Good
Guy

Why
Derek Jeter
so easy
to root for

JUNE 21, 1999

Sports Illustrated

Wipeout!

ERS AND CANADIENS
Dynasties in Decay

Frank Deford Remembers Wilt

Scott Brosius and the Yankees
Barge into the World Series

OCTOBER 25, 19
www.cnnsi.com

OCTOBER 25, 1999

Sports Illustrated

'hy Fight t?
The Yankees will win again

EK JETER Four rings and counting >>>

Enemy ines

pposing
scouts size up
30 teams

The ice of itching

's worth it. Who's not

MARCH 26, 2001

Sports Illustrated

SPECIAL RE...
When coaches...
players become lo...

ROCK
OF AGES

AT 39 YEARS OLD
ROGER CLEMENS
IS MAKING HISTORY

SEPTEMBER 10, 2001

Sports Illustrated

The Playoffs

National League

The Braves' Surprising Sweep

But can Atlanta beat **Arizona** in a matchup of battle-tested aces?

rican League

e Yanks' storic omeback

an **Derek Jeter & Co.** he mighty **Mariners,** all's winningest team?

2001 www.cnnsi.com
: Sports Illustrated

OCTOBER 22, 2001

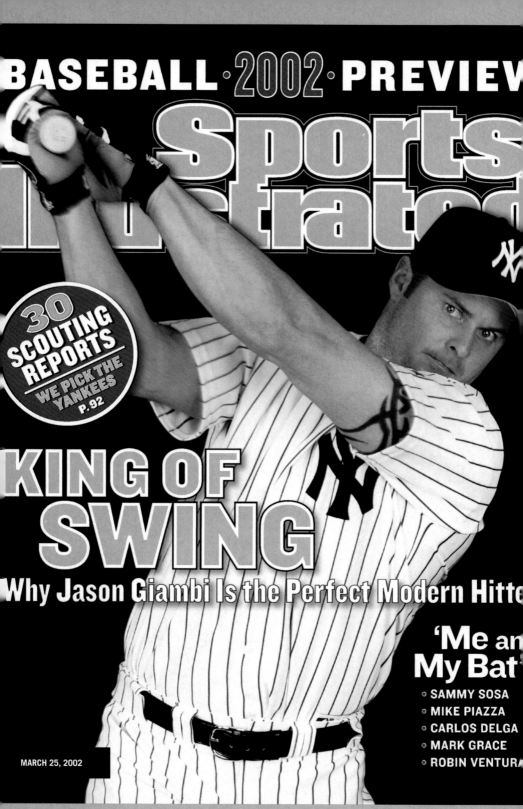

BASEBALL · 2002 · PREVIEW

Sports Illustrated

30 SCOUTING REPORTS
WE PICK THE YANKEES
P. 92

KING OF SWING

Why Jason Giambi Is the Perfect Modern Hitter

'Me and My Bat'

- SAMMY SOSA
- MIKE PIAZZA
- CARLOS DELGA
- MARK GRACE
- ROBIN VENTUR

MARCH 25, 2002

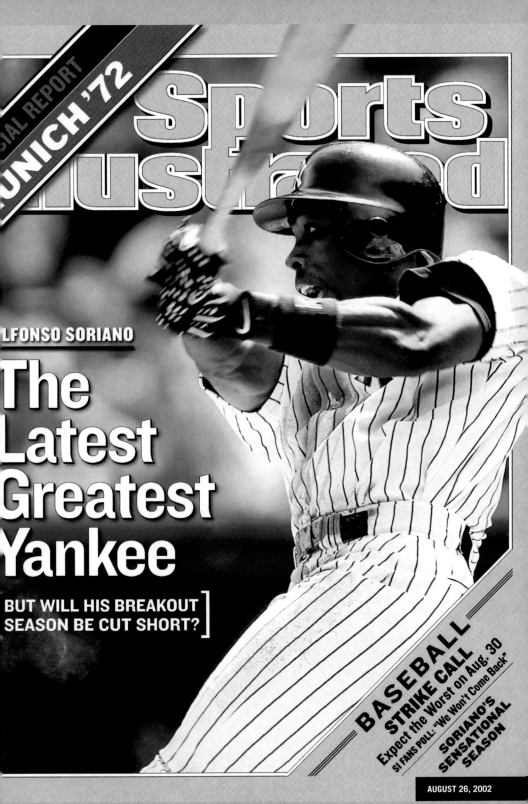

Sports Illustrated

ALFONSO SORIANO

The Latest Greatest Yankee

BUT WILL HIS BREAKOUT SEASON BE CUT SHORT?

BASEBALL
STRIKE CALL
Expect the Worst on Aug. 30
SI FANS POLL: "We Won't Come Back"

SORIANO'S SENSATIONAL SEASON

AUGUST 26, 2002

BASEBALL

2003 PREVIEW

Sports Illustrated

You Can't Have Too Much
PITCHING

(Just Ask George)

60 PAGES OF COMPLETE
SCOUTING REPO

HOW RANDY JOHNSON THROWS HIS
And Other Big League Secre

Yankees owner George Steinbrenner with (clockwise from top left)
Jose Contreras, Andy Pettitte, Mike Mussina and Roger

MARCH 31, 2003

Sports Illustrated

THE ROCKET

ROGER
CLEMENS
AND THE
QUEST FOR

300

Tom Verducci

DOUBLE ISSUE

Sports Illustrated

1954-2004

50TH Anniversary
1954

WILLIE MAYS *made his World Series catch*
ROGER BANNISTER *ran the first 4-minute mile*
ROCKY MARCIANO *was undefeated*
WILT CHAMBERLAIN
was finishing high school
HANK AARON *was joining*
the Milwaukee Braves
ARNOLD PALMER *was turning pro*
MICKEY MANTLE *invented the*
tape-measure home run

Not a bad year
to start a
sports magazine

JULY 14, 2003

DALE JR. WINS THE DAYTONA 500

Sports Illustrated

COLORADO RECRUITING SCANDAL

ELLO, EW YORK

riguez, baseball's best, big move — to third base

TEXAS TWO-STEP
ROD BOLTS FOR THE YANKEES
TTITTE AND CLEMENS AT HOME IN HOUSTON >

2004 www.si.com
Sports Illustrated

FEBRUARY 23, 2004

SMARTY JONES. BELMONT. SATURDAY. HISTORY?

NBA FINAL

How the Lakers
CAN BE BEATEN
BY JACK McCALLUM

Sports Illustrated

THE SLUMP

SOLVING THE BIGGEST MYSTERY IN SPORTS

> > > **DEREK JETER** < < <
Career Batting Avg. .317
Avg. This Season Through May 25 .189
Avg. from May 26 to May 31 .458

JUNE 7, 2004

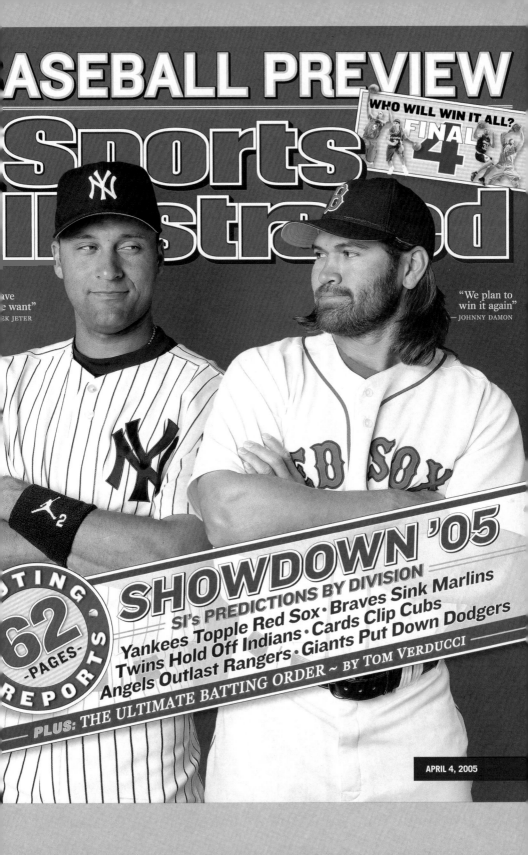

Sports Illustrated

EXCLUSIVE

BOTTOM LINE

The Lucrative Evolution of the Left Tackle

BY MICHAEL LEWIS

Jonathan Ogden

"Alex doesn' know who h We're going to find out who he is in next couple of months."

—JASON G

THE LONELY YANKEE

After a Bewildering Summer, Alex Rodriguez Has to Prove Himself in Pinstripes

BY TOM VERDUCCI

SEPTEMBER 25, 2006

Chapter 7

Fandemonium

Extra Innings

INTERNET, ENTER NOT

Sean Forman

Sean Forman grew up on an Iowa farm with a fascination for statistics. Forman received his fill of Rotisserie and Fantasy baseball as he attended Grinnell College and the University of Iowa. In the early millennium, he started a Web site called baseball-reference.com, a favorite of Yankee fans.

In college I started developing my own system for ranking prospects. I wanted to get the leg up on the rest of the guys in my fantasy baseball league. I started a site called "The Iowa Farm Report," at iowafarmreport.com. It had stats for the big prospects in the minor leagues for several hundred players. I was trying to be like a young Bill James at that time. I had a few hits and did all right.

I was writing for a book called *The Big, Bad Baseball Annual.* The editor saw The Iowa Farm Report and thought it would be interesting for people to read in his book. The last year he did it, they sold only 6,000 copies. It was a Bill James–type book but didn't do anywhere near as well as his books did. I saw there was this database that was publicly available. I thought I could take that and create a set of pages that would be like *The Baseball Encyclopedia.* That was my goal.

Total Baseball had a Web site but it was limited—and hard to use. I was into creating a very useful, very easy-to-use Web site. I read a lot of books about the Web and was interested in it, so I thought it would be the perfect format for a baseball encyclopedia. You have an infinite amount of storage. The encyclopedia is limited to about 2,000 pages. We can have 20,000 pages, and it wouldn't ever get any heavier and there would be no printing costs. We can put it all online, and it's free for us to do that.

There were other advantages. You can create links from a player page to all his teammates to the league leaders to all the home runs he hit that year, and on and on and on. In a baseball encyclopedia, in print, if you see Joe DiMaggio's page, and you want to see all of his teammates, you may have to leaf back to the rosters in the very back of the book, find it, then look up each of those players and leaf back through. I thought this seemed like a format that was custom-made for the Internet.

In late '99 and early 2000, I put together the basic parts of the site in about three months. I was on fellowship at the University of Iowa. I was supposed to be finishing my dissertation. I had a lot of free time all day, and, instead of finishing my dissertation, I worked on this. I couldn't have made this my dissertation because mathematically, this isn't challenging stuff, although there is a lot of execution involved on it. My dissertation was entitled *Torsion Angle Selection and Emergent Non-local Secondary Structure in Protein-Structure Prediction.*

> If you're interested in looking at the 1977 Yankees, we can give you the starting batting order of every game for the Yankees for that season.

I called my site "baseball-reference" because I didn't have a better idea for it. This was in the dot-com boom, and I thought it would be a good idea to have a very descriptive name to describe what it does. In retrospect, it wasn't a brilliant move. My main goal was to make it very easy to use. My goal has always been to make it very fast, very easy to use so that users can get immersed in it and get lost in it. I wanted them to be able to produce the answer almost as fast as they can think of the question.

A Yankee fan would go there and find stats for every Yankee player who has ever played. We can give you things like the opening-day rosters for the Yankees—the Opening Day lineups for the last fifty years. If you're interested in looking at the 1977 Yankees, we can give you the starting batting order of every game for the

Yankees for that season. Say the first game you remember was in 1972, and you remember Roy White hitting a home run, you can go to the player page, go to their game logs, find all the games Roy White hit a home run in and find a box score and a play-by-play account of that game.

You can do things like find a list of teammates that will match Babe Ruth to Derek Jeter, using what we call the "Oracle of Baseball." You type in any two names from baseball history: Babe Ruth, Derek Jeter. Immediately it will bring up a list of five players who were teammates, who, if you go in a chain, would link Ruth to Jeter. For example, Babe Ruth played with Bill Dickey, who played with Yogi Berra, who played with Ed Kranepool, who played with Jesse Orosco, who played with **DEREK JETER***. Obviously there are thousands-millions-billions of such chains. It'll always find the shortest chain between any two players. Four or five players would be the normal links.

We have minor-league stats for the last sixteen years for every one of the Yankee's minor-league affiliates. We have complete draft information for every draft in Yankees history. If you want to see if any first-round draft picks have done as well as Joba Chamberlain, coming out for the Yankees, you could research that very easily. We have a "Stat of the Day" column. If you're interested in finding out some particular tidbit, you can come and ask some of their experts, and, in all likelihood, they'll know how to find that stat for them.

You can e-mail or you can go to the blog and, in the "Comments," you can ask questions and people will typically be able to answer those. If they can't, they'll tell you, but we have a pretty extensive database of material.

We have a subscription area called "The Play Index" and we could generate a list of every walk-off home run in the last fifty years for the Yankees. We can generate a list of all the complete

*****DEREK JETER** was named after Derek Sanderson, former National Hockey League player with the Boston Bruins.

shutouts for starters. Say you're watching a game, and a player has two triples and a double and a home run in the game in Yankee Stadium, you can actually find every time in the last fifty years when that happened previously. It's almost like having your own personalized sports bureau working for you. The Play Index, with all the searchable stuff, is only $29 a year, and you can search it very easily. Almost everything else I've mentioned here is free and will continue to be free.

I was trying to figure out how I was going to make money doing this because, at the time, this was a part-time job. It can cost a lot of money to run a Web server. I hit upon the idea of selling sponsorships. It would be like collecting baseball cards. The idea was that each page has a price based on the popularity of the player or the popularity of the team and how many hits they get. The rates are from $2 to $500 a year. Alex Rodriguez is in the hundreds. Ed Woodson is not. The average cost would be $5 or $10. If a player is available, you can claim him. It's set up pretty easily to do this—it's a two- or three-step process. You sponsor it and pay with PayPal or check. Then you are allowed to put whatever message you want on there.

> The average cost would be $5 or $10. If a player is available, you can claim him.

Across all the sites with basketball and football, as well, we average 20,000,000 page views a month. It's cyclical. I enjoy going to work every day. I'm never at a loss for new ideas and things to put on the site. If viewers suggest something, I'm always happy to consider it. I print them all out and have a big stack of ideas. Yankee fans love baseball-reference.com.

'TIS BETTER TO TRAVEL WELL THAN TO ARRIVE FIRST.

Warren Sherman

Warren Sherman, 62, lives in West Hempstead, New York. He is a 1969 graduate of the University of Cincinnati, with a degree in engineering. Sherman, a CPA, is in the magazine publishing business with Harris Publications.

We grew up in a Yankee household. There were less distractions and things to do in those days—before computers and cell phones. You played ball after school and if you were lucky enough to have a TV, you watched some of the Yankee games on Channel 11. There was no ESPN and all that. It was hard sometimes to follow the news. But, baseball was a big part of my life growing up.

> You end up getting this tremendous, tremendous inside treat of traveling with the team.

I got all entwined in my Yankee Fantasy Camp stuff—between the two Yankee camps, the one that is held now in Jupiter, Florida, which is called Heroes in Pinstripes, which was formerly owned by Hank Bauer and Moose Skowron. Now Moose carries it on. There was Mickey Mantle's camp before Mickey died and was called The Mickey Mantle Week of Dreams. Mickey died, and we encouraged them to keep that camp alive. Between that camp and the one that started in 1997 in Tampa—what we call the Yankee Fantasy Camp, I've been to thirty camps.

We have camp-ending banquets in Tampa. Occasionally, they'll do some fund-raising for the New York Yankee Foundation. They had a fund-raiser and were auctioning off this possibility of bidding on a Yankee road trip. As it started out, you would spend two days with the Yankees, leaving from the Stadium and go on the bus with them to the plane and then go to an out-of-town city.

It turned out that we went on Sunday through Thursday! In July of 2007, we left New York and went to Kansas City for all four games, of which we stayed for three. Yankees won all four games that I was involved in.

> It's funny to watch the players like Johnny Damon and A-Rod going through security.

You end up getting this tremendous, tremendous inside treat of traveling with the team. Keep in mind, through my fantasy camp experience, I knew Ron Guidry; Jay Monahan, the trainer; Steve Donahue, another trainer; Rich Monteleone; Don Mattingly very well. You generally don't know the current players—they're hard to know. We felt honored to be able to fly on a private jet with them. There were fifty-six seats on the jet, and *I had one of those seats*! How do you like that?

As part of the whole package that I won, we were guests at the Stadium on Sunday. After that game, we met the team bus outside the Stadium. With a police escort, we went off to LaGuardia Airport. On the bus, I was sitting with a buddy of mine, but we were right by Ron Guidry. The getaway trip to the airport, the players are on one bus and we were on another with the staff. Joe Torre didn't make the trip that day—he flew out the next morning. We were on with the whole staff, including the coaches—Monteleone, Guidry, Mattingly, the whole deal.

I wasn't comatose . . . but I felt like, "Wow!" My buddy and I kept pinching ourselves saying, "Oh yeah, this is real!"

We got to the airport and were taken onto the tarmac, but you go through complete security. It's real, real security when you get to the plane. It's funny to watch the players like Johnny Damon and A-Rod going through security. It's weird in one sense 'cause you don't think of that. They are just like you and me—you get on an airplane, you've got to be searched.

We got on the plane. The players are creatures of habit. Some of them pair off—like Andy Pettitte and **ROGER CLEMENS*** sat together. The bottom line was you had free access on the plane, and you have a cocktail and they bring you snacks and then they serve dinner. You can roam all around. But . . . *this is the New York Yankees team*! You know all of them better than your family.

> Someone asked me if it was like a dream come true. My answer was, "No." Because it wasn't even on the radar to be a dream.

It was a fun trip. I was chatting with Don Mattingly for a good period of time. I had a couple of laughs with Johnny Damon, and then we landed in Kansas City. I don't remember walking off the plane and getting on the team bus! I said to my friend, "How did we get on this bus?" I just was in such . . . On the bus, you're all together. We took the ride to the hotel. We got off the bus . . . and, you want to know what a big shot feels like: get off the bus—the Yankee team bus—and have the fans waiting. The hotels they go to have good security. If security is not good, after a couple of years, they change to another facility. Also, this helps to keep everybody from knowing where they stay.

We spent a good time in Kansas City. Every day we'd get to the ballpark around 3–3:30 in the afternoon. The first bus to go over to the park would be staff, trainers, and some players who needed to be there for therapy or pregame stuff. We'd go over in the second bus and be there about four hours before game time. We're in the dugout and on the field until the "National Anthem" starts. We got some autographs, but, to me, autographs were secondary to just the fact that you could be on the field, talking to guys like Derek Jeter and getting a few words in with A-Rod and joking with Johnny Damon. Joe Torre was a gentleman and a half sitting in the dugout with us before the game. He chatted with us and seemed

---

*On July 7, 2007, Yankee starting pitcher **ROGER CLEMENS** was older than five of the players playing in the Yankees Old Timers Game that day.

interested in who we were and what we were doing. The whole thing was an enormous, enormous treat . . . to another level.

Someone asked me if it was like a dream come true. My answer was, "No." Because it wasn't even on the radar to be a dream. It's something you could never expect to do . . . and here I did it! I will certainly tell you this. I will make another opportunity—this will happen again! I guarantee it. This was the second trip I took. On the first trip, I went by myself, but the Yankees arranged the hotel for me. I didn't go on their plane that first time.

My father, would he have ever thought I would go on a Yankee road trip someday? Well, he would probably say he would have done that some day, too. My mom knew what a big fan I am, and then to get to go to the camps and play ball and meet these people who are my heroes. Over the years, you get to slowly befriend them. Then, you become friends with them. Now, you've rooted for them . . . you've met them . . . you've played ball with them . . . you're friends! My mother passed away recently and she would have said, "He completed the circle. That's what he did." If she would have known about this trip, she would be hysterical—smiling and laughing for me—that's for sure.

While we were out on the field, we would dress casually. We had to wear credentials around our neck all the time because other-wise they don't know who you are. The players got the drift of who we were quickly. Little by little, we blended in like we belonged to the team. More or less, like administration, as opposed to press. They knew we weren't press. Out there, from the fans, all we would hear is, "Derek!" "A-Rod!" I know Andy Phillips pretty well, as well. He was the young Yankee first baseman. We met at fantasy camp so we had a good time with him, as well as with Miguel Cairo, who was really special but is now no longer with the team. We'd met him a few times in Tampa. That's a "Mr. Personal" guy right there—he's really nice. Being on the field was unbelievable.

> The players got the drift of who we were quickly. Little by little, we blended in like we belonged to the team.

We met Joe Girardi and Ken Singleton and John Sterling. They were doing the YES games that week. Now Joe's the manager. Wow!

After the game, the security guys took care of us very well. They got us down to the clubhouse area. In Kansas City, there was either a mix-up or something happened, but they weren't letting us in the clubhouse. I could live without that. We went down to clubhouse level to wait for the players to come out. We met a bunch of the wives there—A-Rod's wife, Cynthia; Moose's wife; Ron Villone's wife. The wives don't travel on the plane with the team, but they can take the bus back to the hotel with them. I don't know if that's Major League Baseball rules, but it certainly sounds like Yankee rules, which is "team first."

We get on the bus and since we won every game out there, we certainly had some good laughs on the bus going back to the hotel. Then, everybody disperses. People might think, "Do the players go out to dinner together?" No. They break into little groups. They're in the hotel bars and lounges—they don't hide. Some of the bigger names like Derek and those guys will peek in but they don't stay around the lobby . . . they're attacked constantly if they do. We had a good time hanging in the lobby. Sometimes, during the day, because the games aren't until night, we spent time with some of the coaches. We took a side trip to the Negro baseball players Hall of Fame in Kansas City. It was a nice side trip, a special place. You need two hours, and it's amazing.

In the morning, I'd be up at seven and go down to the workout room. My friend and I were on the treadmills. Then about 7:30 or 7:45, in comes Joe Girardi or Ken Singleton. If you hang out a little after 8:00, Johnny Damon came in. Later, after I left, I was told A-Rod came in with his wife and a few of the other players. They do their workouts right there in the hotel gym. It's like business as usual. If you happen to be in there, you say, "Good morning." They're doing their thing, and you're doing yours.

The second day I felt a lot more relaxed. I told my wife I was extremely nervous before I went on the trip. I didn't know what to expect. You want to do everything right. You want to dress like they do. They told us "no jeans on the bus." We asked if we needed a jacket and tie for the plane, and they said, "No." The second half of the season, they relax the rules a little bit, especially when they're going to the Midwest where it may be exceptionally warm.

We didn't take Continental Airlines this time like usual. The second half, they lease planes, and we ended up with the Miami Heat plane. I guess when it's not being used during the basketball off-season, the Yankees were able to lease it for their trip. I saw where Shaq's seat is on the plane. Remember, I said there were fifty-six seats, all like

> **The second half, they lease planes, and we ended up with the Miami Heat plane.**

first-class. There are a couple of card-table setups with seats facing each other. Shaq's seat has at least 50 percent more room than all the others. I couldn't even reach the seat in front of me with my feet and that seat was much bigger. Of course, he's since been traded to the Phoenix Suns.

Your wife or husband generally doesn't go to work with you, but their wives take advantage of some of the cities they may like to visit. Or, some of them are going home—they lived in the area. We didn't push ourselves on them, but after a day or two, we recognized each other, either from the bus or from outside the clubhouse. They were very pleasant and friendly. You might say *surprisingly cordial.*

After the game, the wives are there waiting, and we were talking to them. We're more excited about being there as a fan, but we joked with Ron Villone's wife. I had forgotten her first name. He came into that game that night to get an out. He threw one pitch, got the out and the inning was over. When we left, after the game, they were the last two on the bus. They sat down, and I leaned over—I didn't even know them that well—and said, "Ron, I assume you're a little late because you had to have that arm iced down." His wife got hysterical, and so did he.

> ... the last night was a sellout, which meant close to 40,000. The Royals average maybe 15,000 so that tells you something.

The players are most relaxed when they're on the field and in the dugout. I was watching the camaraderie of the team, which you read about and want to believe, but I see it. It's amazing how it appears that Derek Jeter and Jorge Posada make sure that guys like Cabrera and Cano in particular are doing the right thing all the time. I can't confirm this but it looks like they always go out to dinner perhaps, maybe making sure they follow the Yankees who grew up in the organization as did they and get it done the Yankee Way, whatever that might mean. It's the pride, the tradition, the history of being a Yankee.

Around the lobby, they're pretty friendly. You might bump into them walking around the area and shopping. They try to get away from crowds. Downtown, if they're recognized, they're recognized. But, around the hotel, they try to spend very little time in the hotel lobby. Maybe they'll sign for five to ten minutes, but you know how it is—you can sign 1,000 autographs . . . and the next person in line there will think you're a jerk when you say, "I've got to go." I've seen that in action. The Yankees seem to be well respected in every city I've visited the last few years.

We'd been told that in Arlington, where the Rangers play, and in Tampa, which, of course, is somewhat Yankee territory, they pretty much enjoy the Yankee fans. They've come to root for their team and they have a good time. In Texas in particular I've heard, "You guys are nice. Those Red Sox fans are nasty." There were tons of Yankee fans there in Kansas City. Of the three games we went to, the last night was a sellout, which meant close to 40,000. The Royals average maybe 15,000 so that tells you something. There were chants going on, "Let's go Yankees," that, to me, were louder than the Kansas City fans.

Coincidentally, I saw George Brett and Frank White, and we chatted a little bit. They don't know me, and I don't know them, but they were on that clubhouse level where I was. I bumped into

Buddy Bell. I spoke with some Royals fans. They love the game and just wish they could win. They know they're not going to win. Money comes up quite a bit. They talk about how much the Yankees earn and stuff like that. I said, "Well, the answer is yes. The Yankees and some other teams have the ability perhaps to spend more money. I don't like to think they're buying what they have." When you think about it, I try to explain that "You guys are doing it somewhat in the right way, by bringing up kids from your organization." I said, "Look at the Yankee team." Jeter and Mariano and Pettite and Posada and Andy Phillips and Cano and Cabrera and now the young pitchers—they're all from the organization. That's a great way to build also . . . then, you can fill in the voids. But, the illusion is that the other teams don't have the money. Whether they do or not . . . who knows?

It was only the second time I had seen George Brett in person, I was surprised that he was so personable and friendly. It was "George Brett—Pine Tar T-Shirt Night." Everyone who went in the Stadium got a shirt. It was the twenty-fourth anniversary of the "pine tar" incident. He said to me, "Wait'll next year!" He was kidding, and he looked great. He was tan as could be. It looked to me that TV doesn't do him wonders—he looked a lot thinner and a lot more fit and definitely more personable than I would have thought. Frank White was a dream. He had a smile on his face when he played the game. Those are the kind of guys you like. I didn't mention **GRAIG NETTLES TO GEORGE BRETT***—I don't want to mention that.

My bottom line is that I've been very, very fortunate in my life, but I've done pretty much everything on my own. My dad and mom didn't have much financially . . . but, they had everything! We're the result of that, and I've been very fortunate in my life. Every moment I can talk about this team or this life is a victory for me.

*When the **GEORGE BRETT** "pine tar" game was concluded, Ron Guidry was the centerfielder, and Don Mattingly was the second baseman . . . In 1974, **GRAIG NETTLES** had a broken bat single and six Superballs bounced from inside the bat.

CRAIGSLIST

Craig Crotty

Craig Crotty, 65, has retired in Falmouth, Massachusetts. He grew up on a farm listening to any Major League baseball game he could find on his old Motorola radio.

Most Yankee fans of my age, when they talk about baseball cards, they always talk about the early Topps sets . . . and their quest to get the Mickey Mantle card. Mickey Mantle was not my quest in those cards. It was a bonus baby, a Yankee first baseman from Holyoke, Massachusetts, named Frank Leja. Leja's card was the hardest card I ever had to find in my childhood. We would buy dozens and dozens of packs of Topps baseball cards trying to get this Frank Leja.

Finally, one day, I had a plan. My parents were away for the day, and I decided I would borrow an idea I'd seen from the comic strips—that was to set up a lemonade stand. I went down to the basement, got a frozen can of lemonade, thawed it out, mixed it up, made a cardboard sign, took a card table and a seat and went down to a corner where two gravel roads intersected near this farming community.

> The sign said "Lemonade. All you can drink for one dollar."

About twenty minutes later, the first vehicle came by. It was a tractor driven by an old farmer named August Stender who was taking a load of grain to the mill. He saw my lemonade stand and stopped. He jumped off and said, "I need some cold lemonade." I said, "Well, August, today's your lucky day." Then he saw the sign I had made up. The sign said "Lemonade. All you can drink for one dollar." A bottle of Coca-Cola sold for a nickel in those days. My goal was to make one dollar because if I had one dollar, I could go into town to the

B&F Grocery and buy a whole carton of Topps baseball cards. I knew for sure that if I did that, I would be able to get the Frank Leja card. August stopped, hesitated, pulled out his wallet, gave me the dollar and drank about a half glass of lemonade and left. I quickly took the card table, the sign and the leftover lemonade back up to the house one quarter of a mile away. I rode my bike into town to get my carton of baseball cards. I got the carton, but . . . once again . . . absolutely no Frank Leja cards. About three days later, my father came looking for me—as irate as heck—and said, "Hey, young man, you need to give August Stender his dollar back." I said, "Why? I had a deal that was all the lemonade you could drink for a dollar. I've already spent the dollar." Of course, he knew what I had spent it on. I just got a good strappin' in the meantime. Today, I could have him arrested for child abuse.

In those days, we were growing up right at the right time. There were so many wonderful baseball announcers and Mel Allen and Harry Caray were at the top of that list. A lot of people forget that Curt Gowdy was Mel Allen's sidekick for a couple of years with the Yankees around 1949–1950.

When we grew up, we would go to the ball diamond every spare moment we had and play ball until dark. We didn't need coaches, umpires, or soccer moms yelling at us or yelling at umpires. My kids grew up, went to Little League practice, threw the ball ten times, swung the bat ten times, and went home. Little League has ruined baseball.

Furthermore, in those days, we'd appreciate the one baseball game a week we might be able to see on TV. We all remember the first time we got TV in our house when we'd get up early in the morning to watch "test patterns." Our parents may not have liked our music, but they listened to it nonetheless. Maybe once a year, we'd be able to get a ride on a train. When we eventually started dating girls, they didn't dress like a tarts, and we treated them like ladies. My sons will never know any of those things.

Remember a Yankee pitcher named Bob Turley—Bullet Bob, they called him. The Yankees got him from the St. Louis Browns.

When I was a freshman in high school, everybody was raving about how hard Bullet Bob Turley threw. My high school baseball coach said, "Listen, if you batted against Bob Turley long enough, after a while, you'd hit a foul ball. Then, after another while, you'd hit a fair ball. Eventually you'd get a base hit. You keep on batting against him long enough, and you'll hit it out of the ballpark." He said, "That's true about life. If you get experience and you have perseverance, and you never quit, sooner or later, you can accomplish all your goals." So, Bullet Bob Turley was responsible for one of the greatest lessons I ever learned in my life. . . .

Remember how we used to get the *Famous Slugger Yearbook*s at sporting goods stores? They were put out by Hillerich and Bradsby, the Louisville Slugger people? In the fall, we'd get the *Converse Basketball Yearbook* put out by the Converse Shoe Company. Both books were free.

> The worst things that have happened to baseball are Bud Selig and Donald Fehr.

I'm glad I was born when I was 'cause everything has gone to hell in a handbasket lately . . . I weep for the future. The worst things that have happened to baseball are Bud Selig and Donald Fehr. How the media keeps giving these two guys a free ride is totally beyond me. Selig has screwed up everything from the '94 World Series to the All-Star Game to contraction to expansion to player salaries and, perhaps, worst of all, the total destruction of baseball records. The day Brady Anderson hit his 50th home run was the day that all baseball records became meaningless.

Under Selig's watch, drugs have become rampant—steroids, of course . . . salaries have gone through the ceiling . . . records have become worthless. The only thing his detractors have to say is, "But, attendance has gone up." Why wouldn't attendance have gone up? Since I was born in the early '40s, the population of this country has tripled. There are twice as many Major League teams as there used to be. There are more games being played every year—eight more every year by each team. Selig has brought in so many gimmicks that it's going to turn into the World Wrestling Federation pretty soon. Gimmicks like inter-league play, and the wild card. Another gimmick we can look for him to come up with is something like free beer, naked cheerleaders, and the Beatles singing during the seventh-inning stretch. We've turned the whole thing into a circus with no concern for the records or traditions of the game.

What does the commissioner do all day long anyway? *Seriously*, what does the commissioner do all day long? I don't think he does anything. He doesn't even hand out the fines. He doesn't punish the players. Selig gets paid $14 million in basic "hush money" as I like to call it. He's a total "stooge" for the owners and is one of the worst things ever to have happened to baseball.

> . . . free beer, naked cheerleaders, and the Beatles singing during the seventh-inning stretch.

Then, he had to embarrass the game further before the congressional committee on St. Paddy's Day in 2005 when he sat there and said that he had never heard of steroids until July of 1998. Well, in 1995, he was quoted in *The Sporting News* as saying he wanted to convene a special meeting of the owners back in 1992 to discuss the looming steroid problem. The most galling thing about Selig, besides his pathetic looks, is his continual ignorance of the drug-testing in this country. Until they start testing for HGH, the human growth hormone, they have NO drug-testing policy. Who are they trying to kid with this malarkey that they maintain that they have this terrific policy? They say there is no such test—guess what, there is. It's called a blood test. Just ask the WADA (World Anti-Doping Agency), they've been nailing people in the Olympics with steroids since the 1980s.

What Selig and these other baseball owners don't seem to recognize is the economy goes in cycles. For the last twenty or so years, we've been riding a wonderful crest of a great economic cycle. When the economy starts to go south, which it eventually will, perhaps sooner than later, you're going to see attendance in

Major League Baseball drop like you never dreamed possible before. You might even see teams going bankrupt. It was only a few years ago that teams were already going bankrupt, such as the Arizona Diamondbacks. Selig is just a pathetic loser, and he's dragging baseball into the muck, along with Donald Fehr, who is just reprehensible in his conduct. It's no wonder you never see either of them in public unless they're surrounded by a huge entourage. . . .

The best baseball fans are on the East Coast. They're the most passionate baseball fans besides being the most knowledgeable. The further west you go in this great country, the less passion people have for anything, whether it be baseball, or their jobs, or for life in general. There are only about half a dozen baseball teams that really have great fans. The Yankees, of course, the Red Sox, the Mets, the Phillies, the Cardinals, and the Cubs . . . and that's pretty much it. Name another Major League baseball team that has incredible fans like the Yankees do. You can't do it. . . .

A petulant child like Tony LaRussa with his moronic moves wouldn't last two years in New York. The man has lost over 2,000 games in his career. You have to lose over one hundred games a year for twenty years to lose that many games. The three franchises he's been with in his managerial career all had the best players of the last thirty years during the time he was the manager there. He's won four of his last thirteen World Series games, lost his last three All Star games (with the post season home field advantage at stake) and has lost twenty-one of his last thirty-three NLCS games. He loses two out of every three—16–32.

A friend of mine suggested that other than Mike Sciosia, there may not be a single good manager in Major League baseball today. I'm starting to think he's right. Why do managers use a five-man pitching rotation? It's absolutely stupid that you would take eight starts from your best pitcher and give them to your fifth-best pitcher. It's equally stupid to take eight starts from your second-best pitcher and give them to your fifth-best pitcher. The great Yankee teams through the years of Jack Chesbro, Lefty Gomez, Whitey Ford, etc. always had 4-man rotations.

The fundamentals in baseball today are so bad . . . so bad . . . that I'm not even sure they spend any time at all coaching these guys. There are only about five outfielders in the whole game who can throw hard and accurately. Catchers have just about lost all sight of fundamentals. They don't block the plate anymore. They reach for balls coming in to home plate rather than waiting for the ball to come to them. Outfielders don't catch the ball over the proper shoulder. . . .

> You can call me an "old goat" if you want . . . I'm old enough to be a greeter at Wal-Mart.

You can call me an "old goat" if you want . . . and I am one—I'm old enough to be a greeter at Wal-Mart. But I love baseball the way it was when I was growing up—sneaking transistor radios in the school to listen to the World Series game, collecting baseball cards for fun—not as an investment—doubleheaders, the special "smell" of the new baseball magazines every spring. There are many people my age who can name the starting lineup for the '49 Yankees, the '55 Yankees, the '64 Yankees that couldn't name you half of the starting lineup for the '89 Yankees or the 2004 Yankees.

They say that Barry Bonds has never flunked a drug test. Neither did Jose Canseco, Ken Caminiti, or Jason Giambi. You would have to be a blind moron to realize that Bonds is not on drugs. This is not a court of law. This is a court of public opinion. Plus, Roger Clemens was a buffoon before Congress. In the court of public opinion, the first three witnesses are logic, history, and common sense. Bonds and Clemens will never survive. . . . and where did Clemens find that sleazebag attorney?

Another thing I don't understand is the pitch count. Supposedly we have a pitch count to protect pitchers' arms. But, in reality, the pitch count discourages the development of a strong arm. Walter Johnson, Bob Feller, and Nolan Ryan never had pitch counts. Look at how hard they threw and how long they pitched, and they never had a sore arm. The only way to develop a strong arm is to use it a lot. If you want to protect pitchers' arms, outlaw breaking balls. Even Little League has a pitch count now. When we were young, we'd throw the ball two or three hundred times a day . . . and these kids have a pitch count. We're developing a nation of wusses. Let's give every human being in America a blue ribbon and a certificate suitable for framing so they don't suffer from low self-esteem. In 1974, the Red Sox were playing at the California Angels—Nolan Ryan versus Luis Tiant. The Angels won in fifteen innings 1–0. Luis Tiant pitched the first fourteen innings for the Red Sox and Nolan Ryan went all the way for the Angels. That night **NOLAN RYAN*** threw 235 pitches, and it ruined his career . . . because nineteen years later, he had to retire.

One final thing, it is very hard to watch the baseball scores on Baseball Tonight on ESPN. ESPN keeps going further downhill every year. I don't know who hires the people up there, but he has to be a jock sniffer. Half of his announcers are ex-athletes who butcher the King's English and have horrible voices for television. But, the worst thing is the music/noise they play in the background during interviews or while giving scores. That violates every principle of communication. Why would you have an anchorman talking and putting noise behind him—not only "noise" behind him, but loud noise behind him. It's flat-out stupid. They must have a bunch of kids running that place.

I mean all of this in a positive way, of course.

---

*NOLAN RYAN is the last Major League Baseball player to lose playing time during a season due to military service. When Ryan was with the Mets, he served in the National Guard.

GIVE ME ONLY A MILLION OF YOUR PETE ROSE AUTOGRAPHS: I DON'T WANT TO DEPLETE YOUR INVENTORY

Kelly Eisenhauer

Eisenhauer has been a part-time radio disk jockey, for twenty-seven years. He lives in Lehighton, New Jersey, where he is an English teacher at the local high school. Eisenhauer, 51, origi-nally is from Copley, Pennsylvania, and is a graduate of East Strouds-burg University.

D uring high school, I started collecting Yankee yearbooks. From the yearbooks, I was always fascinated by Babe Ruth and started collecting signatures—autographs. They were quite expensive at that time—back in the '70s. I have Ruth, Gehrig, Mantle, DiMaggio, and a lot of the all-time greats. I had quite a little collection. I was trying to get all the Yankee Hall of Famers. It was pretty tough going back and getting the Herb Pennock's. I had Frank "Home Run" Baker. Some were tough . . . but then forgeries started to crop up in the hobby, and that ruined things. This was before all the PSA-DNA testing.

After collecting all these autographs, it was like a hammer hitting me over the head, and I said, "This is ridiculous. I wouldn't know a fake one from a real one, for some of the obscure players." I then sold all my autographs.

I was always into the Mantle cards, even when there were very few collectors around. There weren't any publications, like *SCD*

(*Sports Collectors Digest*), the No. 1 publication in the hobby. *The Trader Speaks* was probably around. I saw some advertisements and started collecting Mantle cards. Then it became a passion and I wanted to get everything.

Then, *Sports Collector's Digest* contacted me and asked if I would be willing to write a Mickey Mantle checklist. I knew it would take a while to do it, but it was a labor of love. I started to catalog all the Mantle stuff. They did a six-page spread—the highlight of their magazine. I was paid $500 to do the article. It wasn't a lot of money, but it was neat to see my name in print and to see all the collectibles that existed. This was 1984 when that was published.

> I had Whitey and Murcer and Berra sign the dollar bill. Then Gene Michael came in, and I didn't want him to sign that same dollar bill . . .

They asked me to do an update, about seven years later. There are so many Mantle items. There are literally 10,000 to 15,000 different Mantle items out there.

Throughout the years, four of us Mantle "nuts" have all hooked up and we get together. We all get together on Old Timers Day. We use Johnny Blanchard and Don Larsen's tickets and sit in Section 2. The previous two years we were up in the luxury suite with Whitey, Yogi, Bobby Murcer, Gene Michael, and Yogi's and Whitey's wives. It was neat—a highlight.

It was funny because we were friends of Blanchard, who came into the suite a little bit later that day. The luxury box is very small—might seat twenty-five people. Yogi and Whitey and their wives and Murcer were there—you could read on their faces and see them thinking to themselves, "Who the hell are these guys? How did they get in with us?" They treated us very nicely. I didn't have anything in there with me for them to sign and was going to go get a ball. Instead I just got a dollar bill signed. I had Whitey and Murcer and Berra sign the dollar bill. Then Gene Michael came in, and I didn't want him to sign that same dollar bill so I pulled out another one, and he signed it.

The next year we were all together in the Babe Ruth Room, and we had the run of the place. We could go to the Mickey Mantle Room, the Babe Ruth Room, anywhere. All the players were in because it was a rainout so they didn't play the Old Timers game. Gossage was there, Mickey Rivers—all the old-timers—and there was free food and free drinks for everybody. I pulled out the Gene Michael dollar bill and everybody signed it. Gossage signed it twice for me. He said, "I signed this twice." I said, "I'm sorry." He said, "No, no, no that's OK." He was a real gentleman. They thought we were all really close friends of the family or the families. They treated everybody especially nice. It's become a nice camaraderie. We usually get together once a year, if not more.

> I never really wanted to meet Mickey Mantle . . . he was a drunkard and there were horror stories about him.

Those old Yanks are together quite often. In the suite, there's a bar, and then there's a deck outside, through a glass door. The outside is a slanted deck, which looks down on the ball field. They have luxury cushioned seats. Yogi stood at the bar inside and had a drink and watched the game on TV, shooting the breeze with the bartender. Whitey was out socializing. In fact, fans were throwing balls from the left and right sides into where we were and he was autographing them. Murcer was nice—he was my idol growing up, as well. I only saw Mickey play in person two times. I met him four times through the publication and writing and at various shows and it was a dream come true.

I never really wanted to meet Mickey Mantle, even though he was my hero. His past was well known—he liked his alcohol—he was a drunkard and there were horror stories about him. You never knew what kind of mood or frame of mind you were going to come across when you would meet him. I didn't want to be let down so I was a little apprehensive about meeting him.

When I did meet him, he was as nice as could be. I got him on a real good day. Greer Johnson, his manager—well, it was actually his live-in lady—handled everything. She straightened him out a bit. He developed a proper outlook where he realized where his bread was being buttered, and he was nothing but a gentleman . . . so it was awesome. It really was awesome.

Greer was an ex-teacher. She had lived in Georgia. Mickey and his wife, Merlyn, were having problems then. It was a rocky ending when he passed away. Greer wanted to go to the funeral and viewing and the Mantle family didn't want her there. You look at these guys like they're gods. A lot of them are so screwed up that you have to wonder where their priorities are sometimes. . . .

PSA testing is relatively new—maybe for the last five years. It's an authentication process where there are three reputable firms who have exemplars and know what are real signatures, and they will attest to the fact that, even though they weren't there, it's a legitimate, 100 percent authentic autograph. Right now, the going rate is about $75 per item to do this. The true collector wants that guarantee, and that's about the only way they'll buy a signature. There are so many fakes in the hobby that it's gotten out of hand. I look on eBay periodically, and I'll see Mickey Mantle signature on something, and there are ten to fifteen bidders, and it's as fake as the day is long. I've been fooled once or twice, so I'm not infallible, but I'm pretty good. When you realize you have bought a fake, you go right back. There was a guy in Las Vegas who sold a Mickey Charles Mantle baseball. They typically go for $1,200 to $1,500. I bought it for $250. It looked good to me. I saw pictures of it. They sent it to me, and I was pleased. I sent it in to get it authenticated, and it came back as fake. I called them and the guy told me to send it back. He did take it, and I got my money back, but I still lost the $75 I paid to get it authenticated.

> A lot of them are so screwed up that you have to wonder where their priorities are sometimes. . . .

The old yearbooks were fascinating because you could see all the players. It always had the pictures of all your favorite baseball players, and it was very inexpensive. It was "this year's" team. The Yankees were probably the first team to produce a yearbook—their first one came out in 1951. That was a situation where there were actually two yearbooks. It wasn't every year, but right up until 1965 there was a Jay Publications, which made a Yankee yearbook, and then the Yankees made their official yearbook. They were relatively cheap—50 cents or a dollar. I remember watching Channel 11 out of New York, and you could send in your dollar or a check and get your yearbook that way. Also, a lot of the newsstands carried Yankee yearbooks in our area. This was a Phillies and Yankees area. I started a collection of the yearbooks when I was a kid so probably the first ones I got were 1965 or '66. Companies would advertise in sports books like *Manny's Baseball Land.* From there you could get the yearbooks. I did manage to get all of them, and they are still putting them out. Right now, the Yankee yearbook is a major, major publication, and at $25 a pop, they're the most expensive yearbook on the market. They are so thorough and do a major class publication. They've come to a situation where they have five or six pages per player, if they're superstars. They also go to their minor league systems, to their prospects. I used to collect three of each from the late '60s, 'cause I couldn't afford all the '50s ones, but now I've cut back to only two. It all adds up. It's not so much the money—$25—it's an investment, but you don't buy things for an investment—it's something you collect.

Storage is the problem. I go to Wal-Mart or K-Mart or Big Lots and buy huge 21-gallon storage bins. You want to keep them out of the sunlight so they don't yellow. My wife's on my case all the time. You should see my house. I have a shrine of Mickey Mantle and Babe Ruth and Thurman Munson and some other players downstairs. I have two original Yankee seats from the Stadium. I was a collector before my wife and I married, and I actually make money on the deal so she's cool. She understands.

I'm into art—original paintings of Mantle. I probably have twenty-five original 16-by-20 pieces of art. A lot of them came from an artist in the Massachusetts area, Leon Wolf. He does a lot of custom work. They sell in the $400 to $1,000 range. When Mickey died in 1995, he appeared on a special *Sports Illustrated* cover—a black and white picture. I sent him that picture, and he did a mirror image of the cover. He said it gave him nightmares to do and he would never paint another one like that. It turned out beautifully.

HBO contacted me. I have 4,000 to 5,000 pictures of Mantle. It's something I collect, and it's affordable. There are so many out there that you're never gonna get everything. HBO contacted me when they did the documentary, *Mantle,* a fantastic one-hour show, three years ago. They came to my house to shoot my collection. Once there, they realized they would have lighting problems because they needed all the pictures to be the same consistency as far as the lighting is concerned. They asked me if they could take some of the pictures with them—and they took about 500 pictures from my collection. They used 50-plus in the film. I got a byline in the credits at the end of the story.

> **He was the only Major Leaguer who ever owned a Holiday Inn.**

My favorite Mantle picture is a picture from *Sport* magazine of Mickey signing a baseball. There are two young boys real close to Mickey. You can just see their faces radiating that *Mickey is signing a ball for them.* It might be, although I'm not sure, a photo from the real well-known photographer, Ozzie Sweet.

Ozzie Sweet has a coffee-table book with nothing but Mantle pictures, which came out about seven years ago. He came out with another one that has a lot of Mantle pictures in it, but also has Whitey, Yogi, and other Yankees. It's the nicest photography I've ever seen. I think they were so mass-produced that the price has come down, and you can get them on eBay for probably ten bucks. It's well worth it. You name it—if Mickey's on it—people collect it. He's been on Yoo-hoo bottles . . . soda caps . . . knives . . . stationery. He was the only Major Leaguer who ever owned a Holiday Inn. It was in Joplin, Missouri, and was the only one in the entire chain that was named after an individual. It was Mickey Mantle's Holiday Inn.

Jerseys weren't collectible at one time. Nobody collected them when I bought that '59 Mantle jersey in 1984. Tommy Catal, a huge Mantle collector, and I were talking one time and he said he had one . . . and also had the pants. I said, "How much do you want?" He said he wanted $4,000 for the Mantle jersey and $1,000 for the pants, so $5,000. I had been teaching school and my starting salary was $9,700. I went out and took out a loan to pay Tommy off to buy them. That was the pièce de résistance.

I had a museum piece—the dream of a lifetime—Mantle's 1959 uniform—pants and shirt and it was autographed, "Your best friend, Mickey Mantle." Tom Catal had a museum in Cooperstown. I got to be friends with Tom, who sold me the jersey. At that time, it was worth around $10,000 and now it's worth $120,000. I thought it was stupid to have it in my house because somebody could break in and steal it, so I sold it. It's not doing me or anybody any good if it's in my safe. I sold it to the president of the Mark Twain Bank in Kansas City, Missouri. It was a shame, but I felt I had to part with it. From that point on, more or less, everything I have is for sale, except for displayable pieces like the paintings and the memorabilia in my shrine downstairs.

The number of Mantle cards—they're countless, and they're readily available. If you have the money, they're available. The reason why the '52 Topps is so desirable is twofold. Number 1—it's Mantle's first card. Number 2—back in 1952 when baseball cards were more or less just a kid's thing, they were produced in series. You couldn't go out and buy the whole set. You had to collect the whole series. In the '52 year, there were 411 cards. The very last series, which Mickey was in, Card No. 311, which started the last series, was produced and came out on the market during football season in '52, so they weren't bought by the kids because the kids were wanting football cards then.

They are the high-number cards and are called "high series." They were probably produced less than the production runs, but they're readily available. Not everybody had them. They weren't really purchased by the kids back in '52. That continued up until the '60s. A lot of the high numbers, the last series, are more valuable because there were probably less of them produced and few of them have survived.

> The 1951 Bowman was actually Mantle's first card. It's the real true rookie card.

The 1951 Bowman was actually Mantle's first card. It's the real true rookie card. Everything is "condition" these days, and it's a shame. There's a gem mint condition with a rating scale from 1 to 10, with ten being like right out of the pack. People pay 60, 70, 80,100,000 dollars for gem mint cards. They're not that readily available. You don't buy them, and who can afford them? A common card where the corners might be bent or dented are still in the thousands. You can spend 3 to 4,000 dollars just like that. Nobody paid attention to card conditions back then. This has been the last fifteen years where people have become grade-conscious as far as card conditions go.

In times past, you'd hear about "finding stuff in grandma's attic" but that happens less frequently. The hobby has come a long, long way in the last twenty-five years. I'm fifty-two, and we rode around on our bicycles with baseball cards in the spokes. You don't see that anymore. The cards are considered too valuable. Kids have changed. I coached high school baseball. Growing up in the '60s, it was very common for us to have our glove on the handlebar, just looking for a baseball game. Kids don't play baseball anymore around the sandlots. First of all, there aren't that many fields because of real estate value. Kids are too content staying at home playing their video games. It's a part of Americana that is long gone.

Everybody has become wise about the collectibles market. You can go to yard sales and still find some things, but it's less and less frequent. Every once in a while, a treasure is unearthed, and you get a steal—even on eBay. As popular as it is, you can find items that someone won't know what they're selling and some people don't know what they're looking at when they're browsing the Web.

I picked up a great piece that I've never seen before—an advertisement for Timex watches. Mickey was advertising the watches and this was a color transparency that was made for a display piece. The Mantle piece actually folded into a box and it had the picture inside. Then you put a little 2-watt bulb in there. It would illuminate and you would see Mickey in color swimming with a watch attached to the end of the bat. The advertisement itself was a black and white and had appeared in *Life* and *Look* and was very common. But, this was a salesman's sample, a display piece. I never saw anything like that before. I bought the item dirt cheap. With this piece, I was waiting with anticipation. I really wasn't negative. I thought, "This is gonna be something." I couldn't wait for it to come. Sure enough, it was legit. The guy told me he worked for Timex as a salesman and used it to set up displays. People make up stories all the time, but it just seemed right . . . and, it turned out it was.

> Everybody has become wise about the collect-ibles market.

I was looking for a Yoo-Hoo piece. In '59, '60, somewhere around there, there was a piece they put out with all the Yankees— Whitey, Mickey, Yogi, Moose Skowron, Blanchard—it looked good on eBay and I bid and got it for $50 and it might be worth 700 dollars. It turned out it was just a color copy somebody had put on. Then, the person wouldn't take it back. She gave me a hassle. I told her it was a color copy, worth about 50 cents. I had to call eBay, and they did a major investigation, and they worked with me. They knew what was going on. I paid for it via credit card so I told my credit card company it was a fake, and they stopped payment on it. The lady wrote back and said, "You son of a &#^@!" There is some protection you have with eBay. Most of the time, it's pretty good, but there is some phony stuff out there. Knowledge is everything. Education is the key.

Collectors are fanatics. We live and die by them. My wife is a Yankee fan, not by choice, but she has to be. Any time a Yankee game is on, I watch it on TV. The collecting. You idolize the players. Growing up as a fan is something—the All-American dream would be to play for the Yankees. I think everybody wanted to play for the Yankees when they were growing up. Sometimes your hopes are not realized, and you realize it's time to move on. I wanted to play shortstop for the Yankees, but that wasn't going to happen. It's a part of my life. You become so obsessed with them. Whether they won the game last night . . . and how Boston did . . . keeps you healthy.

There is a bar in Hazleton, Pennsylvania called The Sports Page. A friend of mine owned the bar so I would disk jockey there once every month. I look up on the wall, and I see some original pictures of Mickey Mantle that I've never seen before. I said to Danny, the owner, "Where'd you get the pictures of Mantle?" He said, "Oh, Phil Sarno, who covered the Yankees for the *Hazleton Standard-Speaker* took these pictures, and he printed some black and whites for me for the bar. I know you collect Mantle. Do you want them?" I said, "Yeah, I'd love to have them." He said, "You know what. I'll see Phil next week, and I'll find out if he can print you some. Why don't you wait till then 'cause these are framed." I said, "That's fine." Next time I'm up there, I asked Danny if he had seen Phil Sarno, the photographer. He told me he had passed away but that he had Phil's son's name. I said, "OK. I'll let a little time go by, and then I'll call him and see what he has."

> I told him I wasn't going to sell them, that they were in my collection. *Four days later,* they're back.

I met his son, Tom, and we developed a nice friendship. Tom didn't know who Cal Ripken was or Mantle or anybody. Tom did a little black and white photography work and he had his dad's collection. We started to go through these negatives. They were original pictures of Mickey Mantle—probably 120 different pictures. He printed them all for me—8-by-10s. We go through the negatives, and there are other

Yankee players in there as well—Whitey Ford, Yogi Berra, **PHIL RIZZUTO***, et cetera.

Phil was always one of my favorites because of his broadcasting background and was a neat guy. I had Phil's address so I sent him one of the pictures—a picture of Phil with WPIX in the background. I said, "Mr. Rizzuto, would you please be so kind to autograph this for me? I'm a longtime Yankee fan, and you're one of my favorite broadcasters, and I have a background in radio." He signed it and I got it back in about two days. He wrote, "This looks like my first year at WPIX when I started broadcasting for the Yankees."

I wrote him another letter and said, "Mr. Rizzuto, I'm not trying to take advantage of the situation, but I've unearthed a lot of original pictures of you with WPIX when you were covering the Yankees. Would you mind if I send them to you to have them autographed? Take what you want for your own collection, and I can get more made for me—even if it's ten of them, take them, and the rest, if you wouldn't mind, send back to me autographed." I told him I wasn't going to sell them, that they were in my collection. *Four days later,* they're back. He'd signed thirteen of them for me. He told me he kept two of them because they brought back some memories. I said, "Great . . . "

My first Yankee game, when I was nine years old, was in 1965 at Bat Day, when my dad was still alive. He made this large banner on a big white sheet. It had a picture of a cow—my dad was a pretty good artist—with a halo over it. The cow and the halo—and it said HOLY COW! at the top. At the bottom, THE YANKS ARE MOO-VING! I said to Mr. Rizzuto, "This is really near and dear to me. If I send this to you, would you mind signing it?" He told me to send it. I told him I had a painting. He said for me to send it, too. Bottom line was—he autographed twenty-five to thirty things for me—never charged a dime. I told him I felt like I was

---

*PHIL RIZZUTO was the first mystery guest on the TV show *What's My Line?*

---

taking advantage of him, "I appreciate this so much. You are the epitome of class." He said, "I'm just glad I can help you out."

> He had donated the whole check to the school. It gives me goose bumps just talking about it.

The last correspondence I did to him, I said, "It's not much, and I know your autographs go for much, much more, but I'm going to send you a check for $50." I sent him the check, and months went by, and it didn't cash. Finally, maybe six or seven months later, the check is cashed. Our bank doesn't give copies of checks anymore. They just give photocopies. I put in a request and told them I wanted the original check. I got that check through some work. I turned it over to see that he had endorsed it and it was stamped, "St. Joseph's School for the Blind in Jersey City, New Jersey." He had donated the whole check to the school. It gives me goose bumps just talking about it. Now, in this day and age, where all these athletes are so money-conscious and money-hungry, you have a Hall of Famer, who's beloved by everybody in Yankee history, who signed twenty-five to thirty different things for me and then takes his donation and donates it to the school for the blind. That's a neat story. I still have every picture he signed. I wouldn't dream of selling anything. That is the epitome of class. Just a nice man. Leon Wolf painted a picture that I had Phil autograph for me, and he said, "I like this picture." I told him I would take some pictures of it and send him the negative. He wanted to use it when people asked for his autograph— have some pictures made up so he could autograph them and send it out to them. So, I sent him that negative. I don't know if he ever followed through with it or not, but it was something to help him out. And, also, he had autographed the painting. What a neat man!

ROOTIN' FOR THE YANKEES IS AN ITCH THAT DOESN'T GO AWAY WITH ONE SCRATCH

Jay Knight

Jay Knight, Fairleigh Dickinson graduate, was born in the Bronx, but grew up in Newark. In 1978, he moved to Delray Beach, Florida, to become CEO of a huge medical firm. Now retired, he watches every Yankee game, which helps him in his fight against lung cancer.

To say I am a Yankee fan is the understatement of a lifetime, but I didn't know it until the summer of 1950. I was five years old and on vacation with my parents, aunts, uncles, and all my cousins. We were all staying in small bungalows in the Catskills, when my oldest cousin who was nine at the time asked me what baseball team was my favorite. I didn't have the slightest idea of any team, let alone, a favorite. So, being five, I did what I thought was the smart thing to do, I ran inside and asked the first person I saw, my mother, what baseball team I should like. Her response was typical: "Go ask your father." He was fishing with my uncles. I told her I needed to know *now* so I could tell my cousin who was waiting outside. Her answer was one only my mother could give. "Well, I only know of the New York Giants, the Brooklyn Dodgers and the New York Yankees." I asked her, who was the best team, she said "How should I know, maybe, maybe I think, maybe the Yankees," and the rest, as they say, is history . . . as of that July 1950, I became a devoted Yankee fan.

> So, being five, I did what I thought was the smart thing to do, I ran inside and asked the first person I saw, my mother, what baseball team I should like.

The next day we packed up the car and headed back to Walton Avenue in the Bronx. The entire ride home I drove my father nuts asking questions about the Yankees and baseball in general. He wasn't that knowledgeable but he gave me enough information to keep my interest going. He told me about the Babe, Lou, Joe D. and his favorite, the Scooter—my father was only about 5-8, maybe 150 pounds soaking wet. I guess that's why he liked Phil Rizzuto so much. After begging for about two more years to go see the Yankees, my father finally gave in and we took the long walk to the ballpark. We strolled into the Stadium; I could not believe my eyes. The enormity of the ballpark, you could smell the freshly cut grass before you saw it. How smooth the grass in the outfield looked. We had paid our 50 cents to get in the bleachers, my butt hurt by the second inning . . . they were just hard unforgiving planks to sit on, no backs at all, but I didn't care—I was having the time of my life. What I could not understand, was how the batter, could be half way to first base, when we would hear the sound of the ball hitting the bat. Boy, those bleachers were a long way away from home plate, and everyone looked so small.

> . . . those bleachers were a long way away from home plate, and everyone looked so small.

My father and I went to many games after that, always sitting in the same area in the bleachers. We moved to Newark, New Jersey, when I was eight. I assumed my life was over. It was so far away we couldn't walk to the Stadium. I knew my father couldn't and wouldn't spend the money to drive to New York, and I thought I would never see my Yankees again. Well, he found a way. We took the bus to Grand Central station and the trains to the Stadium from there. We couldn't go as often as I would have liked, but somehow my father managed to get us there about two times a year, and we still sat in the same area in the bleachers. This ritual continued until I was about thirteen. One of my mother's friends who knew of my love for the Yankees—I'm sure everyone knew—got four box seats to a Sunday doubleheader through a friend of hers. She drove my parents and me to the Stadium in her 1958 fire-engine-red Chevy convertible. Wow, what a day! We rode with the top down, in the coolest car I had ever seen. This was the first time I could hear the sound of the ball hitting the bat when it happened, the players were so close I could almost reach out and touch them. I could not believe how big my idol Mickey Mantle was; he had forearms like Popeye. Mickey hit a home run in the first game left-handed and a home run in the second game right-handed. I was so excited I don't even remember who we played or if we won or lost. I think I died that day and went to heaven.

As time went by I became a true fanatic. I would walk around the house with a no-windup pitch and make my mother guess who I was. She got good. After a couple of tries she would guess "Bullet Bob Turley." I would stand as a left-handed batter and swing over my head. In one second she would say "Yogela"—she made them all Jewish, Mickela Mandela, Vity Fordowitz—I must have driven her nuts, but she knew more about the Yankees than any other mother in our neighborhood. When the Yankees lost or Mickey had a bad day, I would literally get sick to my stomach. It got so bad my mother had to take me to the doctor—diagnosis: a nervous stomach. His solution—don't let me watch or listen to the games. Guess what? I would have rather been dead.

In the early '60s, I would bring a small transistor radio to school hidden in my pocket—there was a thin wire attached that was under my shirt and connected to my ear. I am sure most of my teachers knew what I was doing; they just ignored it as long as I did my work, and they all knew I was a Yankee fanatic. There was a memorable day during the World Series—they had day games then. There I was, sitting in class, with the radio on and the earpiece in the perfect position. Nobody even knew it was there—I had painted the earpiece the same as my skin tone. Mick swings, and there goes a long drive to deep right field—that ball is "going, going, gone." It was a two-run homer. For the moment I forgot where I was. I jumped into the air and started yelling, "Yes! Yes! Yes!" Mr. Martino, my chemistry teacher, yelled back, "No! No! No!" That incident was the end of my transistor radio—I was told my face was as red as a beet. There was a similar incident that happened around the same time. Mickey caught his foot in the centerfield fence—I believe it was Baltimore—he was going to be out for about six to eight weeks with a broken foot, and boy, was I depressed. They called the Mick's name to pinch hit in the ninth inning, it was his first at bat in six to eight weeks. We were behind, I just started to clap and scream uncontrollably when he hit the game-winning homer and started jogging around the bases with his head down, elbows up, as only he could. I must have gone nuts about the time Mel Allen said, "How about that." Ida Dolinz was our landlady; she was an immigrant, who spoke broken English. Both my mother and I understood what she meant when she came knocking on our door, saying "Iv, ya dunt make him schtop mit da bangin', and da noise makin', I'm goin' to told you to leaf mine house." I had converted my mother into a true and devoted Yankee fan, but as she said, we needed a place to live. Boy, was it tough to hold back my verbal enthusiasm in that house.

> "Iv, ya dunt make him schtop mit da bangin', and da noise makin', I'm goin' to told you to leaf mine house."

In the early '70s my brother-in-law Barry was dating a wonderful woman name Patricia Burke. She was living in Connecticut and my wife and I were living in Livingston, New Jersey. I had yet to make any connection to whom she was related. One cold day towards the end of March, Barry called and wanted to know if I wanted to go to Opening Day at Yankee Stadium, "First class, all the way." Even before I could say yes, it hit me right between the eyes, could Patricia be related to Mike Burke, the president of the Yankees? Well, knock me over with a feather—she was his daughter. I guess it pays to talk to everyone about how much I love the Yankees. Barry said there was only one glitch, I would have to take my wife, his sister. This was going to be a double date and my wife, Carol, isn't the biggest baseball fan. I only had to beg and grovel for about fifteen minutes till she gave in. It was going to cost me, but I didn't care. I was going to see the Yankees on

Opening Day, and I was going to be sitting with Mike Burke in his box. As luck would have it, it was one of the coldest days in April, the temperature dropped into the mid to upper 20s; with the wind chill, it felt numbing. The seats were alongside the Yankee dugout; I could have reached out and touched the players—if I took my hands out of my pockets, that is. Around the third inning we couldn't clap for fear that our fingers would fall off. Mike could see how uncomfortable we were and called an assistant over. He instructed him to take us up to his private office to watch the game on closed-circuit TV. We were taken to an area of the Stadium I had never seen before. We went down a long dark corridor to a freight elevator, the old-fashioned kind, with wooden gates that closed from the top and bottom and met in the middle. When we arrived on the right level—I was so excited and cold I don't remember the level—we continued down another dark passageway until the assistant stopped to unlock an unimpressive door. When the assistant opened the door, we entered a palatial office, the likes of which I had never seen. You could not imagine how contemporary, well lit, and beautifully furnished it was, Mike had an enormous modern wood desk with a phone— just the receiver—built into the wall, the dialing mechanism was on the desk. How cool it was to see; we were in awe. There was a luxurious leather couch off to the side, it was so soft, and we sank into the cushions and did not want to move. The assistant set up the closed-circuit TV for us, ordered food, gave us programs and a yearbook; he smiled and left to go back to the freezing cold of the day. The food was delivered in about twenty minutes; a five-star restaurant could not have prepared a more delicious meal. As we sat on the couch, eating everything in sight, I just had to call my office and let someone know what I was doing. I raised my bloated body and waddled to Mike's desk, I zipped the phone from the wall, put my feet on the desk and started to dial, as my eyes gazed on a baseball on the edge of the desk. It was signed by the entire 1961 team, with Mickey Mantle on the sweet spot. I had just finished dialing my office when the door opened, and a cold, shivering, red-nosed Mike Burke walked into his office. I am sure my heart missed a beat as I tried to take my feet off his desk without knocking everything over. I started to apologize, but before I could, Mike just said, "Relax, continue your call, I'll sit on the couch." Even freezing, this man exuded class. Barry suggested to Mike that he play Yankee trivia with me. Barry bragged that I was an expert. Mike said to me, "Do you really think you know more than the president of the Yankees?" Being young and too scared to back off, I said, "Go for it." Mike said, "Great, what do we play for?" I suggested the ball on his desk; I told him I would give everything for that ball. Mike just smiled and said, "I did. I bought the team." He then said, "A good meal." He looked at me and said, "A done deal." What could I say? "Sure, no problem." The trivia game lasted for about forty minutes, I answered every question he threw at me. He missed just one. He held out his hand and said, "You win. Pick a restaurant." We left before the end of the game, one of the greatest days of my life was ending, so I thought. The next day there was a knock on my door, the delivery man gave me a package about 4 inches by 4 inches, I had no idea what was inside, I unwrapped the paper, ripped open the cardboard package, there was a note, "To a better Yankee fan, thanks for the game"—it was signed "Mike." Yes, it was the ball that was on his desk. I still get the chills even though it's been over thirty-five years since that day.

In 1978 my family and I moved to Plantation, Florida. A few months before the move I asked my then seven-year-old son if he would like to go to see the Yankees at the Stadium. It was the first time he showed any interest; I jumped at the opportunity to have him join me as a fan and made some phone calls to get the best seats I could. It was not going to be the bleachers for my son, in hindsight it should have been. I got a call back from someone I knew at Revlon; they gave me two tickets to their luxury suite. As we drove to the Stadium, I decided to take my son through my old neighborhood on Walton Avenue in the Bronx. Another mistake! He wanted to know how anyone could live there—not a good start. As we walked around the exterior of the Stadium, trying to get to our entry gate, I looked down and saw a gleam in the eyes of this seven-year-old I had never witnessed before. As we walked into the Stadium his eyes opened even wider, he had the same look I must have had almost twenty-seven years before. He even said, "Dad, look how green the grass is," just like I said to my father—I got the goose bumps. We went up another level to the luxury suite. As we entered, a butler asked if we needed anything—the inside area was loaded with food and drink. We just wanted to see the game. We walked through the inside area, to the seats that are outside but covered heated and/or air-conditioned. This child was spoiled rotten before the game even started. It must have been the third inning and Cory asked for a hot dog. I signaled the butler and within five minutes, he served Cory his hot dogs from a silver tray on beautiful china. Great, how do you top this? Now he thinks this is the way everyone goes to a baseball game. . . .

> The next day there was a knock on my door, the delivery man gave me a package about 4 inches by 4 inches. . .

It was a Sunday like any other Sunday. The date was August 13, 1995, and it was about 8:00 a.m., I was in what we called the computer room. I was doing some work for the office, trying to save myself some time on Monday, when my son Cory came into the room, and asked if I was OK, and, did I need a hug. First, for my then twenty-four-year-old son to be up on a Sunday at 8:00 a.m. was in itself very unusual, for him to be asking if I was OK, and, especially, did I need a hug, my first thought was, am I dying? I said "I'm OK, why do you ask?" His arms were still outstretched, awaiting a hug. I swallowed hard and asked him what was going on. He gave me a bear hug, and said, "Mickey passed away late last night." I knew how very sick Mickey was, but I never wanted to face the reality that my childhood hero was no more. As I let my emotions go, and, as Cory sensed I would, the tears started to flow. I, along with my son, knew that, for me, it would never be the same again.

All those nights as a teenager hiding under the covers, so my parents wouldn't know I was listening to the radio. Looking up, asking a higher power to let the Mick hit one out so we could win the game . . . and it happened so many times. These were the kind of thoughts that ran through my head. In the end, the Mick showed his true colors. His last speech, requesting people to become organ donors, and not to look at him as a role model, truly demonstrated to everyone, how the Mick overcame his indiscretions and why he was, and always will be, my hero. I will remember him, as he was, not what he had become, not the frail shell of a man, but the powerful and graceful athlete I will never forget.

> All those nights as a teenager hiding under the covers, so my parents wouldn't know I was listening to the radio. Looking up, asking a higher power to let the Mick hit one out so we could win the game . . . and it happened so many times.

As it turned out, due to many reasons, we did not get back to the Stadium for another twenty-three years. One of my great friends and business associates, Bob Regolia, of Pennington, New Jersey, connived with my son for us to fly into Newark airport. Bob met us, took us to a hotel where we dropped off our bags. He took us for lunch at Mickey Mantle's restaurant. I was already as happy as I could be—I thought. After lunch, we then rode the No. 4 train to the Stadium. We ate dinner in the fancy restaurant inside the Stadium. We had box seats just a few rows up from the field, between home and the edge of the visitors dugout. We could see the spin of the ball, the perspiration dripping from the players; it was almost like being in the game. We won the game in the top of the ninth with a play at the plate. Wow! It was one of the most exciting games we have ever seen. My son and I talked about it all night long. Bob informed us we would be picked up at 11:00 a.m., for a surprise road trip. Bob kept driving and I was to try to guess where we were going when I saw the sign to Montclair . . . I knew we are going to Yogi Berra's museum. What an absolute joy! The museum was great—playing trivia with two of Yogi's sons was amazing. They got me though—the question I did not know the answer to was, "Who was playing first base for the Yankees on Yogi Berra Day?" It's an answer I will never forget. It was Marvelous Marv Throneberry.

Eating lunch at Mickey Mantle's . . . dining in a wonderful restaurant I never even knew existed in the Stadium . . . seeing a great game . . . seeing the Yankees win . . . then touring Yogi Berra's museum . . . talking with Yogi's sons . . . being with Bob, a great friend . . . and spending quality time with my son—Priceless!

I am fifty-eight and my love for the Yankees has never wavered, not even after Mickey retired and the team went downhill. Now everything is not the same as when I was young. I cannot recite every player's stats as they happen like I could when I was sixteen, but my appreciation for the Yankees and the beauty of the game is stronger then ever.

I would like to thank my son, Cory, for continuing the Yankee fan tradition and passing that Yankee pride on to his children. I would especially like to thank my late mother and father for helping me become a Yankee fan, and to **GEORGE "THE BOSS" STEINBRENNER*** for always keeping Yankee fans' dreams for a World Series win alive.

*In a 2007 *Sports Illustrated* poll of 464 Major League ballplayers, **GEORGE STEINBRENNER** was voted the "best owner" by 41 percent of them—more than double the next highest vote-getter. He also finished sixth as the "worst owner.". . . Andy Pettitte was selected by 55 percent of the players as having the best pickoff move.

YANKEE MEMORIES ARE FREE AND THEY'RE WORTH EVERY PENNY

Irv Miljoner

Irv Miljoner, 55, is an officer for the U.S. Department of Labor, in charge of enforcing all labor laws. He grew up in Brooklyn and now resides in Oceanside, Long Island. Miljoner's parents survived the Holocaust.

It's a major mystery how a kid from Brooklyn can become a Yankee fan. Having been just, just, just too young to be a Brooklyn Dodger fan, I was in that purgatory time period that lasted only four years or so when there was only one team in New York City . . . that was the Yankees. It was before the Mets came into being.

I'm actually a child of the streets—I grew up, learned about life, in the schoolyards. My parents were refugees. I always felt a little different in many ways from a lot of other kids. My assimilation, my growth, my acceptance came via all those variations of baseball that were played in the schoolyard—stickball, punchball, slapball—all of those.

Now, where I really got to pretend to be a Yankee was in stickball. We played stickball against the schoolyard wall. We'd take chalk and draw a strike zone, a rectangular box, or a square box, on the wall. The batter would stand in front of that. We stand 40 or 50 feet away. Using that same kind of rubber Spalding ball, we'd fire strikes. Hopefully, our pitches hit the drawn strike zone. We'd use broom handles as bats because we couldn't afford the "actually made and sold" stickball bats from the toy stores and sporting good stores. They would have cost us about a buck apiece, and most of us couldn't afford that so we just used broom handles. We might put some electrical tape around the base of our "bat" for a better grip. I'm telling you, to this day, I remember the euphoria of connecting with a fastball. With that hard rubber ball, and with that broomstick or stickball bat, you can hit a rubber ball, even at age ten or twelve or thirteen, 300 to 400 feet. That meant hitting it over the schoolyard fence, across the street and onto the roofs of the homes across the street. We were never short of balls because if you ever needed a ball, you'd just climb up onto the garage roofs or the other roofs of homes to replenish our supply of balls. It was great.

Another game we did, we could play with as few as two people—one-on-one. Mostly, I played one-on-one or two-on-two. I remember going through the lineup and being Richardson and Kubek and Maris and Mantle, Tom Tresh, Pepitone, and on down the line. I'd switch-hit—turn around, bat lefty. Of course, Mantle and Tresh were switch-hitters so it gave me the option. When I was Roger Maris, I'd turn around and bat lefty, and Joe Pepitone and all of them.

There were two Mickey Mantle Days—one was three or four years before he retired. There was another Mickey Mantle Day commemorating his retirement in 1968 or '69.

> My bar mitzvah day was Mickey Mantle Day, September 18, 1965. What's a guy gonna do?

The first one—they just gave him a day. It was thought that he wouldn't play certainly not for more than a year or two longer. While he was still playing, they wanted to honor him with a day. He had not yet hit his 500th home run because he ended at 535. He probably had about 450 at that point. His knees were awful. So, toward the end of that 1965 season, they had a Mickey Mantle Day.

My bar mitzvah day was Mickey Mantle Day, September 18, 1965. What's a guy gonna do? My bar mitzvah day was of great significance to my parents, holocaust survivors, to see their son bar mitzvahed in some fancy hall on the Lower East Side. When I found out it was Mickey Mantle Day, I actually told my parents and requested that my bar mitzvah be scheduled for a different day.

My parents did not understand what this thing called baseball was. I was just a poor little tenement boy from Brooklyn. What are these things I'm getting into? Who was Mickey Mantle? They knew who Mickey Mantle was because those were the two most common words uttered by me in my household. My parents speaking Yiddish and me replying "Mickey Mantle." We had a big fight over it. I had to go to my bar mitzvah. I still have an old 16 mm film that was made then. I had it converted to video about ten years ago.

I do remember disappearing from my own bar mitzvah and frantically searching the halls of the catering facility looking for a television to watch Mickey Mantle Day, but, alas, I missed it. I was absent without leave from my own bar mitzvah searching for Mickey Mantle. I may have become a man that day, but I missed Mickey Mantle, so it's a great lament of mine. Luckily there was another Mickey Mantle Day on the year he retired, and I was able to watch that one on TV.

I went to a lot of Yankee games. We could get into the bleachers with our student card, called the G.O. card. Every New York City public school had a G.O. (general organization), something like a student organization, and every kid was able to join. I think it cost about 50 cents to join. You got a button that said, "G.O." and it made you feel like you were part of a student organization. It also gave you a student ID and at Yankee Stadium, you could get into the bleachers for 50 cents with that G.O. card. I went to a lot of games that way—took the subway up from Brooklyn to the Bronx, which was a long, long schlep. When I say long—I mean an hour-and-twenty-minute ride on the subway. You got a lot for your nickel. It was wonderful to go to those Yankee games.

Mantle, to all of us, was larger than life. Mantle was from a place called Oklahoma, which might as well, to me being a poor little tenement boy from Brooklyn, have been Outer Mongolia. The visage of him, this strong, strapping guy with incredible power was like Paul Bunyan. He was Paul Bunyan to little tenement boys from Brooklyn. I'm looking at a picture of him right now warming up in the on-deck circle, swinging two bats. He was a hero. He was Superman. He was invincible. He was strong. He was fast. He hit longer home runs than anyone else. He spoke with a little bit of a twang that I'd never heard from any other human being. The exotic hero.

> Mantle was from a place called Oklahoma, which might as well, to me being a poor little tenement boy from Brooklyn, have been Outer Mongolia.

Bob Costas delivered the eulogy at Mickey Mantle's funeral. He answered that question of why? How much it meant for a generation of street kids from New York City to have somebody to look up to—a larger-than-life hero. Mickey Mantle died in 1995—within a couple of days of my mother passing away. I was going through my mother's things after she passed away, and found a lot of things she had kept from when I was a kid. Among the things I found was a facsimile of the Mickey Mantle jersey with No. 7 on it. I had it as a kid. I sent in some box tops to get it somehow. It was a cheesy little thing, but she had kept it—which shocked me. It was tattered and had holes in it.

My first trip to Yankee Stadium, I hopped on the subway from Brooklyn with a couple of classmates. I was probably about eleven years old, and we had the G.O. card and just took the ride on the subway. I was surprised at the size of the ball players. In retrospect, they all seemed so big as an eleven-year-old, for the first time in Yankee Stadium. . . . I wasn't into getting autographs, but I had thousands of baseball cards—many thousands.

My father, when we moved, threw out my shoesboxes full of baseball cards. I had Mickey Mantle rookie cards. I had it all. They were precious to me, but not in the sense of monetary value. I'd read their statistics over and over again. I'd take my baseball cards with me to the schoolyard to play stickball. It was the early '60s.

To me, the Yankees are the most identifiable, quintessential symbol of New York. I am a quintessential New York guy. I was one of the last of my contemporaries to move from my old neighborhood in Brooklyn. To this day, when people ask me where I'm from, my answer is, "Not Long Island, it's Brooklyn. I live on Long Island, but I'm from Brooklyn." The Yankees symbolize New York to me; therefore, they symbolize my home, my being, my essence, my universe, my whole life. Baseball was something I could relate to. I idolized the ball players. It was something I could do—I played ball. I never played baseball in Brooklyn— never played baseball, meaning hardball on a field. I played a lot of softball and all those other variations when I was younger.

> The Yankees symbolize New York to me; therefore, they symbolize my home, my being, my essence, my universe, my whole life.

The Yankees represent who I am, where I'm from, and what I love. As I got older and I have friends all around the country now, including many in New England who absolutely hate the Yankees, but they're very good friends of mine. I don't hate Boston, as a matter of fact, the Boston Red Sox, that is—never did, never will. I never root for them . . . I root against them, but I don't hate them in the way they hate the Yankees. There's something about being either loved and admired or hated and disdained— there's not a middle ground, and that has always been fascinating to me. Seemingly, when it comes to the Yankees, if somebody has a feeling or an opinion about it, it's one of those extremes. To me, that's fascinating. There are people who are not sports fans who don't think about the Yankees, but, if you do, in most cases, you either hate them or love them. Being the little tenement boy from Brooklyn, it was an anomaly in later years to hear them being described as aloof and businesslike, and they are in many ways, and regal and aristocratic. I never thought of them in any of those terms. I definitely didn't think of them as being aristocratic. After all, Joe Pepitone lived in my neighborhood—how aristocratic could he be?

YADA, YADA, YADA

In 1980, I was a staff writer for a Catholic newspaper upstate. I was looking for an angle to get into Yankee Stadium. I wanted to do a story on the Baseball Chapel, which was big in those days. I wanted to talk to Catholic players to see whether or not they attended the Baseball Chapel services. My editor told me to go for it. I contacted the Yankees press office and asked if I could have a press pass to come down and get into the clubhouse. I thought it would be difficult, but they said, "Sure." They set aside two tickets and two passes, so the question was who to take with me. My children were too young. I asked the advertising manager I worked with if he wanted to go with me and he said he did. I said, "Pretend you're the photographer," so we hung a camera around his neck. We went down, showed our passes, and got into the clubhouse. We were really left alone. I thought somebody would walk around with us, but they just said, "Do what you want to do." I began buttonholing some of the more famous players. I asked them, "Do you attend Baseball Chapel? And, if you do, why?"

I got brushed off by Reggie Jackson. Gossage told me to get lost. Several of the other players were very friendly and willing to talk about it. I would ask them why they attended. One common answer was they had no other way to get to church because of day games, and they wanted to maintain some sort of religious connection and that was the best way to do it. I found most Catholic players tended not to attend. A couple did, but it was more Protestant-oriented. The Catholic players more often went to Mass when they could. Toward the end of the time I was in the clubhouse, Yogi Berra walked out. I asked him if he went to the chapel. He said, "My chapel is the Catholic Church." So I had the ending of my story. Tommy John was someone who was strong in it. Rudy May was the friendliest guy and talked to me the longest.

I was trying not to be a fan and to maintain some journalistic distance, but I stepped over the line. At the end of each interview, I would ask for an autograph. I asked Rudy May for an autograph, and he said, "Why don't I get you an autographed baseball with everybody on it?" My reaction was, "Wow." I thought, "Now, I've really gone too far," so I asked him to just give me a ball. He took a practice ball and gave it to me. I still have it.

I got all these autographs and rubbed elbows with these players in the clubhouse, and then we were allowed to go down the ramp into the dugout and out onto the field, with the one rule being you weren't allowed into fair territory. Batting practice was going on and you could get hit. I didn't care. I went out and stepped over the line just so I could say I had been in fair territory in Yankee Stadium. Throughout all this, my friend, Jon, was very aloof. He stood in the corner in the clubhouse and didn't mingle. He had a camera. He could have taken pictures, but he didn't. The camera was a ruse, but I thought maybe he'd take a couple of pictures. When I started to head toward the field, he said, "I'm going to go to our seats." This was kinda ticking me off. I'm thinking, "Gee, I picked you, a good Yankee fan, to come down here and it's like you don't care." I didn't say this, but I was annoyed. I went out on the field and talked to a couple of opposing players about chapels. They were playing Cleveland. Andre Thornton was very strongly affirmative about his faith. I wrapped up my interviews and put the notebook away, found our seats, and we stayed for the game.

> Batting practice was going on and you could get hit. I didn't care.

We were driving home, and he said, "Thanks for taking me." I said, "Well, you seemed like there was something wrong, and you really weren't into it." He said, "Well, it's just that I've been there before."

Jon, a guy who never talked about himself—still doesn't at age eighty-two—was in Italy in World War II. I tried to get him to talk about it, and he won't. The other day I called him when the Yankees were playing and asked if he was watching *The War* on PBS. He said that he had seen a little bit but he didn't want to sit down and watch it. I used this as an opening and said, "I'm just wondering whether you thought it was accurate or not." For the first time, he talked a little bit about the war. This was after knowing him almost forty years.

Going back to the baseball game, I said, "What did you mean when you said you'd been there before?" He told me he had grown up in New York City and his father was a policeman. His normal patrol was Times Square. He got to know a lot of characters, including Jack Dempsey. When they had events at Yankee Stadium, his dad would often be assigned there, and Jon got to go with him.

At that point, I had known him for ten years and he'd never said anything like that. I said, "What do you mean—you would go to the games?" He said, "My father would have to be on patrol so the team kinda adopted me." I said, "The team? Like, who?" He said, "Gehrig and Ruth." I said, "Adopted you in what way?" He said, "I would be in the clubhouse, and they'd want to get a cake for somebody's birthday. They'd give me money, and I'd run to the nearest bakery and get a cake and bring it back to them, and they'd give me a tip." I said, "You've got to be kidding me. You knew these people!" Here I had been trying to impress him with Tom Underwood, one of the Yankee pitchers in that period.

He said, "Not only that, but Grover Cleveland Alexander used to stay with us." I said, "What are you talking about now?" He said, "My father, when he was on his beat in Times Square . . . Alexander, when he was drinking, would be falling down and in need of a place to sleep it off. My father would bring him home. I'd wake up in the morning, and there he would be at our breakfast table."

> He said, "Not only that, but Grover Cleveland Alexander used to stay with us."

The point of all this is that some people live humble lives. I was going to come home and crow to everyone I knew, "I shook hands with Ron Guidry." Here's a guy who *knew* Babe Ruth, Lou Gehrig, and whoever else was on that team . . . who had Grover Cleveland Alexander in his house and never said a word.

—JAMES BREIG, 62, editor, Albany, New York

I'm sure I'm prejudiced in this, but I think fans my age who grew up with the Yankees of the late '60s and early '70s have a certain bond to that team that maybe fans who came along later when the Yankees were starting to become good again don't have. You had to be a real fan to go to Yankee Stadium and to watch the games on TV and listen on radio when they were that bad, and they were pitching Bill Burbach and Thad Tillotson and Dooley

Womack and the lineup with Jerry Kenney and others—they were so bad. To be a fan back then, you *really* had to be a fan. You weren't a front-runner. People my age who were Yankee fans I think probably have real strong memories of that and a nostalgic feeling about those teams. You knew you were a fan if you were rooting for them because they were terrible.

In 1969, when the Mets won the World Series, I was thirteen. I remember distinctly having conversations with my Met fan friends that year toward the end of the season when the Mets were on their way to winning the pennant and everything. Comparing position for position, actually making the argument that the Yankees were better than the Mets . . . and the Yankees were awful. I'm looking back on it and thinking, "Oh, God, I was totally blinded by love." I would say, "Look. Joe Pepitone is better than Ed Kranepool at first base. And, Horace Clarke is better than Ken Boswell, or at least as good. Bud Harrelson versus Gene Michael. Good-fielding, poor-hitting shortstops. Ed Charles at third versus Jerry Kenney—I don't see where Ed Charles is that much better. Jerry Grote or Jake Gibbs." Where we lost them would be on the pitching staff, but I would always argue that Stottlemyre was as good as Tom Seaver, which, of course, was absurd. Position by position you can see it, but when you get to the pitching staff, that's where it changes. As good as Stottlemyre was, and I think had he been with the great Yankee teams, he could have been a Hall of Fame pitcher. You had Stottlemyre, Peterson, Stan Bahnsen, and then after that nothing. The Mets had Seaver, Koosman, Gentry, **JIM MCANDREW***, a young Nolan Ryan who hadn't come into his own, but he'd come in from the bullpen and scare the hell out of you for three innings.

The Met fans and I would argue like crazy about it. I was standing my ground. I wasn't giving in. The Yankees were as good as the

---

*In the first forty-six years of Mets history, no Met pitcher threw a no-hitter. . . .In the early 70s JIM MCANDREW of Lost Nation, Iowa, retired twenty-seven Montreal batters without a hit in one game for the Mets. After Mack Jones tripled with two outs in the second inning, no Expo hit safely until Jones tripled again off McAndrew with two outs in the eleventh.

Mets . . . even though the Mets won 100 games that year and the Yankees probably finished below .500, damn it, the Yankees were as good—I didn't care what they said. Then, of course, I had to root for the Orioles in the World Series. After Game 1, I was figuring out, "Aw, this is going to be a sweep. The Orioles are so much better." And, they were. You look back on it now, and how did the Mets win that? What a great team the Orioles had. The Mets beat the Cubs by eight games that year—just blew right past them.

> You look back on it now, and how did the Mets win that?

Remember that game at Shea when Seaver had retired twenty-five in a row, and Jimmy Qualls broke up his perfect game in the ninth inning. When the black cat walked . . .

—MARK BRAFF, P.R. firm owner

I saw a few episodes of the TV series, *The Bronx is Burning*. It was fantastic. They really captured the essence of how crazy it was back in the summer of '77—not just for the Yankees—for New York in general. It's interesting because I had a newspaper route in the summer of '77, delivering the newspaper every day. I would find a nice shady tree and lean my bike with its big basket full of newspapers against it . . . and I would read the sports. The first thing I'd turn to and read was about the New York Yankees and how they were doing.

The summer of '77—the blackout, the looting that happened, the tremendous heat wave we had, the mayor's race between Ed Koch and Mario Cuomo, and, of course, the Yankees. The Bronx burning was in the news all the time because of all the arson there. Even during the World Series of 1977, when the Yankees were playing the Dodgers, ABC was covering it, and they panned the cameras from the Goodyear Blimp to show a building burning down a few blocks from Yankee Stadium. I remember hearing Howard Cosell saying, "That's an arson just a few blocks from the Stadium."

—MATTHEW DONNELLY, college professor

I'm a big baseball nut. The Yankees just excite me. Up in this area where we live, we used to get the Yankees on TV every day. I think that had a lot to do with me becoming a die-hard Yankee fan because my father watched them . . . we watched them as children. Then, as the years go on, the YES Network was formed.

They took it off the cable companies up here, and the only way you could watch it is you would have to buy DIRECTV. I tried to get petitions signed to send to Major League Baseball to try to get baseball back in this area.

I contacted Major League Baseball. I spoke to the secretary to the commissioner. She explained to me that the only way we could get them here where we are is we would have to get the Philadelphia Phillies to relinquish their rights for us to watch them as Yankee fans. There's no way that's going to happen because they're not going to let Yankee fans watch the Yankees here in Phillie country—they want you to watch the Phillies. I was up against the wall.

They did tell me there was only one other way we could try that might work—if you can get enough signatures, a petition signing, where they would make a decision. I went out and got close to 3,000 signatures from the area here. I turned it in to Major League Baseball, and I didn't get one answer from them. They never even sent me a letter back saying, "Thank you. We're reviewing it. We'll get back to you." They never even acknowledged me after I had sent all those out to them, and that really upset me. They tell you to do that, and I did it and got all those signatures. We took petitions out to get signatures and to not even hear a word from them. . . . Nothing. That ticked me off.

I was really upset, so I called back and said, "I'm a big Yankee fan. I love the Yankees. I loved them as a child. How can I get the Yankees?" They said, "Sir, you're going to have to buy DIRECTV, and then you have to go out and buy the MLB package." I said, "Oh, OK, so it all boils down to money. In order for me to watch my Yankees, here in my area, I've got to go out and spend money for a dish, which was around a hundred bucks, and then on top of that, I've got to go and buy this MLB package, which is another $180. I was getting it for free, and now you're making me spend almost $300 just to watch my favorite team. Whatever happened to freedom of choice here in America? How can you dictate to me, a Yankee fan, and tell me I have to watch the Phillies in my area? I don't even like the Phillies. You're turning baseball fans away from the game. Yankee fans like myself—we're not going to watch the Phillies. We're gonna turn baseball off. You should be trying to promote baseball, not turn people away from it." I was on the phone for about half an hour on this. I was getting loud with her because I was getting upset. I said to her, as my closing statement, "Do you know why baseball is in the condition it is today?" She said, "No, sir. Why?" I said, "Because of your boss, Mr. Selig—he's a business person. He couldn't care less about the average-Joe baseball fan. What about a father and a mother who are out working trying to support their family . . . and their kids love baseball? You're making them go out to buy a dish and a Major League package, which they can't even afford, just to watch baseball? How fair do you think that is? You should be promoting baseball, not turning people away. That ain't right. That's why baseball is in the condition it is today—because of your boss. He's a business person, and all he sees is dollar signs. He don't care about the average baseball fan." And I hung up on her.

> . . . she said, "I'll look into it and get back to you." Never heard a word.

When I had mentioned I hadn't had a response from the 3,000-signature petition I had sent them, she said, "I'll look into it and get back to you." Never heard a word. She just blew me off.

—CHUCK FRANTZ, Northampton, PA

I was on stage in 1991 when this huge guy stood up and said, "Hugh Fink, you stink." I tried to ignore him, but he kept yelling, "Hugh Fink, you stink." I proceeded to completely destroy this guy, who stormed out of the room to audience applause.

Four years later, when I was a writer on *Saturday Night Live*, I was introduced to David Wells, the Yankees' star pitcher, who was going to appear in a sketch. He said, "Hugh Fink, holy _ _ _ _! Did you perform in Vegas at the Tropicana Hotel? You _ _ _ _ _ _ _ humiliated me. I was drunk and I stood up and heckled you, and you just _ _ _ _ _ _ _ nailed me."

I asked, "You sure it was me?"

He said, "Hugh Fink, you stink."

—HUGH FINK, comedian

IN THE WORLD OF THE BLIND, THE ONE-EYED MAN IS KING

Mike Sayre and Aiden McGuire

Aiden McGuire

Aiden McGuire works for the advertising, marketing and PR firm Mark Russell and Associates in Syracuse. He's a graduate of LeMoyne College and a life-long Yankee fan.

Mike Sayre and I met twenty-two years ago when we were kids, growing up around the corner from each other. We were childhood buddies and went to the same elementary school. Over the years, we developed a strong friendship and would always look out for each other. I knew, growing up, that Mike had congenital glaucoma. I never treated Mike differently than any of the other kids on the block. He was always one of the boys, one of our friends. We all made sure, even though there were some things he couldn't do, to include him in everything we did as kids. Growing up together, we were very close all through high school. We'd go to the same parties together. We'd double date and each take a girl to the prom in a limo.

Over the past year, Mike's glaucoma caught up with him, and he lost all vision in his right eye. Mike was a little hesitant to tell me about it. I'm not sure if it was a guy thing, where guys really don't want to talk about stuff like that, but one night we were watching a Yankee game. He pulled me off to the side and told me what the doctors had told him—that he had lost all vision in his right eye. For him to tell me, that took a lot. As his best friend, I was heartbroken for him. It's always been tough not being able to do enough for him. I can't give him his vision back so it was very frustrating to me that I could only do so much at my end.

I went to bed, after talking to him, and when I woke up the next morning, the first thing that popped into my mind was to write the Yankees a letter to tell them Mike had been a die-hard Yankee fan his entire life and that his passion for the Yankees runs very deep. They're the team he has always followed, and, over the years, that's how I became interested in baseball, too.

I went to work that morning and looked up the Yankees address and started writing a letter to them. I told them about Mike, about his medical condition, and about our friendship. I told them about his determination and how he doesn't let anything get in his way. I told them how much it would mean to me if Mike were able to go down to Yankee Stadium and experience the team he's been so passionate about up close and personal. I knew deep down inside that if I was able to convey that to the Yankees, maybe they could have a special day for him.

About a month and a half went by, and a letter came from the Yankees. I opened it up, and they told me that they'd love to make it work, would love to help out. They asked me to call them. I called them, and they helped me get tickets to the game . . . these tickets turned out to be two of **GEORGE STEINBRENNER'S*** personal tickets behind home plate. These are tickets he gives out to friends or business associates.

I was very surprised to hear back from them. When I wrote to the Yankees, I wrote fifteen letters in all. I wrote one letter to every executive on the team. I wrote the same letter to every one of them. I thought the odds of one getting through were so small that it couldn't hurt to contact a bunch of people. Sonny Hight was the one who wrote back to me. He said, "Let's make it happen."

> ***GEORGE STEINBRENNER'S** original Major League target was the Cleveland Indians in 1972. The Indians were owned by Vernon Stouffer. Steinbrenner, a Cleveland native, has owned part of the Chicago Bulls since their inception. . . . In 1989 Steinbrenner was given a presidential pardon by Ronald Reagan.

When you think about all the junk mail we get at our homes, and to have somebody actually open a letter, read it, and react to it, especially the Yankees, it was truly incredible. I'm sure they get tons of letters like that. I'm sure I'm not the only friend out there who's trying to do something special for their buddy. For them to go above and beyond was remarkable. In my head, I wanted to put together a "day" that Mike would never forget. To do that, I knew I'd have to go above and beyond just taking him to a game.

> When I wrote to the Yankees, I wrote fifteen letters in all. I wrote one letter to every executive on the team.

I sat down with pen and pad and jotted down ideas on how to do that. I wrote JetBlue and told them the story and the kind of day I was trying to put together for Mike and what the Yankees had agreed to do. I didn't ask for anything at all . . . I just wanted to know if they wanted to be a part of it. I left it up to them what they might want to do. About a week went by, and they called and told me they would love to help out and offered us round-trip tickets on them.

The trip developed legs of its own in no time. I wrote to the Peninsula Hotel, a five-star hotel in New York City, and told them about Mike and the Yankees and JetBlue. They wrote back saying they'd love to be a part of it, too. They gave us a suite for the night we were in New York. The cost to stay there would have been $1,000 a night. For them to do that for Mike was incredible.

I wanted Mike to have something to keep afterward to help him remember what a day we'd had so I wrote to the president of Louisville Slugger telling them Mike's story and what everybody else had agreed to do for him. I asked if they'd like to be a part of it, and, sure enough, Mark Redmond wrote me back and said, "Absolutely." They customized a bat for Mike—the same bat A-Rod, Jeter, and Giambi used . . . the black Louisville Slugger baseball bat with the silver writing. They inscribed Michael's name, date of our trip, June 29, 2007, and they put the Yankee logo on it. They surprised me with a bat also. I had no idea they were doing it—they put IN RECOGNITION OF AIDEN J. MCGUIRE, ONE AWESOME FRIEND, with the date on it.

I wanted to make it as over-the-top as possible. I wanted to have Mike dressed appropriately when we went there so I wrote Majestic Athletics and told them about Mike and his story and what a fan of the Yankees he was. I told them I was giving him a day that was a once-in-a-lifetime experience. They stepped up to the plate and mailed a Don Mattingly jersey for Mike.

The one other thing was that I wanted was for Mike to be able to go on the field and meet his all-time favorite Yankee, Don Mattingly. For that to happen, I knew I'd have to pull some strings. I was told by the Yankees that kind of thing was reserved for Make-a-Wish cases—people who are terminally ill. I went online and found the company that represents Don Mattingly, Iron Clad Authentic, and spoke to Mattingly's agent. I told him about Mike and what all was happening and that meeting Don Mattingly would be the icing on the cake. His agent ended up arranging the details. He told Don Mattingly what I was doing, and we were able to secure an on-field meet-and-greet with him.

One more detail to the trip, I contacted the president of the Glaucoma Research Foundation, based in San Francisco. I told them what I was doing and wanted to know if he would be able to find any companies or corporations who might want to make a donation to their organization in honor of Mike. After a bunch of back-and-forth dialogue, he called me back and told me he was able to contact executives at the Pfizer Corporation, and they donated $1,000 to the Glaucoma Research Foundation in Mike's name in honor of our trip.

I was on my way to work one day and was walking into our building in downtown Syracuse. I noticed a limo in front of our building. I walked up to the driver, Ron Curcio, and jokingly said to him, "Hey, I'll be down in about twenty minutes." He laughed, and we started a conversation. It turned out he lost his best friend to cancer a month and a half before. I told him all the details about Mike's trip and asked him if it would be possible for a limo to pick up Mike and me at his house in Syracuse and take us to the airport the morning of our trip. He said he was so blown away by what we were doing that he would personally drive us to the airport.

The morning of the trip, I woke up and met Sarah Qwak, a reporter for *Sports Illustrated* at her hotel. She had flown out the day before, and we rode in the limo to pick up Mike. I walked up to Mike's front porch with this reporter from *Sports Illustrated*. Mike was standing there with his backpack on. He was under the impression we were going to go to Yankee Stadium on the bus. That was the cover for the trip. I'd had to tell his parents about the trip to make sure he didn't have doctor appointments or any conflicts. They knew all about it well before the trip but were able to keep it a secret from him, his friends, and his family. Mike looked puzzled and wondered who the girl was. He thought I was bringing a date on the trip.

> He was under the impression we were going to go to Yankee Stadium on the bus.

We were all there in his living room, and I said, "I know you've had a tough year, Mike. A few months ago, I wrote the Yankees a letter and told them about you and how much I wanted to put together a special day for you. I'm not going to tell you everything at once—just let it unfold as the day goes on." It was funny because everything that happened that day was pretty much how all the letters went out and how everything came together.

His initial reaction was, "You're joking?" He said he didn't know if I was pulling his chain, or whether or not he should cry. I could tell he was overwhelmed, which is exactly what I wanted to happen. I wanted to totally give him a day that would be unbelievable to him. His mom was crying . . . his dad, a big tough guy, was even choking up a little bit . . . his older brother was there crying. Everybody took pictures and said their goodbyes.

The limo driver rolled out the red carpet for him, and the three of us got into the limo. At that point, Mike still had no idea what was going on. He knew we were going to a Yankee game, but he didn't know the details of the trip. For all he knew, we were taking a six-hour ride down the Thruway to Yankee Stadium. As we approached the airport, I said to him, "Do you know where we are? Do you know where we're going right now?" He said, "Yeah. We're going to Yankee Stadium." I said, "We are, but we're right outside the airport." He got a big grin on his face and said, "What did you do?" I told him I had written to JetBlue—at that point, he's shaking his head and smiling—and they're flying us there.

> We'd never been in a hotel where someone walks up with you and shows you the room and walks you through all the amenities.

We fly into JFK and catch a cab to our hotel. I tell about how the hotel is going to put us up for the night. That whole time, Mike was speechless. He wasn't giving the reporter much, but I didn't blame him—he was overwhelmed over what was happening. We pulled up to the hotel. Mike and I get out of the limo, and we look up at the incredible building—gold-plated signs everywhere and the railings were gold-plated. Mike just kept shaking his head. He knew he was in for something big, but he didn't realize how big. We walked into the hotel lobby, and, clearly, we looked out of place. We both had on shorts and flip-flops and Yankee jerseys . . . everyone else had on business suits and wore ties.

We checked in and a young lady walked us up to our room. We'd never been in a hotel where someone walks up with you and shows you the room and walks you through all the amenities. We walk in and see a tub filled with beer and ice. There were slippers next to the beds. It was beyond belief.

At that point, Mike was calling all his family and friends to tell them about what had happened. We hopped on the "D" train and went to Yankee Stadium. They gave us press passes. Mike still doesn't know that he's moments away from meeting Don Mattingly. We were escorted down onto the field.

All throughout the trip, the whole thing I wanted was for Mike to be able to go onto the field. I didn't care if it was just for a moment, or if he had to be off the side, or out in the outfield, I just wanted him to know what it felt like, for one moment, to be at Yankee Stadium and to be closer than anybody has ever been. They walked us right down onto the field. Mike was able to watch his favorite Yankees walk up right past him, up the tunnel into the dugout. He watched Mattingly throw batting practice and saw other players giving interviews. We were able to take some pictures of everything happening.

When batting practice ended, **DON MATTINGLY*** walked over with a bag in his hand. I didn't know whether to take pictures or to film the event, but I grabbed my camcorder when I saw Mattingly come up and introduce himself and talk to Mike. Mattingly knew the details of the story from his agent. He went right up to Mike and told him, "I'm really happy you guys are here. I think what you're doing is wonderful." He talked to Mike for ten to fifteen minutes. Mike was beyond happy—beyond overwhelmed! He was face-to-face with his all-time favorite Yankee. I think it finally hit him right there that he was in for a special day. He just kept shaking his head and saying, "Unbelievable." After Mattingly talked to him, Mike turned to me and said, "You really didn't have to do this. I don't deserve it." I looked at him and said, "No. You do deserve it. You've been an incredible friend." I've always admired Mike for his positive attitude especially considering what he has. He's better than a lot of people I know who don't have any impairment.

After the Mattingly meet-and-greet, Roger Clemens came over and talked with Mike. Then, after that Andy Pettitte came over. Joe Torre came over. Then we were escorted out to Monument Park where he was able to take pictures.

> ***DON MATTINGLY** hit 6 grand slams in 1987, an all-time Major League record for one season. Mattingly never hit a grand slam before or after that season.

Immediately following that, we're taken to our seats behind home plate. We both had hot dogs and a beer. You couldn't have asked for anything better. It was at that one moment—that one moment in time—that Mike forgot about everything. He forgot about all the doctors' appointments . . . forgot about everything he was going through over the past half a year. He lived for that moment at Yankee Stadium. Looking at him and talking with him, it was clear that this was a moment in his life that he'd never forget. And, that was what I had set out to do.

> Looking at him and talking with him, it was clear that this was a moment in his life that he'd never forget. And, that was what I had set out to do.

Sports Illustrated did an article our trip. Rick Reilly asked Mike how he could ever repay me. His answer: "Do you know any Laker Girls?" Mike was kidding of course, but those six words traveled all the way to the Los Angeles Lakers organization, who worked with Mike in secrecy for 3 months to surprise me with a trip of my own. Mike surprised me one day after work and told me we were flying out to LA to see the Lakers play. It was his way of thanking me for giving him a day he'll never forget. The NBA's Lakers flew us out to LA and put us up at the Beverly Hilton hotel. Our first NBA game, our first trip to California.

November 29th, 2007 was the big day. We were interviewed and featured on FOX Sports Net, TNT, NBA TV and some local media outlets. Mike surprised me with lunch with the Laker Girls, too! I was so shocked to be having lunch with six gorgeous women. It was truly a dream come true. And I owed it all to my best bud Mike.

Later that night, we received a private tour of the Lakers practice facility, and were given court side seats at the Lakers game, a few feet away from Jack Nicholson. After the game, Kobe Bryant gave us his game worn shoes and signed them both for us.

The PGA Tour heard about Mike and I and invited us to Florida to watch THE PLAYERS Championship at TPC Sawgrass. They gave Mike a private tour, let him ride with the superintendent as he set up the course and gave him an all-access pass. Phil Mickelson was fantastic to us.

Looking back on it, I'm very glad I did it. To have everybody come together the way they did for a complete stranger was very heart-warming. I tend to lose sight of the fact that there are really good people out there. Good people who will go above and beyond for a complete stranger and who are compassionate and under-standing of the relationships best friends have with each other.

Say what you want about Baltimore. Frankly, "losers" comes to mind.

TO BE CONTINUED!

We hope you have enjoyed *For Yankee Fans Only-Volume II!!!* You can be in the next edition if you have a neat story. You can e-mail it to printed page@cox.net (please put YANKEES in the subject line and include a phone number where you can be reached), or call the author directly at (602) 738-5889. The author can't type, has never turned on a computer and has never seen the Internet, so it you need an immediate response, use the phone rather than email.

In addition, we'll be putting together *For Brooklyn Dodgers Fans Only*, so if you are a Brooklyn Dodgers fan and have a great story, e-mail that as well to printed page@cox.net (please put BROOKLYN DODGERS in the subject line and include a phone number where you can be reached),

Note: There were no actual METS fans harmed during the making of this book.

Other Books by Rich Wolfe

Da Coach (Mike Ditka)
I Remember Harry Caray
There's No Expiration Date on Dreams (Tom Brady)
He Graduated Life with Honors and No Regrets (Pat Tillman)
Take This Job and Love It (Jon Gruden)
Been There, Shoulda Done That (John Daly)
Oh, What a Knight (Bob Knight)
And the Last Shall Be First (Kurt Warner)
Remembering Jack Buck
Sports Fans Who Made Headlines
Fandemonium
Remembering Dale Earnhardt
For Yankees Fans Only
For Cubs Fans Only
For Red Sox Fans Only
For Cardinals Fans Only
For Packers Fans Only
For Hawkeyes Fans Only
For Browns Fans Only
For Mets Fans Only
For Notre Dame Fans Only—The New Saturday Bible
For Bronco Fans Only
For Nebraska Fans Only
For Buckeye Fans Only
For Georgia Bulldog Fans Only
For South Carolina Fans Only
For Clemson Fans Only
For Cubs Fans Only—Volume II
For Oklahoma Fans Only

Questions? Contact the author directly at 602-738-5889.

Sample Excerpts From This Book

. . . I stumbled upon the entrance to the Yankee dugout. I looked around, and there wasn't anybody in the Stadium—not a soul. I said to myself, "There's nobody here. It's my one opportunity." So I went out and stood on the pitcher's mound. I wanted to see what it feels like to be on the pitcher's mound at Yankee Stadium. Now, I'm in a suit and tie looking around. It was eerie and scary— in that empty Stadium. I knew I had to do it—I ran around the bases—first, second, third, and home. I said, "Now I know what it feels like to hit a home run at Yankee Stadium." I actually did that, as an adult, at twenty-eight years old! Don't tell anybody that. . . .

. . . Mantle hit the game-winning homer and started jogging around the bases with his head down, elbows up, as only he could. I must have gone nuts about the time Mel Allen said, "How about that." Ida Dolinz was our landlady; she was an immigrant, who spoke broken English. Both my mother and I understood what she meant when she came knocking on our door, saying "Iv, ya dunt make him schtop mit da bangin', and da noise makin', I'm goin' to told you to leaf mine house." I had converted my mother into a true and devoted Yankee fan, but as she said, we needed a place to live. . . .

. . . The next year, my dad took me to my first game at the Stadium. I was overwhelmed to walk down the runway into the Stadium and see the expanse of grass come into full view. The sheer size of the Stadium . . . the incredible green of the grass . . . the blue seats . . . the famous facade—all joined together to assault the senses of a nine-year-old boy. . . .